FAST TRACK TO A 5

Preparing for the **AP***
English Language and
Composition Examination

To accompany
The Riverside Reader
Alternate Edition, 1st Edition
by Joseph Trimmer and Heather Milliet

Steve Olson
La Porte High School, La Porte, Texas

Eveline Bailey
La Porte High School, La Porte Texas

McDougal Littell   A Houghton Mifflin Company
Evanston, Illinois   Boston   New York

*AP and Advanced Placement Program are registered trademarks of the College Board,
which was not involved in the production of and does not endorse this product.

CONTENTS

ABOUT THE AUTHORS

STEVE OLSON has taught for twenty-five years at La Porte High School in La Porte, Texas. He has taught AP English Language and Composition, English Literature, and Macroeconomics. However, English Language has been his primary focus for the last eighteen years. He has been a grader for the English Language and Composition exam for the past fourteen years and a consultant for the College Board for the last ten years.

EVELINE BAILEY has been teaching English for ten years. For the last five years, she has taught AP English Literature and Composition at La Porte High School. Eveline also teaches Composition and Rhetoric at San Jacinto College. Eveline has a master's degree in English Literature from the University of Houston and is currently a PhD candidate in English Literature at UH.

PREFACE

We have a mantra written on the whiteboard in our classroom: *Read Critically! Think Rationally! Communicate Effectively!* These are laudable goals and our society would do well to heed them. Today's media rarely encourage thoughtful debate or complex discussion. With the advent of talk shows and reality television, communication has become little more than shouting matches and slogan writing. It appears that Americans have forgotten altogether the fine art of reflection. *Read Critically! Think Rationally! Communicate Effectively!* is what the Advanced Placement English Language and Composition examination is all about.

The AP English Language exam has been significantly changed over the past five years, in particular for the 2007 exam. It has been redesigned to emphasize argumentation and the analysis of argument, and its focus has moved from style analysis to rhetorical analysis. The test asks students to take seriously the issues that affect their generation and to become part of a thoughtful, educated community of people who believe that ideas are foremost and solutions are possible. Furthermore, the skills emphasized on the exam are essential to virtually every aspect of a solid college education.

This edition of *Fast Track to a 5* includes chapters on all of these important test elements and offers specific resources for improving the skills needed to pass the examination. The book also provides a number of sample essays and passages for multiple-choice study. Finally, and most significantly, it stresses the importance of reading, thinking, and communicating. We hope that *Fast Track to a 5* not only helps students succeed at the test, but also supports their development as skilled rhetoricians and communicators.

We had valuable assistance in writing the book. We want to thank Margaret Lannamann, our muse and our editor. We also want to thank the editors at Houghton Mifflin who supported this project, and Brook Bullock and Angelia Greiner for their valuable insight into our writing and our ideas.

Steve Olson and Eveline Bailey
La Porte High School
October 2007

Part I

Strategies for the AP Exam

PREPARING FOR THE AP* EXAM

Advanced Placement courses and tests have become the standard in academic preparation for college. Each AP discipline is designed to provide the student with the best material and training not only to succeed at this particular level of skill or knowledge, but also to prepare for the rigors and challenges of the first year of college.

The English Language and Composition test fits all of these criteria. The fundamental skills are basic but demanding. You must learn to read critically, engage a text with full comprehension of the issues raised, synthesize various sources and opinions about an issue, and be able to challenge, validate, or debate the issues with a degree of knowledge and commitment. In short, you must learn to think rationally and write clearly.

The series of *Fast Track to a 5* books is designed to assist students by providing them with the tools necessary for success on a particular AP test. This book is devoted to the necessary skills of critical reading, rational thinking, and effective communication. It will improve your ability to read critically and argue effectively. It is designed to be a resource in your efforts to study for that very challenging exam—an exam that has undergone significant changes recently as the College Board endeavors to emphasize the communication skills most needed in our society.

What passes for debate and discussion in the media frequently involves rudeness, shouting matches, interruptions, and a lack of appreciation for what is being said. This book and the discipline it nurtures seek to do just the opposite. You will evaluate information about several sides of an argument, and you will be encouraged to reflect before responding. You will then propose reasonable resolutions to problems and cultural concerns.

Finally, a strong response to this exam requires a sophisticated level of communication. It demands from you the ability to compose your ideas and feelings and express them coherently and with academic rigor.

Fast Track to a 5: Preparing for the English Language and Composition Exam can be used alone or in conjunction with Joseph Trimmer's *The Riverside Reader, Alternate Edition,* a collection of carefully selected pieces of largely nonfiction prose designed to expand your ability to read, critique, and synthesize arguments. *The Riverside Reader* also contains valuable information on writing strategies. We have used several passages from the book to help

---

* AP and Advanced Placement Program are registered trademarks of the College Board, which was not involved in the production of and does not endorse this product.

create some of the multiple-choice questions and essay prompts for the sample tests.

WHAT'S IN THIS BOOK

As you might have gathered from the introduction, the English Language and Composition test is very much a skills-based examination. There is a working vocabulary you will need in order to succeed, but it is relatively small. Knowledge is not the foremost component to the test—skills are! This study guide is designed to improve those essential skills. It will help you employ them more effectively and more quickly on a timed test.

Following the introductory material you are reading now is a diagnostic test. It includes fifty-two multiple-choice questions and three sample essays. Use the diagnostic test to determine your current abilities and to identify those skills in which you need the most improvement.

After the diagnostic test, you will find a section called "Things You Should Know," which includes "A Working Vocabulary of Fundamental Terms" (an annotated glossary of all major and minor concepts) and a brief chapter on tone and mood, including a tone word list. You will find yourself referring to these sections often.

Following "Things You Should Know," the book is divided into separate chapters on strategies for managing the multiple-choice test questions, the synthesis question, the rhetorical question, and the general argument question. Each of these chapters follows a set pattern. We offer insight into the makeup of each of these types of questions. More importantly, we provide strategies to help improve your overall score in each of these four areas. We follow our introductory notes to each chapter with a sample question that is annotated and discussed in detail. In the case of the multiple-choice chapter, we give you a passage and a whole set of questions about that passage. The multiple-choice selection is followed by a dissection of the correct answers, while the essay sections provide a grading rubric and an analysis of several sample student essays. These discussions are specific and should support both the development of your skills and an awareness of your shortcomings.

We conclude with two complete practice tests. The key word here is *practice*. Practice is an absolute necessity if you are to succeed at the English Language and Composition test. In our classrooms in the spring, students take a multiple-choice test or write an essay at least three times a week for approximately six to eight weeks prior to the exam. That may not sound appealing, but we've discovered a rather bizarre and somewhat delightful truth: this test (and any course that offers instruction about it) is more like football than, say, chemistry. Rather than memorize facts to regurgitate on a test, you must practice, practice, practice in order to gain and nurture the skills and abilities you need to do well. We hope that this book genuinely encourages useful practice and provides effective feedback on how well you are doing.

The most important thing we want to hear from our students after they have taken the exam is, "It was hard, but nothing happened that was out of the ordinary. I was prepared." We hope this book provides you with that same feeling, and that when you leave the test you will feel that what happened in the exam room was exactly what you expected. You were ready!

PREPARATION

All of the books in the *Fast Track to a 5* series advise you to set up a review schedule. However, your review schedule really depends on how much time you have. If it is spring when you are reading this and the test is very close (perhaps one or two weeks away), we strongly recommend that you at least take the practice tests, making very sure to read our discussion of the correct answers. Also, read the essay prompts and the scored sample essays we provide. It will be very helpful for you to know what the graders are thinking when they read your essays.

If you purchased the book in the fall and plan to use it throughout the year as a vehicle for further study and review—especially if you are taking a high school class in English Language and Composition—then you can work systematically through the whole book. In fact, we wrote the book with this approach in mind. Take the diagnostic test in the fall, write the sample essays, and evaluate how well you did. Then work through the chapters in the order they are presented, or use them in relation to the material you are practicing in your class. For example, if your class is working on multiple-choice questions, work through our multiple-choice chapter. If your class is working on and practicing the general argument question, read and work on our sample essays in that particular chapter.

You can also take the book with you to class. If you don't have a good working knowledge of the vocabulary you may encounter on the exam (or if you suffer from CRADTS—*Can't Remember A Darn Thing Syndrome*), you may wish to have this book with you simply to use the chapter called "A Working Vocabulary" as a backup to any question about terminology that might arise.

If for some reason you are on your own, or are a senior in English Literature and Composition and are taking the Language test for the second time without the support of the Language class (most students take the English Language and Composition test the first time as juniors in high school), then parcel out your time and use this book as a steady but systematic approach to the test. Take the diagnostic test in the fall. In February, begin working through the chapters, completing one every two weeks. The last week before the test, take the final practice test, reread the vocabulary, work on your memory bank of examples (more about that later), and then get a good night's sleep and eat a decent breakfast the morning of the test. Good luck, and as we said earlier, we hope that you leave the test having confronted exactly what you expected.

TAKING THE ENGLISH LANGUAGE AND COMPOSITION EXAM

Advanced Placement tests have been given since 1956. They arose quite simply as an opportunity to allow students in high school to test out of certain required lower-level college courses. As of 2007, more than twenty-five AP exams were offered in art, music, social studies, English, foreign languages, science, and mathematics. When the authors of this book first started grading the English Language and Composition examination in the early 1990s, there were approximately 65,000 examinations. In 2007, we graded nearly 300,000 tests. What a testament to today's young scholars!

THE BASICS

The AP examinations are given during the second and third weeks of May on high school campuses worldwide. The methods of grading and scoring will be discussed in detail in subsequent chapters, but for now just know that the exams are scored in June by AP teachers and college professors. Students receive their scores in the middle of July. When you are ready to apply to college, you can have the College Board send your scores to the colleges of your choice.

SCORING

When you receive a copy of your score, it will simply be reported to you as a 1, 2, 3, 4, or 5. You will not know your scores on the two separate sections of the test. You can pay additional money to find out that information if you wish, but most people don't do this. Each score represents a level of qualification to potential colleges about your skills:

- a 5 means you are exceptionally well qualified;
- a 4 means you are well qualified;
- a 3 means you are qualified;
- a 2 means you are possibly qualified;
- a 1 means no recommendation.

Our advice to students in an AP course is always to take the test. Although a score of 2 does not usually provide college credit, two university studies found that the students who had the highest grades in their own first-year college composition programs were students who had taken the English Language and Composition Exam while in high school. What does this mean to you? Even though you may not get a score of 3 or higher when you take the exam, you are certainly far better prepared for college as a writer and a thinker!

If you do receive a score of 3, 4, or 5, check with the universities you are considering. Usually their websites will tell you what credit your score may earn at those colleges.

WHO SHOULD TAKE THE EXAMINATION

If you are currently enrolled in an English Language and Composition (or English III AP) course, you are being given a year's instruction in the necessary skills. Most students who take the class will take the test. Some will take the test because it is mandatory at their school for AP students to take the exam. Other students will take the test because they feel the instruction has been sufficient for them to be successful. However, a formal year-long course is not a necessity. Any high school student may take any AP examination in May and can retake any exam. Occasionally, students choose to retake the English Language and Composition test in May of their senior year because they received a score of 2 the previous year and they hope to achieve a higher score.

HOW MUCH DOES THE EXAMINATION COST?

To take the test, you need to sign up in February or March with your school counselor or designated AP coordinator at your campus. Each test costs approximately eighty-five dollars. However, please note that many states and school districts offer a variety of financial incentives for taking the test, so it rarely costs you that much money.

WHEN IS THE EXAMINATION GIVEN AND WHAT DO I NEED TO BRING?

The English Language and Composition test is nearly always given in the morning and lasts approximately three and a half hours. Bring a form of identification (usually your driver's license or your school ID card is sufficient), a pair of good pencils, and two good black pens. Also, you may bring gum or candy that can be unwrapped easily (and quietly!) to keep your mouth from drying out. We also recommend that students bring a sweater or sweatshirt since you never know how cold any particular testing room is going to be.

Inside the testing room, you are not allowed to have anything with you at the desk, including a cell phone. Even if it is turned off, it should not be on your person. Some proctors will allow you to have capped bottled water on the floor beside your desk, but that rule changes from year to year.

AN OVERVIEW OF THE MULTIPLE-CHOICE QUESTIONS

The test is divided into two sections: a series of multiple-choice questions, followed by three essay questions. First we'll discuss what will happen when you take the multiple-choice portion of the test.

Once the testing space has been organized, you are in your seat, and everyone has been accounted for, the proctors will pass out your Scantron and the multiple-choice portion of the test. The proctor will say "Begin," and you will have sixty minutes to complete this section. The proctor will usually give a warning five minutes before the end of the section. However, be sure you have a watch, or sit where you can clearly see a clock in the room, since you will need to budget your time in order to read the four passages of nonfiction prose and answer the questions that accompany them. One of the passages is usually an excerpt taken from a British writer from the seventeenth to nineteenth centuries. Another passage is typically written by an American writer from a particular ethnic background. A third passage will include footnotes, and the last passage will generally be contemporary. Take note of our qualifiers: "usually," "typically," and "generally." We mean for you to understand that these categories, while standard, should be accepted with caution; there have been exams in the past in which all four passages were considered "contemporary," which means they had been written within the last fifty years.

Ordinarily, there are fifty-three to fifty-five questions. You should be able to read, analyze, and answer the questions for any given passage in fifteen minutes. We will discuss how to manage your time and will provide techniques to help you when we study the multiple-choice section in detail.

This portion of the test counts for 45 percent of your total score. Your objective is to answer approximately 50 percent (or more) of the questions correctly. Yes—the test is that rigorous! You are aiming for thirty correct answers out of the fifty-plus questions asked. Moreover, as with the SAT, the College Board takes off a quarter point for each wrong answer. As we will discuss later, you should never randomly guess an answer. However, you will learn effective strategies for removing poor distractors. (A distractor is a possible answer that seems to be correct, but is either wrong or is not as good as another answer.) By doing this, you will be down to choosing between two—or at the most three—possible answers. The odds will then be in your favor for guessing.

THE BREAK

When the multiple-choice portion of the test is over, you will be given a fifteen-minute bathroom and water break. We recommend you drink regular ol' water that is fortified with two hydrogen molecules and one oxygen molecule in order to maintain your focus and well-being, rather than sugary sodas or energy drinks with jitter-causing caffeine in them. However, be careful not to overdo it—a potentially great essay can be ruined by an extra trip to the bathroom to dispose of your water molecules. If you need an energy boost, a healthful power bar or nutritional snack will provide it. Finally, if you are allowed to go outside during your break, do so. Get some fresh air and stretch.

AN OVERVIEW OF THE ESSAY QUESTIONS

Once everyone has returned to the testing room and settled down, the proctor will hand each student a green booklet. It will have three essay questions in it. Two of the questions, the rhetorical analysis essay question and the general argument essay question, will each take up a single page, whereas the new synthesis essay question will include six or seven short passages plus a visual (graph, table, photograph, or cartoon) dealing with the same topic or issue (the format is similar to those you may have seen on the AP U.S. History, European History, and World History exams). You have FIFTEEN MINUTES to read the passages that accompany the synthesis essay. Use your time well. Make critical notes and jot down ideas in the green booklet, possibly even an outline, as you read the passages. Annotate the synthesis question first. If you have any time remaining, read the rhetorical analysis question and, last, the general argument question. The best strategy for the fifteen-minute reading time is to have the synthesis question outlined and ready to write with the rhetorical analysis percolating in the background of your mind.

After the fifteen minutes, the proctor will hand you a pink booklet. This is where you will write your essays. Each page in the pink booklet has a box in the upper right-hand corner where you will indicate which essay question you are answering (one, two, or three). You do not have to write the essays in any particular order. If, after the test, you remember that you failed to put the number of an essay in the box, DO NOT PANIC! Graders will read all the pages in the booklet in order to find your essay. You will not be penalized for your error.

Once you receive the booklet for your essays, you have TWO HOURS to complete all three essays. That is only forty minutes per essay. You have never in your life written so much so fast. It is, therefore, absolutely necessary to budget your time. If, for example, you have written a *good* second essay that could be a *great* essay if you had ten more minutes to finish that last point, stop anyway. Even if you could raise your essay score by a single point, you would then take away valuable time from your third essay, costing you much more than the loss of a single score point.

When your two hours begin, set your green booklet to the side but still in sight to keep track of your ideas, organization, and quotations. Do not agonize over the spelling of one word or your exact phrasing. Graders know and are repeatedly told to evaluate the essay as a rough draft. We know you do not have time to go back to edit for correct usage and clarity in all things. Just keep going. Most proctors will let you know when forty minutes and then eighty minutes have passed. They will sometimes let you know when you are down to your last five minutes. At the conclusion of the two hours, turn in your booklet.

You will no doubt be exhausted. The last three and a half hours will have passed very quickly, and rarely does a student feel that the test was a breeze. The exam asked from you just about everything you had to offer, and you gave it. That is an awesome feeling! Whereas most examinations are usually within our reach and we finish them with time to spare, that does not often happen with this exam, which is a good thing. You indeed will have been "tested" and found equal to the task.

SOME ADDITIONAL INFORMATION ON SCORING

As we have told you earlier in this chapter, the College Board reports your score to you as a 1 to 5, and we have explained what those scores indicate. On the English Language and Composition Exam, how that number is defined varies slightly from year to year, but you might like to know how it is arrived at.

As we have said, the multiple-choice portion counts for 45 percent of your score. The College Board takes the number you got right and subtracts one-fourth of the number that were incorrect. Therefore, no blind guessing at the end of the test! (We will tell you specifically when to guess and when not to guess in the multiple-choice chapter.) If you got 32 correct and you missed 16, your raw multiple-choice score would be 28. That score is then multiplied by a number that is in the neighborhood of 1.2. This number changes somewhat each year, based on the number of total questions on the test. So your multiple-choice score in this scenario would be about 28 x 1.2, or 34.

Your essays are scored on the basis of a rubric that ranges from 1 to 9. Essays with scores of 1 to 4 are unacceptable and weaker essays. Scores of 5 to 9 are given for essays that are acceptable to excellent. You will find detailed rubrics explaining what each of these numbers means in the essay chapters. The three essays together count for 55 percent of your total score. In that mysterious realm of math, each of your essay scores is multiplied by 3.3 (again this number may be adjusted very slightly from year to year). For the sake of argument, say that you scored a 4, a 6, and a 7 on the three essays. Each of those would be multiplied by 3.3 and your essay result would be approximately 56. Add that to your multiple-choice score of 34 and the result would be 90.

Every year there is a total scale from zero to approximately 145 (a perfect total score). That scale is curved somewhat each year. THIS IS VERY, VERY APPROXIMATE, but generally a score in the low 70s produces a 3, a score in the low 90s produces a 4, and a score above about 105 produces a 5.

The math is approximate because it changes slightly from year to year. YOU DO NOT GET THE DETAILS from the College Board. All you get is your score, but it is nice to have a little knowledge about how this was achieved. Just be aware that if you can do better than 50 percent on the multiple-choice questions and earn fifteen total points on the essay (receiving at least a 5 on all three essays), you will pass the exam with a score of 3 or better.

Turn now to the next chapter and take the diagnostic test. Check your answers and evaluate your strengths and weaknesses. Then begin working through the chapters to help you develop more efficient strategies. When you face that test in May, you will be ready: it will not be an intimidating beast of a test, but a demanding challenger—one you can vanquish.

A DIAGNOSTIC TEST

You can evaluate your specific strengths and weaknesses by taking the diagnostic test in this chapter. However, as we have explained, the test is difficult. We certainly don't want to make you anxious, but we have worked hard to make our questions reflect as closely as possible the nature of the actual tests. Don't be surprised if some of these questions are tough to figure out.

OPTIONS FOR TAKING THE MULTIPLE-CHOICE TEST

You do *not* have to take the test under standard test conditions for it to help you—no matter what the conditions, it will still give you a feel for what to expect.

TAKING THE MULTIPLE-CHOICE TEST IN ONE SITTING

One option is to sit down and take the multiple-choice test in an hour and then check your answers. Afterward, look at our discussions of the right answers and try to follow our reasoning. Remember: in order to evaluate critical reading skills, many of the questions will be interpretive and will require you to make subtle distinctions. Only one answer will be correct and can be supported by details found in the text. At the same time, one or two distractors will sound plausible. You must learn to distinguish among those subtle differences. That is the nature of critical reading.

TAKING THE MULTIPLE-CHOICE TEST IN FOUR FIFTEEN-MINUTE BLOCKS

Alternatively, you can take the test in four fifteen-minute blocks. After you have read each passage and answered the related questions, stop, check your answers, and read our discussion of those questions. Do this four times in a row, or on four separate occasions. You should try to complete each section in fifteen minutes, but what's most important is that you finish all the questions for that section. If it took you longer than fifteen minutes, it's a good idea to make a note of how long it took you.

WRITING THE DIAGNOSTIC ESSAYS

When you get to the essays, write each one without paying attention to the amount of time you need to complete it. Don't do all three at once unless you are masochistic, grounded for the entire day, or facing some other deadline you want to avoid. Instead, in an hour or less—preferably less—write just one of the essays. Repeat this process until you have done each one and then read both our analysis of each essay question and our suggestions as to what will most likely produce upper-half and lower-half scores. We will provide specific sample essays of each kind in the later chapters, but here we focus on what you should consider in your approach to each of the essay questions.

One important thing to remember: in order to pass this test, you must practice. This is a skills-based test. To improve those skills, you have to practice them, just as you would do to get better at baseball, volleyball, or the violin. It is hard to motivate yourself to write essays when you know no one is there to grade them. We can't send a personal trainer to your house to make you write the practice essays. All we can tell you is that writing them and then reflecting on how you did is the best way to prepare for this test. There are twelve questions in this book. Writing all of them will take you a long way toward successfully passing the test. Feel good about your work and then check out our ideas on possible approaches to the essays.

Above all, have fun. Don't stress out. Do the tests by section. Check your answers and your essays and then take a look at the annotated answers when you are ready for detailed assistance on each part of the test.

DIAGNOSTIC TEST

AP ENGLISH LANGUAGE AND COMPOSITION
Section I: Multiple-Choice Questions
Total time: 1 hour
Number of questions: 52

Directions: This part consists of selections from prose works and questions on their content, form, and style. After carefully reading each passage, choose the best answer to the accompanying questions.

Note: Pay particular attention to the requirement of questions that include the words NOT, LEAST, or EXCEPT.

Questions 1–14 are based on the following passage from "Stone Soup" by Barbara Kingsolver. Read the passage carefully before you choose your answers.

It's awfully easy to hold in contempt the straw broken home, and that mythical category of persons who toss away nuclear family for the sheer fun of it. Even the legal terms we use have a suggestion of caprice. I resent the
5 phrase "irreconcilable differences," which suggests a stubborn refusal to accept a spouse's little quirks. This is specious. Every happily married couple I know has loads of irreconcilable differences. Negotiating where to set the thermostat is not the point. A nonfunctioning marriage is a
10 slow asphyxiation. It is waking up despised each morning, listening to the pulse of your own loneliness before the radio begins to blare its raucous gospel that you're nothing if you aren't loved. It is sharing your airless house with the threat of suicide or other kinds of violence, while the ghost
15 that whispers, "Leave here and destroy your children," has passed over every door and nailed it shut. Disassembling a marriage in these circumstances is as much *fun* as amputating your own gangrenous leg. You do it, if you can, to save a life—or two, or more.
20 I know of no one who really went looking to hoe the harder row, especially the daunting one of single parenthood. Yet it seems to be the most American of customs to blame the burdened for their destiny. We'd like so desperately to believe in freedom and justice for all, we
25 can hardly name that rogue bad luck, even when he's a close enough snake to bite us. In the wake of my divorce, some friends (even a few close ones) chose to vanish, rather than linger within striking distance of misfortune.
But most stuck around, bless their hearts, and if I'm any
30 the wiser for my trials, it's from having learned the worth of steadfast friendship. And also, what not to say. The least helpful question is: "Did you want the divorce, or didn't you?" Did I want to keep that gangrenous leg, or not? How to explain, in a culture that venerates choice: two terrifying

35 options are much worse than none at all. Give me any day the quick hand of cruel fate that will leave me scarred but blameless. As it was, I kept thinking of that wicked third-grade joke in which some boy comes up behind you and grabs your ear, starts in with a prolonged tug, and

40 asks, "Do you want this ear any longer?"

Still, the friend who holds your hand and says the wrong thing is made of dearer stuff than the one who stays away. And generally, through all of it, you live. My favorite fictional character, Kate Vaiden (in the novel by Reynolds

45 Price), advises: "Strength just comes in one brand—you stand up at sunrise and meet what they send you and keep your hair combed."

Once you've weathered the straits, you get to cross the tricky juncture from casualty to survivor. If you're on your

50 feet at the end of a year or two, and have begun putting together a happy new existence, those friends who were kind enough to feel sorry for you when you needed it must now accept you back to the ranks of the living. If you're truly blessed, they will dance at your second wedding.

55 Everybody else, for heaven's sake, should stop throwing stones.

1. Taken as a whole, the passage is best described as a(n)
   (A) technical analysis of social values
   (B) critique of a hypocritical society that condemns divorce
   (C) series of admonitions and predictions
   (D) discussion of the complexities accompanying the decision to divorce
   (E) evaluation of divorce and remarriage

2. Which of the following best summarizes Kingsolver's belief about divorce?
   (A) "You do it, if you can, to save a life—or two, or more." (lines 18–19)
   (B) "We'd like so desperately to believe in freedom and justice for all, we can hardly name that rogue bad luck, even when he's a close enough snake to bite us." (lines 23–26)
   (C) "Give me any day the quick hand of cruel fate that will leave me scarred but blameless." (lines 35–37)
   (D) "Once you've weathered the straits, you get to cross the tricky juncture from casualty to survivor." (lines 48–49)
   (E) "Everybody else, for heaven's sake, should stop throwing stones." (lines 55–56)

3. All of the following are metaphors EXCEPT
   (A) "stop throwing stones" (lines 55–56)
   (B) "linger within striking distance of misfortune" (line 28)
   (C) "they will dance at your second wedding" (line 54)
   (D) "A nonfunctioning marriage is a slow asphyxiation" (lines 9–10)
   (E) "you're on your feet at the end of a year or two" (lines 49–50)

4. In the context of the paragraph, "specious" (line 7) means
   (A) hollow
   (B) false
   (C) misleading
   (D) valid
   (E) justifiable

5. The writer "resent[s] the phrase 'irreconcilable differences'" (lines 4–5) because it suggests
   (A) legal jargon
   (B) the syllables suffocate just as divorce suffocates
   (C) the words can never be clearly defined
   (D) an excuse for something that is inevitable in any relationship
   (E) that what makes men and women different is negative

6. The images in lines 10–16 ("It is waking . . . nailed it shut") combine to form an impression of
   (A) passion and optimism
   (B) fear and menace
   (C) isolation and desperation
   (D) nostalgia and whimsy
   (E) hopelessness and despair

7. The pronoun "it" in line 10 ("It is waking . . .") refers to
   (A) "nonfunctioning marriage" (line 9)
   (B) "slow asphyxiation" (line 10)
   (C) "irreconcilable differences" (line 5)
   (D) "spouse's little quirks" (line 6)
   (E) "loneliness" (line 11)

8. Which of the following best describes the effect of the sentence in lines 16–19, "Disassembling a marriage . . . or two, or more"?
   (A) It implies evidence of the speaker's personal experience with the subject.
   (B) It characterizes the speaker as somewhat critical of the subject.
   (C) It intimidates the reader with its unexpected candor.
   (D) It provides evidence that the speaker is directing remarks to an audience of doctors.
   (E) It alerts the reader to a recurring image in the following paragraphs.

9. The phrase "airless house" (line 13) is most intensely and metaphorically connected to which word?
   (A) "pulse" (line 11)
   (B) "gospel" (line 12)
   (C) "asphyxiation" (line 10)
   (D) "venerates" (line 34)
   (E) "whispers" (line 15)

10. All of the following words sustain the primary tone of the first paragraph EXCEPT
    (A) "asphyxiation" (line 10)
    (B) "suicide" (line 14)
    (C) "despised" (line 10)
    (D) "stubborn" (line 6)
    (E) "gangrenous" (line 18)

11. The phrase "hoe the harder row" (lines 20–21) is an example of
    (A) personification
    (B) irony
    (C) metaphor
    (D) assonance
    (E) jargon

12. The phrase "within striking distance" (line 28) metaphorically implies a relationship between our narrator and
    (A) "destiny" (line 23)
    (B) "bad luck" (line 25)
    (C) "snake" (line 26)
    (D) "divorce" (line 26)
    (E) "misfortune" (line 28)

13. The presentation of material in the second paragraph (lines 20–28) is characterized primarily by
    (A) descriptions followed by amplifying statements
    (B) subtle and digressive rebuttals of earlier assertions
    (C) facts followed by wide-ranging analysis
    (D) generalizations followed by personal commentary
    (E) clichéd formulas followed by personal testimony

14. The narrative style of the passage is best described as
    (A) ornamental and reflective
    (B) pragmatic and personal
    (C) scathing and irreverent
    (D) patronizing and pretentious
    (E) solemn and detached

Questions 15–26 are based on Benjamin Franklin's letter to President George Washington regarding the new Constitution. Read the passage carefully before you choose your answers.

Mr. President:

I confess that there are several parts of this constitution which I do not at present approve, but I am not sure I shall never approve them; for having lived long, I have experienced many instances of being obliged by better information, or fuller consideration, to change opinions even on important subjects, which I once thought right, but found to be otherwise. It is therefore that the older I grow, the more apt I am to doubt my own judgment, and to pay more respect to the judgment of others.

Most men indeed as well as most sects in Religion, think themselves in possession of all truth, and that wherever others differ from them it is so far error.

5

10

15 Steele a Protestant in a Dedication tells the Pope, that the only difference between our Churches in their opinions of the certainty of their doctrines is, the Church of Rome is ***infallible*** and the Church of England is ***never in the wrong***. But though many

20 private persons think almost as highly of their own infallibility as of that of their sect, few express it so naturally as a certain French lady, who in a dispute with her sister, said "I don't know how it happens, Sister but I meet with no body but myself, that's

25 always in the right. 'Je ne trouve que moi qui aie toujours raison.'"

In these sentiments, Sir, I agree to this Constitution with all its faults, if they are such; because I think a general Government necessary for us, and there is no

30 form of Government but what may be a blessing to the people if well administered, and believe farther that this is likely to be well administered for a course of years, and can only end in Despotism, as other forms have done before it, when the people shall become so

35 corrupted as to need despotic Government, being incapable of any other.

I doubt too whether any other Convention we can obtain, may be able to make a better Constitution. For when you assemble a number of men to have the

40 advantage of their joint wisdom, you inevitably assemble with those men, all their prejudices, their passions, their errors of opinion, their local interests, and their selfish views. From such an assembly can a ***perfect*** production be expected? It therefore

45 astonishes me, Sir, to find this system approaching so near to perfection as it does; and I think it will astonish our enemies, who are waiting with confidence to hear that our councils are confounded like those of the Builders of Babel; and that our States are on the point

50 of separation, only to meet hereafter for the purpose of cutting one another's throats.

Thus I consent, Sir, to this Constitution because I expect no better, and because I am not sure, that it is not the best. The opinions I have had of its ***errors***, I

55 sacrifice to the public good. I have never whispered a syllable of them abroad. Within these walls they were born, and here they shall die. If every one of us in returning to our Constituents were to report the objections he has had to it, and endeavor to gain

60 partisans in support of them, we might prevent its being generally received, and thereby lose all the salutary effects and great advantages resulting naturally in our favor among foreign Nations as well as among ourselves, from our real or apparent

65 unanimity.

Much of the strength and efficiency of any Government in procuring and securing happiness to

70 the people, depends, on **opinion**, on the general opinion of the goodness of the Government, as well as of the wisdom and integrity of its Governors. I hope therefore that for our own sakes as a part of the people, and for the sake of posterity, we shall act heartily and unanimously in recommending this Constitution (if approved by Congress and confirmed 75 by the Conventions) wherever our influence may extend, and turn our future thoughts and endeavors to the means of having it **well** administered.

On the whole, Sir, I can not help expressing a wish that every member of the Convention who may still 80 have objections to it, would with me, on this occasion doubt a little of his own infallibility, and to make **manifest our unanimity**, put his name to this instrument.

15. At the conclusion of the letter, Franklin is recommending that the delegates
(A) approve the Constitution unanimously
(B) approve the Constitution but only after changes have been made
(C) approve or disapprove according to their personal beliefs
(D) disapprove the Constitution unanimously
(E) disapprove the Constitution but still seek approval by the states

16. Franklin says that increasing age is accompanied by
(A) surety and conviction
(B) willingness to compromise
(C) a lessening of influence
(D) a distrust of all argument
(E) doubt and uncertainty

17. The first paragraph has a long sentence followed by a relatively brief one. The purpose of this brief sentence can best be identified as doing which of the following?
(A) It counters the first sentence.
(B) It extends the argument of the first sentence.
(C) It provides an authoritarian validation of the initial premise.
(D) It begs the question about a word used in the first sentence.
(E) It functions as a transition to the second paragraph.

18. The purpose of the second paragraph is to provide examples of differences of opinion. The tone of the paragraph is
(A) contemptuous
(B) passionate
(C) satiric
(D) bantering
(E) foreboding

19. Paragraph three provides an example of a(n) _____
     argument.
     (A) bandwagon
     (B) ignorant
     (C) slippery slope
     (D) false analogy
     (E) ad hominem

20. The allusion to "Builders of Babel" (line 49) suggests that
     (A) any assembly of men will inevitably produce confusion
     (B) the new Constitution will defy God
     (C) the new Constitution has been pieced together and will
         gradually crumble over time
     (D) putting the new Constitution together has been time
         consuming
     (E) other documents based more on the Bible would be better

21. The fifth paragraph includes an example of
     (A) onomatopoeia
     (B) periodic sentences
     (C) apostrophe
     (D) hyperbole
     (E) personification

22. "Salutary" as employed in line 62 most likely means
     (A) cooperative
     (B) useful
     (C) beneficial
     (D) convenient
     (E) sick of

23. Franklin regards the attitude of other nations toward the young
    United States as one that can be characterized as
     (A) anticipating our success with hope
     (B) anticipating our success so we can pay our bills
     (C) filling their own coffers with our unprotected natural resources
     (D) waiting for our demise so they can pick up the vulnerable
         pieces
     (E) looking forward to our civil rebellions in order to sell us arms

24. What common aphorism would best express Franklin's attitude?
     (A) A stitch in time saves nine.
     (B) He who hesitates is lost.
     (C) Nothing is perfect.
     (D) Death comes to us all.
     (E) Two steps forward and one step back.

25. Franklin first explicitly states his support for the Constitution in
    paragraph
     (A) 1
     (B) 2
     (C) 3
     (D) 4
     (E) 5

26. Franklin's letter is written in a style that has many qualifying clauses. All of the following serve to qualify information in the sentence EXCEPT
   (A) "for having lived long" (lines 4–5)
   (B) "to pay more respect to the judgment of others" (lines 10–11)
   (C) "who in a dispute with her sister" (lines 22–23)
   (D) "if they are such" (line 28)
   (E) "if well administered" (line 31)

Questions 27–39 are based on the following excerpt from *The Real Thing* by Christina Slade. This particular chapter is titled "News as Soap Opera." Read the passage carefully before you choose your answers.

In 1998 and 1999, the State of the Union was again overshadowed; this time by the even less salubrious events of the Monica Lewinsky case.[1] In 1999 it was the curiously modern event of the Internet release of the documents put
5 forward as evidence in the case to impeach the President. Materials had been released which had the potential of unprecedented public importance, yet had an unprecedentedly private flavor. By 2000, in fact, the State of the Union had become a sideshow: the last quack of the so-
10 called "lame duck presidency." The good economic news and worthy programs announced by Clinton were rarely mentioned in the press coverage; the focus was on the forthcoming presidential election.

The issue here is not that the media is failing to tell the
15 truth. For the reports on Monica, O.J. and the State of the Nation are *true*. Few claims made on the television news are made without evidence. What O.J.'s judge, Monica, and Starr said are accurately reported, with all the objectivity which has become the hallmark of contemporary
20 journalism. Yet the feel is at best insalubrious; the overall impression is of news that is not true.

There is an increasing tendency for news to adopt the generic conventions of the soap opera.[2] Soap opera's repertoire of plots, from romance to violence, are domestic
25 in focus and designed so that the story goes on forever. The characters are also from a limited repertoire, with good looks and sporting prowess pitted against evil and the terrors of female sexual aggression. O.J. fits the mold, whereas the State of the Union, dealing with the large
30 public issues of the economy, education, and health does not. And competition it is—as the commentators the next day made clear. Networks and cable channels are out for consumers' blood. Television sells consumers to advertisers, not news to citizens, and consumers prefer

[1] Carlos Fuentes (1998) actually called the Monica Lewinsky case "a global telenovela."
[2] John Ellis's *Visible Fictions* (1982) is a notable precursor to the argument I propound here, but with a different focus. Catherine Lumby's *Gotcha* (1999) contains an excellent recent exposition similar to the views about news I develop here.

35   O.J.[3] In the event, there was a twist to the final score. For an unprecedented number of viewers saw the State of the Union simply because they were already tuned in, waiting for the O.J. result. Happily, the result was delayed, and the President was nearly finished when he lost the limelight.

27. The title of the article best suggests which of the following?
    (A) News has evolved into soap opera.
    (B) People prefer news that is about sex and scandal to news about international conflicts and environmental damage
    (C) News is more important than soap operas in the ratings.
    (D) Newscasters use the news to advertise other programming.
    (E) Soap operas now include major world and national events to attract viewers.

28. The words "salubrious" (line 2) and "insalubrious" (line 20) are used to suggest
    (A) destruction and restoration
    (B) sensual awareness and mental awareness
    (C) growth and decay
    (D) catharsis and repression
    (E) health and illness

29. All of the following are negative metaphors EXCEPT
    (A) "final score" (line 35)
    (B) "sideshow" (line 9)
    (C) "consumers' blood" (line 33)
    (D) "soap opera" (line 23)
    (E) "tuned in" (line 37)

30. The sentence "Materials had been . . ." (lines 6–8) creates its paradoxical nature through
    (A) the use of "yet" instead of "but"
    (B) parallel use of "unprecedented" and "unprecedentedly"
    (C) a contrast between public and private
    (D) the indefinite nature of the noun "materials"
    (E) a metaphor of food implied in the word "flavor"

31. The word "sideshow" (line 9) evokes all of the following for the State of the Union EXCEPT
    (A) circus
    (B) freaks
    (C) insignificant
    (D) exhibition
    (E) historic

---

[3] Ralph Begleiter of CNN claimed at a Media Studies Forum, New York (20 February 1997) that CNN's ratings quintupled as a result of their choice to run the first O.J. trial. The public taste for the trial proved utterly insatiable.

32. Footnote 1 suggests that Carlos Fuentes
    (A) wrote about the Lewinsky scandal for a largely corporate audience
    (B) was quoted by Christina Slade
    (C) wrote in 1998 and was prophetic about the Clinton scandal
    (D) implies that the Clinton scandal had an international impact
    (E) was misquoted by others but quoted correctly by Slade

33. Footnote 2 suggests that
    (A) both Ellis and Lumby would agree with Slade's argument
    (B) both Ellis and Slade got similar ideas from Lumby
    (C) Lumby's work is not copyrighted
    (D) the issue of news as something other than news began with the actual advent of television in the 1950s
    (E) *Visible Fictions* and *Gotcha* are novels about the television news industry

34. Footnote 3 informs us of all of the following EXCEPT
    (A) Begleiter spoke at a Media Studies Forum
    (B) Begleiter worked for CNN
    (C) Begleiter made a speech on February 20, 1997
    (D) The CNN decision to show the O.J. Simpson trial was a smart one
    (E) CNN had little influence on subsequent news television

35. The word *"true"* (line 16) is in italics because the news on television is
    (A) false
    (B) only sometimes true
    (C) always true
    (D) true but does not always tell the whole truth
    (E) true but only when it is about political events

36. Slade reminds us that television news is primarily a
    (A) vehicle of entertainment
    (B) transition to entertainment programming
    (C) travesty
    (D) routine for providing good feelings
    (E) source of valid information

37. In her brief discussion of soap operas, Slade suggests that the soaps feature all of the following EXCEPT
    (A) conventional romance
    (B) handsome men and attractive women
    (C) unusual or bizarre story lines
    (D) evil linked to powerful female aggression
    (E) domestic crises

38. The use of the word "score" (line 35) is a pun on which of the
following?
I.   Simpson's football career
II. The outcome of a political debate
III. Television ratings
(A) I only
(B) III only
(C) I and II
(D) II and III
(E) I and III

39. "Happily" (line 38) carries what tone?
(A) Exuberant
(B) Sardonic
(C) Bitter
(D) Candid
(E) Passionate

Questions 40–52 are based on the following excerpt from Judith Ortiz Cofer's "The Myth
of the Latin Woman: I Just Met a Girl Named María." Read the passage carefully before
you choose your answers.

This is what I have gleaned from my discussions as an adult
with older Puerto Rican women. They have told me about
dressing in their best party clothes on Saturday nights and
going to the town's plaza to promenade with their
5   girlfriends in front of the boys they liked. The males were
thus given an opportunity to admire the women and to
express their admiration in the form of *piropos:* erotically
charged street poems they composed on the spot. I have
been subjected to a few piropos while visiting the Island,
10 and they can be outrageous, although custom dictates that
they must never cross into obscenity. This ritual, as I
understand it, also entails a show of studied indifference on
the woman's part; if she is "decent," she must not
acknowledge the man's impassioned words. So I do
15 understand how things can be lost in translation. When a
Puerto Rican girl dressed in her idea of what is attractive
meets a man from the mainstream culture who has been
trained to react to certain types of clothing as a sexual
signal, a clash is likely to take place. The line I first heard
20 based on this aspect of the myth happened when the boy
who took me to my first formal dance leaned over to plant a
sloppy overeager kiss painfully on my mouth, and when I
didn't respond with sufficient passion said in a resentful
tone: "I thought you Latin girls were supposed to mature
25 early"—my first instance of being thought of as a fruit or
vegetable—I was supposed to *ripen,* not just grow into
womanhood like other girls.
      It is surprising to some of my professional friends that
some people, including those who should know better, still
30 put others "in their place." Though rarer, these incidents
are still commonplace in my life. It happened to me most
recently during a stay at a very classy metropolitan hotel

favored by young professional couples for their weddings. Late one evening after the theater, as I walked toward my room with my new colleague (a woman with whom I was coordinating an arts program), a middle-aged man in a tuxedo, a young girl in satin and lace on his arm, stepped directly into our path. With his champagne glass extended toward me, he exclaimed, "Evita!"

Our way blocked, my companion and I listened as the man half-recited, half-bellowed "Don't Cry for Me, Argentina." When he finished, the young girl said: "How about a round of applause for my daddy?" We complied, hoping this would bring the spectacle to a close. I was becoming aware that our little group was attracting the attention of the other guests. "Daddy" must have perceived this too, and he once more barred the way as we tried to walk past him. He began to shout-sing a ditty to the tune of "La Bamba"—except the lyrics were abut a girl named María whose exploits all rhymed with her name and gonorrhea. The girl kept saying "Oh, Daddy" and looking at me with pleading eyes. She wanted me to laugh along with the others. My companion and I stood silently waiting for the man to end his offensive song. When he finished, I looked not at him but at his daughter. I advised her calmly never to ask her father what he had done in the army. Then I walked between them and to my room. My friend complimented me on my cool handling of the situation. I confessed to her that I really had wanted to push the jerk into the swimming pool. I knew that this same man— probably a corporate executive, well educated, even worldly by most standards—would not have been likely to regale a white woman with a dirty song in public. He would perhaps have checked his impulse by assuming that she could be somebody's wife or mother, or at least *somebody* who might take offense. But to him, I was just an Evita or a María; merely a character in his cartoon-populated universe.

Because of my education and my proficiency with the English language, I have acquired many mechanisms for dealing with the anger I experience. This was not true for my parents, nor is it true for the many Latin women working at menial jobs who must put up with stereotypes about our ethnic group such as: "They make good domestics." This is another facet of the myth of the Latin woman in the United States. Its origin is simple to deduce. Work as domestics, waitressing, and factory jobs are all that's available to women with little English and few skills. The myth of the Hispanic menial has been sustained by the same media phenomenon that made "Mammy" from *Gone with the Wind* America's idea of the black woman for generations; María, the housemaid or counter girl, is now indelibly etched into the national psyche. The big and the little screens have presented us with the picture of the funny Hispanic maid, mispronouncing words and cooking up a spicy storm in a shiny California kitchen.

40. Cofer suggests that the primary purpose of the passage is to
    (A) explore the cultural differences that lead to particular stereotypes of Latin women
    (B) analyze the myths of Latin women
    (C) compare stereotypes of the Latin woman with the black woman
    (D) describe the incidents that occurred in the speaker's past
    (E) show readers how to deal with anger that stems from unfair treatment

41. Which of the following best describes the tone of the passage?
    (A) Baffled
    (B) Critical
    (C) Disdainful
    (D) Objective
    (E) Moralistic

42. The function of the opening sentence might best be described as
    (A) anticipating a possible fallacious claim
    (B) qualifying a culturally accepted statement
    (C) rebutting an common argument
    (D) stating an immediate objection
    (E) establishing her credibility for the discourse that follows

43. In the context of the paragraph, "things can be lost in translation" (line 15) evokes which of the following meanings?
    I.   Cultural
    II. Linguistic
    III. Political
    (A) I only
    (B) II only
    (C) I and II only
    (D) II and III only
    (E) I, II, and III

44. Cofer's comparison of Latin girls to ripened fruit and vegetables (lines 24–27) does all of the following EXCEPT
    (A) suggest that Latin girls are not intellectually stimulating
    (B) introduce one of several cultural stereotypes that appear in subsequent paragraphs
    (C) imply an economic value on Latin girls' sexuality
    (D) recall the cultural clash referred to earlier in the passage
    (E) emphasize the dehumanization of Latin girls

45. In line 30, the commonly used phrase "in their place" most correctly refers to
    (A) education and racial status
    (B) political and national status
    (C) political and economic status
    (D) racial and economic status
    (E) national and education status

46. The author's description of the hotel at which she is staying as "a very classy metropolitan hotel favored by young professional couples for their weddings" is employed to
    (A) emphasize the inappropriate behavior of the man
    (B) illustrate the author's wealth
    (C) imply that the author is attending a wedding
    (D) underscore the irony inherent in the situation
    (E) suggest that the author is attempting to escape her cultural roots

47. All of the following are used by Cofer to criticize the propensity toward ethnic stereotyping EXCEPT
    (A) "ripen" (line 26)
    (B) "professional friends" (line 28)
    (C) "those who should know better" (line 29)
    (D) "after the theater" (line 34)
    (E) "Evita!" (line 39)

48. In the context of the paragraph, the author's reference to the man as "Daddy" (line 46) serves to do all of the following EXCEPT
    (A) create ironic tension between the man's parental role and his inappropriate public behavior
    (B) identify the subject of the sentence
    (C) refer to the child's presence and the father's relative incompetence as a parent
    (D) emphasize his drunkenness
    (E) show the author's contempt for the man

49. Cofer's advice to the child "never to ask her father what he had done in the army" (line 56) implies chiefly that
    (A) the girl will be appalled at the violence and abuse her father has suffered
    (B) the man was an instrument of the government that strove to suppress third-world countries
    (C) the man probably has viewed and treated women as nothing more than sexual objects since his young adulthood
    (D) the girl would learn that her father sees her as a commodity rather than a person
    (E) the girl would find the psychological reason for her father's drunkenness

50. The sentence that begins in line 69 ("Because of my education . . .") marks a shift from
    (A) discursive reflection to direct argument
    (B) an historic perspective to a modern one
    (C) an unqualified claim to narrative description
    (D) exaggerated pathos to didactic logos
    (E) a cynical viewpoint to an objective one

51. A central contrast presented in the passage is that between
    (A) men and women
    (B) stereotypes and reality
    (C) Caucasians and Hispanics
    (D) women and culture
    (E) the educated majority and the illiterate minority

52. The author's primary purpose in referring to "Mammy" from *Gone with the Wind* is
    (A) to bring literary culture to her essay
    (B) to remind readers of the hardships faced by minorities
    (C) to compare the stereotypes of Hispanic maids to the previous ones of black maids
    (D) to show the pervasiveness of the media's influence in society's thinking
    (E) to show a valid form of work available for women with little education

English Language and Composition Exam
Section II

Question 1

Reading time: 15 minutes
Suggested writing time: 40 minutes

(This question counts as one-third of the total essay section score.)

Directions: The following prompt is based on the eight accompanying sources.

The question requires you to integrate a variety of sources into a coherent, well-written essay. Refer to the sources to support your position; avoid mere paraphrase or summary. Your argument should be central; the sources should support this argument.

Remember to attribute both direct and indirect citations.

INTRODUCTION

Plastic bags, plastic wrap, plastic sheeting, and the like are all very much a part of our commercial culture. However, nearly all the plastic materials we use every day are nonbiodegradable. They will remain in landfills for centuries. Plastic also litters the landscape and causes havoc for marine life. It is also more expensive to recycle than it is to make in the first place. Recently, there have been significant politically legislated efforts to reduce the amount of plastic used. Most notably, Ireland placed a fifteen-cent tax on every plastic bag removed from a store.

ASSIGNMENT

Read the following sources (including any introductory information) carefully. Then, in an essay that synthesizes at least three of the sources for support, take a position that defends, challenges, or qualifies the claim that legislation should be initiated in the United States to impose a tax on plastic bags in order to reduce their use.

Refer to the sources as Source A, Source B, etc.; titles are included for your convenience.

  Source A (BBC News)
  Source B (Wikipedia)
  Source C (Environmental Literary Council)
  Source D (Starr)
  Source E (Gay)
  Source F (Grassroots Recycling)
  Source G (Oxo-biodegradable Plastics)
  Source H (Institute for Lifecycle)

Source A

"Why can't we recycle all this plastic?" BBC NEWS Magazine. 19 September 2003.

Why can't we recycle all this plastic?

BBC News Online

A trip to the shops these days is likely to result in almost as much packaging as food. And once used, these wrappers, bags and trays are destined for the bin. Ever tried to find a place to recycle plastics in the UK? It's a fruitless mission.

Shopping list: Nectarines, kiwifruit, avocado, goat's cheese, baked potatoes, sliced ham, olives, and cheesecake for afters.

Rubbish generated: four plastic bags, clingfilm, six plastic pots, trays—one polystyrene foam, two plastic and one pulped cardboard—a cake-shaped plastic box with plastic windows, all packed in a plastic carrier bag.

So what to do with this lot once lunch has been scoffed? Straight into the bin it goes. While we are encouraged—and soon will be required by law—to recycle our waste, it is not always straightforward to put this into practice.

One tray made from cardboard is biodegradable and can be composted (by those with gardens). While the local supermarket has a collection point for carrier bag recycling, no other type of plastic is accepted.

Down the road at the recycling centre, there are bins for newspapers, aluminum cans, glass, even clothing and shoes, but not plastics. The local council is not much help either; plastic isn't included in the curbside collection.

Source B

"Plastic Shopping Bag" <u>Wikipedia.</u> http://en.wikipedia.org/wiki/Plastic_shopping_bag.
18 April 2007. 4–5.

Solutions by country

Australia

In Australia shoppers are now encouraged to buy bags called "green bags," which cost a few dollars, but can be reused many times. The bags are coloured depending on the company that sells them. Some "green bags" are insulated for carrying hot or cold items.

Ireland

On March 4, 2002, the Republic of Ireland introduced a 15 cent levy on every plastic shopping bag. This led to people cutting down on plastic bags by 95% and using reusable bags. The money gathered by the levy was used to raise money for environmental initiatives.

Japan

Almost any store you visit in Japan, from convenience stores to street vendors, will also net you a free plastic bag for your purchase. Although there are some supermarkets (like *Kyoto Co-op)* which charge for plastic bags, this is by no means the norm. Many supermarkets (like *Izumiya)* will give you extra points on your point-card if you bring your own bag.

Germany

Generally, most German supermarkets charge between 5 and 10 cents per single-use bag, depending on the type of bag. Most shops also offer cloth bags or sturdier, woven plastic bags for about €1, encouraging shoppers to re-use them. Many high-street retail shops will provide plastic bags free of charge. Most people will re-use single-use shopping bags, i.e. for collecting deposit bottles or using them as bin liners.

United States

Plastic bags largely displaced paper bags as the most common type of shopping bag during the late 1980s and early 1990s. There has been no broad government action against the litter problem, although some local governments have enacted ordinances, and many stores allow customers to return the bags for recycling. Empty bags carried on the wind are popularly known as "urban tumbleweed."

On March 27, 2007, the City and County of San Francisco became the first city to ban a certain kind of plastic bag. Starting in July 2007, all large supermarkets in the state of California will be required, by law, to take back and recycle shopping bags.

Source C

"Paper or Plastic," <u>Environmental Literacy Council.</u>
http://www.enviroliteracy.org/article.php/1268.html. 18 April 2007.

Both paper and plastic bags have to be transported to stores, which requires energy and creates emissions. In this comparison, plastic is preferable because plastic bags are lighter in weight and more compact than paper bags. It would take approximately seven trucks to transport the same number of paper bags as can be transported by a single truck full of plastic bags.

The disposal of bags entails additional environmental aspects. If landfilled, plastic bags are more environmentally benign than paper, as they require less space; paper occupies approximately half of overall landfill volume. Plastics (not just bags) generate 14 to 28 percent of the volume of trash in general, but because much of it can be compressed, only 9 to 12 percent of the volume of waste in landfills. Although plastics do not biodegrade, modern landfills are designed in such a way that *nothing* biodegrades, because the waste is isolated from air and water in order to prevent groundwater contamination and air pollution. As manufacturers have continued to make their plastic packaging thinner and lighter to save materials, the percentage of landfill volume taken up by plastics has remained steady since 1970 even as plastics have become more widely used.

Source D

Starr, Roger, "The Effectiveness of Recycling Is Exaggerated." From *Garbage and Waste*. Ed. Charles Cozic. San Diego: Greenhaven Press, Inc., 1997. 145.

Other industry leaders suggest that the recycling business needs what they call "a level playing field." By this they mean that products made with recycled material should be as readily acceptable to potential buyers as anything made from previously unused fibers and chemicals. Their specific proposal, already adopted by some governmental institutions, gives a new slant to the meaning of "level." It suggests that all local and state governments, together with the national government, be required to purchase and use a defined percentage of their office supplies and other sundries made from recycled materials. They recommend further that governments be allowed to accept bids, even though the asking prices for recycled products are as much as 15 percent higher than those of competitive virgin products. Such price concessions favoring recycled products are already offered by some local governments. While they demonstrate that recycling is not the cheap and easy matter that would make a substantial market share easy to obtain, this favoritism is simply a tax that prefers one class of producer over all others.

Source E

Gay, Kathlyn. *Global Garbage*. New York: Impact Books, 1992. 118.

Still, there are many debates over the types of products that are truly "green." For example, there is no consensus on whether paper products are always better to use than plastic materials. It is common knowledge that plastic materials clog landfills because they do not biodegrade and may be intact for centuries. Plastic manufacturing also generates hazardous waste. But paper products account for most of the material dumped in landfills, and they are compacted so tightly, without air and light, that they cannot break down either. Paper mills also generate many toxins.

Martin B. Hocking, a chemistry professor at the University of Victoria in British Columbia, compared the manufacture of polystyrene cups with those made of paper. In a report in *Science*, Hocking concluded that plastic cups used fewer raw materials and generated less waste. "Six times as much wood pulp as polystyrene is required to make a cup," Hocking found, and manufacturing a paper cup consumes more energy and water. He also noted that resins used to waterproof paper cups make them impossible to recycle.

Source F

"Paper or Plastic?" Grassroots Recycling Network.
http://www.grrn.org/resources/paper_plastic.html. 18 April 2007.

Paper or Plastic? (Either is good if reused)

In 1980, many supermarkets switched from using paper bags to plastic since the plastic (polyethylene) bags are less expensive. Because many customers complained, grocery stores now give a choice between paper and plastic. Some shoppers choose paper assuming it is an environmentally better alternative. But is this the case?

In a comparison of the two types of grocery bags, Franklin Associates[*] concluded that the manufacture of plastic bags produced considerably less air pollution, waterborne wastes, and industrial solid-waste than the manufacture of paper. Because plastic bags are lighter, they also produce less post-consumer solid waste, taking up less space in landfills. Researchers found that plastic sacks have these advantages even when grocery store clerks pack less in each bag, thereby using 1.5 or 2 times as many plastic bags to pack the same groceries as paper.

Energy-wise, it is a tie. Plastic bags required slightly less energy to manufacture at a use rate of 1.5 to 1 compared with paper and more energy at a use rate of 2 to 1. Paper bags are better because they are made from wood, a renewable resource, while plastic bags are made from petroleum. Also paper grocery bags are recycled at a higher rate and are reused more frequently, since many home kitchen trash containers are designed with paper grocery bags in mind.

In the end, it is a toss-up whether paper or plastic grocery bags are better for the environment. The important thing is to reuse paper and plastic bags over and over. Best still is to bring your own cloth bags or ask store clerks to hand you easily transportable items without bags.

[*]Brower, Michael & Leon, Warren (1999). *The Consumer's Guide to Effective Environmental Choices—Practical Advice from the Union of Concerned Scientists,* Three Rivers Press, New York, pp. 132-133.

Source G

"Biodegradable Plastics." Oxo-biodegradable Plastics Institute. www.oxobio.org. 20 April 2007.

Purpose: This paper has been prepared by the Oxo-biodegradable Plastics Institute (OPI) in order to provide a non-technical overview of degradable plastics that, it is hoped, can provide some assistance to policy makers in their consideration of the way in which these materials can contribute to the environmentally sound management of solid waste in their jurisdictions.

Introduction: Products made from plastics have been widely used since about the 1950s. The number of applications for these products has continued to grow as science has yielded resins and resin blends with enhanced properties and also the technologies to process these resins into products and to use them. Some of the general features of plastics that make them attractive for many of the common uses with which they are associated, including packaging, are strength and toughness, durability and long life, light weight, excellent barrier properties for water and gases, resistance to most chemical agents, excellent processability, and low cost. These properties that make plastics the material of choice for many applications are also problematic at the end of the useful life of these products, particularly single use products such as bags and other forms of packaging. Their inherent inertness allows them to persist in the environment and their low cost makes them highly disposable.

Plastics, while they are ubiquitous, are not the major constituent of municipal waste streams. A recent study in California found that 9.6% of landfilled waste was plastic and only a fraction of this was packaging materials. Waste paper products, organic matter and construction waste together accounted for almost ¾ of total waste. Nonetheless, discarded plastic products are unsightly and cause other problems when ingested by wildlife or when as bags, they form a barrier between the environment and the refuse they contain and limit the ability of the contained material to biodegrade.

Jurisdictions around the world have used a variety of strategies to deal with this issue, particularly as it relates to plastic bags. Taiwan has banned plastic bags, Ireland taxes them, California mandates the use of a fraction of recycled materials in their manufacture, Europe has mandated their exclusion from the organic refuse stream which is destined for composting, others consider the use of biodegradable technologies. There are pros and cons associated with each of these strategies— environmental and/or economic. OPI represents an industry that offers a viable alternative that fits in this overall spectrum—relatively low cost degradable products that safely return to the environment in certain disposal situations via a scientifically well understood route.

Source H

Institute for Lifecycle Environmental Assessment.
http://www.ilea.org/lcas/franklin1990.html. 20 April 2007.

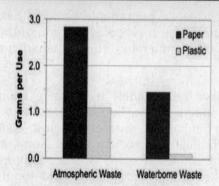

Figure 1 – Grams of atmospheric and waterborne waste at current recycling rates. Atmospheric waste contributes to smog and acid rain. Waterborne waste disrupts associated ecosystems.

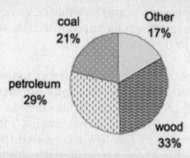

Figure 2 – Energy distribution for paper bags at current recycling levels.

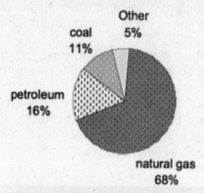

Figure 3 – Energy distribution for plastic bags at current recycling levels.

Question 2

Suggested time: 40 minutes

(This question counts as one-third of the total essay section score.)

The passage below is an excerpt from an essay by John Donne. It appeared in a larger collection of essays, *Paradoxes*. Read the passage carefully. Then, in a well-written essay, analyze the rhetorical devices Donne uses to craft his justification for and delight in women's changeableness.

From *Paradoxes*
A Defence of Women's Inconstancy

That women are inconstant, I with any man confess. But that inconstancy is a bad quality I against any man will maintain; for every thing, as it is one better than another, so is it fuller of change. The heavens themselves continually turn, the stars move, the moon changeth, fire whirleth, air flieth, water ebbs and flows, the face of the earth altereth her looks, time stays not, the colour that hath most light will take most dyes; so in men, they that have the most reason are the most alterable in their designs, and the darkest and most ignorant do seldomest change. Therefore women changing more than men have also more reason, they cannot be immutable like stocks, like stones, like the earth's dull centre. Gold that lieth still rusteth, water corrupteth, and air that moveth not poisoneth. Then why should that which is the perfection of other things be imputed to women as greatest imperfections? Because thereby they deceive men? Are not your wits pleased with those jests which cozen your expectation? You can call it pleasure to be beguiled in trifles, and in the most excellent toy in the world you call it treachery. I would you had your mistresses so constant that they would never change, no not so much as their smocks, then should you see what a sluttish virtue constancy were. Inconstancy is a most commendable and cleanly quality; and women in this quality are far more absolute than the heavens, than the stars, than moon, or anything beneath it, for long observation hath picked certainty out of this mutability. The learned are so well acquainted with the stars signs and planets that they make them but characters to read the meaning of the heaven in his own forehead. Every simple fellow can bespeak the change of the moon a great while before hand. But I would fain have the learnedest man so skilful as to tell when the simplest woman meaneth to vary. Learning affords no rules to know, much less knowledge to rule the mind of a woman. For as philosophy teacheth us, that light things do always tend upwards, and heavy things decline downwards, experience teacheth us otherwise, that the disposition of a light woman is to fall down; the nature of women being contrary to all art and nature. . . .

To conclude, therefore, this name of inconstancy which hath been so much poisoned with slanders ought to be changed into variety, for the which the world is so delightful, and a woman for that the most delightful thing in the world.

Question 3

Suggested time: 40 minutes

(This question counts as one-third of the total essay section score.)

The passage below is an excerpt from "So what do you have to do to find happiness?" by Dorothy Wade. Her article primarily discusses the work of Martin Seligman (author of *Authentic Happiness*) and others who believe that humans are hard-wired for negativity. Read the passage carefully. Then write an essay in which you support, refute, or qualify the observation that happiness is a short-lived and fleeting human condition. Support your position with evidence from your own reading, observation, and/or experience.

> Survival in a time of adversity forged our brains into a persistent mould. Professor Seligman says: "Because our brain evolved during a time of ice, flood and famine, we have a catastrophic brain. The way the brain works is looking for what's wrong. The problem is, that worked in the Pleistocene era. It favoured you, but it doesn't work in the modern world."
>
> Although most people rate themselves as happy, there is a wealth of evidence to show that negative thinking is deeply ingrained in the human psyche. Experiments show that we remember failures more vividly than successes. We dwell on what went badly, not what went well. When life runs smoothly, we're on autopilot—we're only in a state of true consciousness when we notice the stone in our shoe.
>
> Of the six universal emotions, four—anger, fear, disgust and sadness—are negative, and only one, joy, is positive. (The sixth, surprise, is neutral.) According to the psychologist Daniel Nettle, author of *Happiness* and one of the Royal Institution lecturers, the negative emotions each tell us "something bad has happened" and suggest a different course of action. Fear tells us danger is near, so run away. Anger prompts us to deter aggressors. Sadness warns us to be cautious and save energy, while disgust urges us to avoid contamination.

STOP

END OF EXAM

Answers and Explanations for the Diagnostic Test

Using the table below, score your test and determine how many questions you answered correctly and incorrectly. Then look over the answer explanations.

Answer Key for Multiple-Choice Questions

1. D	2. A	3. C	4. C	5. D	6. E
7. A	8. A	9. C	10. D	11. C	12. C
13. D	14. B	15. A	16. E	17. B	18. D
19. C	20. A	21. E	22. C	23. D	24. C
25. C	26. B	27. B	28. E	29. E	30. C
31. E	32. D	33. A	34. E	35. D	36. A
37. C	38. E	39. B	40. A	41. B	42. E
43. C	44. A	45. D	46. D	47. B	48. C
49. C	50. A	51. B	52. D		

Answers and Explanations for Multiple-Choice Questions

1. **Answer: D** Throughout the passage, Kingsolver discusses the many complex personal issues and questions that arise when one must consider divorce. She does not analyze social values, critique the hypocrisy of her society, predict, or evaluate divorce in any measure.

2. **Answer: A** The force of the passage arises from the author's conviction that divorce does not happen because of "irreconcilable differences" (lines 4–5), but because there is emotional, mental, or physical danger present in the marriage that is harmful to the spouses and any children in the home.

3. **Answer: C** All of the answer choices are metaphors except C, since the author is literally accepting that it is quite feasible that friends will dance at one's second wedding.

4. **Answer: C** In context, "specious" best means misleading. Kingsolver tells of her discontent with the phrase "irreconcilable differences" and states that every couple has such differences. Thus, her meaning best implies that it is a misleading phrase, rather than a false one.

5. **ANSWER: D** Kingsolver explicitly declares that all marriages have irreconcilable differences. Therefore, to use that as an excuse for divorce is both hypocritical and contrary to common sense. She prefers honesty to excuses.

6. **ANSWER: E** The images and feelings of loneliness, being unloved, suicide, potential violence, and an inescapable coffin coalesce into hopelessness and despair about one's situation.

7. **ANSWER: A** To determine the correct answer to this question, substitute each answer choice for the pronoun and decide if the sentence retains the same meaning. In this case, a "nonfunctioning marriage" is one in which a person wakes up feeling despised and lonely.

8. **ANSWER: A** The effect of these lines is to show the reader that Kingsolver has personal experience with divorce. It does not show her as critical of divorce; it is not meant to intimidate the reader; the author is most definitely not speaking to a group of doctors; and although the "gangrenous leg" reappears in subsequent paragraphs, it is not meant to emphasize the image.

9. **ANSWER: C** Airlessness implies suffocation, which most closely ties to asphyxiation.

10. **ANSWER: D** The tone of the first paragraph derives its strength from the repetitive imagery of death, disease, and loss. The word "stubborn" implies impetuous behavior instead of despair.

11. **ANSWER: C** While this is a common phrase, a cliché, you are not offered the answers of aphorism or cliché. Since it means to follow the more difficult path in life, it is clearly a metaphor and none of the other answers apply.

12. **ANSWER: C** The author refers to bad luck and misfortune as a snake, a metaphor that is further carried out by the knowledge that snakes strike their prey; thus, one must stay out of striking distance of a snake in order to remain safe from its venom.

13. **ANSWER: D** Kingsolver begins the paragraph with vague generalizations about single parenthood and society's beliefs, but ends the paragraph with personal remarks about her own divorce and the friends she lost as a result.

14. **ANSWER: B** The author is practical and personal in discussing her own divorce and the effect it had on her life. Answer A is not correct because the writer's style is not ornamental—her writing style is neither lavish nor complex. Finally, although the writer may offer a few scathing remarks, her overall style is not ornamental, scathing, pretentious, or detached. As a special note, be aware that the College Board likes to use the word "ornamental," which, as you might guess, describes writing that is particularly complex, fancy, and difficult. It is the opposite of "plain style."

15. **ANSWER: A** Franklin makes it clear in the third paragraph that, despite his objections, he favors the constitution, and in the last paragraph, he says that it should "manifest our unanimity."

16. **ANSWER: E** In the first paragraph, Franklin clearly expresses increasing doubt in his own opinion as he ages. The good distractor here is B, for Franklin's doubt makes him willing to compromise. This type of question demonstrates how there can be two or more answers with plausible distractors. However, the right answer will always be supported by a close reading of the text.

17. **ANSWER: B** This is a question with another good distractor, E. However, the second sentence clearly elaborates on the point made in the first sentence. The second paragraph develops an inductive argument on religious righteousness and infallibility, which Franklin calls into question. But the better answer is B.

18. **ANSWER: D** The best way to characterize the second paragraph is to say that it has a kind of gentle humor. Those who think they know the truth also think that others do not. So who is right? Franklin finds such religious feuding somewhat, as he would say it, "French." The best word for humor here is "bantering."

19. **ANSWER: C** This question is a reminder that learning some of the common fallacies of logic is a good thing for this test. However, you need to know only the most common ones. Slippery slope is also called "the domino effect." If one thing happens (i.e., I give you my car keys), an extreme result will follow (i.e., I am likely to never see the car again). Franklin notes that all "poorly administered" governments inevitably slide into a form of "despotism."

20. **ANSWER: A** The College Board expects students to be conversant in common allusions from history, mythology, and the Judeo-Christian tradition. The Tower of Babel is in Genesis and describes an arrogant humanity building a tower to the heavens. God destroyed it and scattered humankind and afflicted peoples with different languages so they could not communicate. Hence, the answer is A.

21. **ANSWER: E** Franklin's opinions "were born" and "shall die." That is a personification of his ideas.

22. **ANSWER: C** Because it's paired with "great advantages," "salutary" must be a positive word. D is neutral and E is negative. Plug in each of the three positives; "beneficial" is the best fit.

23. **ANSWER: D** The answer is in the fourth paragraph, where "our enemies" are anticipating the destruction of this American republic. The language is clearly negative, so A and B are out. Of the negatives, there is no clear language about "natural resources" or the "selling of arms." Answer D is the best answer by a process of elimination.

24. **ANSWER: C** Franklin loved aphorisms—cute, quick truisms. There are two right answers. There is a sense in Franklin that we need to get this done, so B looks good, but there is also a sense from him throughout this letter that he will accept it because there is no way that it will ever

satisfy everyone. We will take what we can get. Hence the better answer is C.

25. **ANSWER: C** This is a straightforward question. He clearly defines his acceptance of the document in the third paragraph.

26. **ANSWER: B** A "clause" has a verb and can be "independent"—which means simply that it's a complete sentence—or "dependent"—which means that it cannot stand alone. The last seven words of the sentence you just read are a dependent clause. "Which" implies that it is not a complete thought in and of itself. The last seven words are also "qualifying" since the clause helps clarify what the word "dependent" means. This question reminds you that the AP test will ask about grammar terms. As you look at the answers, you will recognize that all of the answers except B are "qualifying clauses." Answer B is an infinitive, which does not help clarify or add information to the noun.

27. **ANSWER: B** This is one of those questions with two possible right answers. C, D, and E are ideas that cannot be extrapolated from the article, so you are left with A or B. The title of the chapter alone seems to suggest A. However, the excerpt clearly identifies a viewership that sees the news as a kind of entertainment. Therefore, B is the answer that best identifies the intention of the author.

28. **ANSWER: E** Notice in line 2 that "salubrious" has the adverb "less" in front of it as it refers to Monica Lewinsky. Therefore, the word requires a positive connotation. "Insalubrious" in line 16 is in a sentence that suggests the news is not good. A, C and E all suggest antonyms of one another. Only C and E have the positive and negative words in the right order. Growth just does not work in line 2, so the best answer is E.

29. **ANSWER: E** If you paid attention to "EXCEPT," you were looking for something neutral or positive as the answer. Only E fulfills that criterion.

30. **ANSWER: C** Here's another question with only one right answer and a tempting alternative. Paradox creates contradiction within the structure of a sentence or a couple of sentences. B's use of the adjective and adverb is a brilliant twist of language by the author, but it does not create a paradox. However, the opposition of "public" and "private" to describe the same thing is certainly a paradox.

31. **ANSWER: E** To some extent, this takes us back to question 29. Always notice if one question can help you with another. The word "sideshow" is clearly pejorative. Although "circus" is not always negative, in references to politics it is. "Exhibition" and "historic" are not necessarily negative, but "historic" is almost always positive. It must be the answer.

32. **ANSWER: D** This is our first footnote question and there will always be a few footnote questions on every test. This one is relatively easy as the use of Spanish in the footnote best identifies D as the right answer.

33. **Answer: A** This footnote suggests that Slade wanted us to know about both of these works because both developed ideas similar to her own concerning how the news has turned into entertainment.

34. **Answer: E** Noting once again the "EXCEPT," this is not a difficult question. The footnote tells us a great deal about that speech, but nowhere do we find any indication that CNN had little subsequent influence.

35. **Answer: D** This is a typical question, in which all the answers look fairly reasonable. You must read carefully to find the answer that completes the idea. Slade wants us to realize that the news is biased for ratings and filtered for excitement. What we are told is the truth, but a truth prejudiced to provide—how shall we say it—nasty pleasure.

36. **Answer: A** While Slade tells us that the news is "primarily" true, she more importantly reminds us that television is about ratings and advertising revenue, which translates into answer A.

37. **Answer: C** The answer to this question relies on your ability to do a close reading of the paragraph. You would see that Slade writes that a soap opera's plot centers on domestic romance and violence and the characters have "good looks and sporting prowess pitted against evil and the terrors of female sexual aggression." While we may agree that soap operas have unusual or bizarre story lines, Slade does not specifically mention this in her paragraph.

38. **Answer: E** A suggestion on how to handle Roman numeral questions: Cover up the answers and systematically rule the Roman numerals "in" or "out." Slade certainly intends the "score" to reflect both football and television ratings. I and III are therefore "in." II is "out," even though the news media love to score debates. However, this was not a debate.

39. **Answer: B** Since "sarcastic" is not present, you need something as close as possible. The College Board loves upper-level vocabulary, especially on tone. Learn those words in the tone chapter. "Sardonic" is the closest in meaning to sarcasm.

40. **Answer: A** The passage clearly states that the author understands "how things can be lost in translation" and that when a "Puerto Rican girl dressed in her idea of what is attractive meets a man from the mainstream culture . . . , a clash is likely to take place." The author then elaborates on the types of clashes that may occur, such as the episode with the young boy who kissed her at a party, her encounter with the drunken man in the hotel, and her ruminations on the media's cultural stereotypes of Latin women.

41. **Answer: B** The author maintains a critical tone throughout the passage as she discusses the myths behind the cultural stereotypes of Latin women. Evidence may be found in the speaker's use of such comments as "I was supposed to *ripen*, not just grow into womanhood like other girls" (lines 26–27), "those who should know better, still put others 'in their place'" (lines 29–30), "stood silently waiting for the man

to end his offensive song" (lines 53–54), "I was just an Evita or a María: merely a character in his cartoon-populated universe" (lines 66–67).

42. **ANSWER: E** In the opening sentence Cofer establishes credibility for her invective against the stereotypes surrounding Latin women by stating that she is a woman who has firsthand knowledge of the lifestyles and trials of Latin women through the many personal discussions and stories she has heard from Puerto Rican women.

43. **ANSWER: C** The phrase "lost in translation" refers to both cultural and linguistic as implied by the writer's discussion of custom and ritual, as well as the more concrete notion of the difficulties of translating meanings of words across languages.

44. **ANSWER: A** The writer's comparison of Latin girls to fruits and vegetables obviously has nothing to do with the girls' levels of intelligence; rather, it serves as a metaphor to illustrate the stereotypes of Latin women as products or goods in a society that is, by definition, not their own.

45. **ANSWER: D** "In their place" refers to the racial position of Hispanics in mainstream American society and the economic status of Latin women as "domestic" workers (lines 71–78). The author does not discuss the political or national status of Hispanics in America, nor does she expound on the educational status of Hispanics in general.

46. **ANSWER: D** The author's description obviously underscores the irony of the situation in which she finds herself, the irony being that such a gross offense as the one perpetrated by the man could occur in a "classy" location frequented by educated "professional" people.

47. **ANSWER: B** The phrase "professional friends" remains neutral in this context as a mere descriptor of the people who find it difficult to fathom that racial stereotyping of the kind discussed by the author still occurs in mainstream society.

48. **ANSWER: C** Although it is apparent that the daughter is present and the father is arguably an unfit parent, the primary purpose for the word "Daddy" in this particular manner is not to remind the reader of the daughter's presence.

49. **ANSWER: C** The implication is that the father would have treated women in other cultures callously when he was traveling in the military, especially since he behaved so abhorrently toward the speaker while he was in his own country and society.

50. **ANSWER: A** The writer is moving from a personal discussion of her experiences as a Latin woman in the United States to a direct argument about the origins and causes of the cultural stereotype of Hispanics in America as sustained by the media.

51. **ANSWER: B** The writer often points out the differences between the "myth" surrounding the racial and social positions of Latin women in the United States and the reality that she experiences as an educated, professional Latin woman.

52. **ANSWER: D** The author obviously intends to use this example to show that the media is as responsible for the persistent myth of Hispanic women as domestic workers as it is for creating "America's idea of the black woman for generations" (lines 81–82).

EXPLANATIONS AND RUBRICS FOR ESSAY QUESTIONS

ESSAY QUESTION 1: UPPER-HALF PAPERS: SCORES OF 5–9

This is an example of the new synthesis question, for which you must make your own argument and then support that argument with at least three of the sources you read on the subject. Upper-half essays present the student's own opinion. The quoted passages from the prompt are part of the argument and provides a seamless and sustained point of view. Sources used are both correctly cited and integral to the student's argument, but the student's argument must be central. The writing is clear but not necessarily flawless. In the essay to this particular prompt, each student forms and shares an opinion about taxes on plastic bags and uses sources for and against that position or to argue in conjunction with it.

ESSAY QUESTION 1: LOWER-HALF PAPERS: SCORES OF 1–4

You are guaranteed to have written a lower-half paper if you did not quote and correctly cite at least three sources. However, bear in mind that most lower-half papers do quote the sources but then offer no discussion incorporating them. The sources are not integrated into the student's argument, or the student does not present his or her own argument, merely summarizing what the sources seem to say. Lower-half papers also demonstrate an incompleteness of argument. These essay writers don't seem to understand the nature of the issue or take it personally, stating, for example, that no one can make them use a plastic bag. They may turn the essay into a diatribe on littering or even advertising. Writers of these papers will not have done what they were asked to do.

ESSAY QUESTION 2: UPPER-HALF PAPERS: SCORES OF 5–9

Upper-half paper writers understand the task being asked of them. They analyze the strategies Donne employs to develop his satiric argument that women's inconstancy (fickleness) is a valuable part of their personalities and that men should appreciate it. Donne uses a substantial number of literary devices, and writers of upper-half papers identify and discuss the effect of any number of devices, from diction to parallel syntax to argument from nature. Writers of upper-half papers effectively integrate examples from the essay itself into their own analyses and produce a thoughtful examination of Donne's strategies.

ESSAY QUESTION 2: LOWER-HALF PAPERS: SCORES OF 1–4

Lower-half paper writers may have misunderstood the prompt and argued for or against Donne's position. Or they may have understood the task but misinterpreted what Donne wrote. However, the biggest and most obvious weakness in lower-half papers is that their writers did not successfully identify any strategies and found the essay confusing. Therefore, they may quote Donne but then simply summarize what he is saying rather than analyze how he says it. Lower-half papers are often too brief in their analysis and/or poorly written. Any of these elements can produce a lower-half score on the analysis essay.

ESSAY QUESTION 3: UPPER-HALF PAPERS: SCORES OF 5–9

Upper-half paper writers understand the claim being made by Wade, incorporating the work by Seligman: Human beings are basically designed to anticipate the negative and will rarely trust happiness. Writers of these papers will argue coherently for or against this observation by offering specific examples from their own lives and from what they understand of the lives of others. Upper-half paper writers might also qualify this observation historically or culturally and relate these thoughts to an optimistic or pessimistic view of human nature. Upper-half papers do not need to be perfectly free of errors, but they are generally clearly written, and the relationship between the examples and the writer's argument is clearly defined.

ESSAY QUESTION 3: LOWER-HALF PAPERS: SCORES OF 1–4

Writers of lower-half papers will misunderstand the prompt to say that we are all happy all the time. More than likely these papers will provide little evidence, evidence without development, or evidence that hardly seems related to the issue. They may be too brief or, in the worst cases, poorly written. Papers that score a 2 are often characterized by a simple restatement of what was set forth in the prompt and offer no original ideas.

COMPUTING YOUR SCORE ON THE DIAGNOSTIC TEST

Please keep in mind that these numbers are subjective. Two variables affect the computation every year: the number of the multiple-choice questions and the difficulty level of the essays. There is a slight curve created every year in terms of the numbers. Having said that, remember that earning 15 points on the essays and getting 50 percent right on the multiple-choice questions will generally produce a score of 3.

SCORING THE MULTIPLE-CHOICE SECTION

_____ − (1/4 × _____) = _____
number   number   multiple-choice score
correct   incorrect

SCORING THE FREE-RESPONSE SECTION

_____ + _____ + _____ = _____
Question 1   Question 2   Question 3   total essay
(0–9 score) (0–9 score) (0–9 score)   score

COMPOSITE SCORE

1.29 × _____ = _____
         multiple-choice   weighted section I
            score   score

3.05 × _____ = _____
         free response   weighted section II
            score   score

_____ + _____ = _____
weighted section I   weighted section II   composite score

You now have a number between 0 and about 150. Each year that scale is adjusted. Generally it goes like this:

0–49 = 1   50–75 = 2   76–94 = 3   95–110 = 4   112–150 = 5

Part II

The AP English Language and Composition Exam

THINGS YOU SHOULD KNOW

BRIEF NOTE ON TONE

One of the clearest indicators that the AP English Language and Composition exam has changed significantly is that three years ago this section would not have had "brief" in the title. When we, the authors, first started grading the examination, the essay portion included two passages that required style analysis and only one passage of general argument. Rhetorical analysis replaced one of the style passages, and the synthesis question the other. A test originally designed to evaluate the student's ability to read and understand the mechanics of mood and tone has become an examination that evaluates the student's ability to read and understand the mechanics of argument.

However, style analysis and an understanding of tone have not disappeared from the test altogether. If you need additional help identifying and dealing with tone, there is a portion of the rhetorical analysis chapter that focuses on diction and imagery. It is also important to remember that most imagery, while it supports tone, serves the purposes of various figures of speech. Still, in any argument, and certainly in a pathos argument, the tone established by the diction is often used not only to manipulate an argument, but also to coerce a reader or listener into accepting a particular argument.

There are still questions in the multiple-choice portion of the test that consider the overall tone of the piece and ask you to choose an appropriate answer from several tone words. One of these types of questions appears in nearly every passage, so it is still worthwhile to learn the central vocabulary of a good tone list.

So what is tone? Essentially, tone is the connotative impact of language. Words such as "lazy," "meandering," "casual," "torpor," and "drowsy" create a sense of lassitude and passivity. On the other hand, a harsh tone is evoked by "dismemberment," "calamitous," "growl," and "shatter." Tone is not a complex issue. You just need to be attentive to the language of a piece, particularly its connotative associations.

Mood, on the other hand, is the relative atmosphere created by a piece. When you hear a piece of music, it puts you in a certain mood. Writing can do the same thing!

For purposes of this test, mood and tone are used almost indistinguishably. They are interlocking, linked by the College Board in questions about attitude or perspective. When you analyze a piece, be watchful for the author's attitude toward the subject, in particular toward positions that do not agree with his or her own. On the multiple-choice portion, just remember what attitude or tone questions are essentially asking you: to detect possible bias or to distinguish between logical and emotional arguments.

The one obstacle we face—and it is one we have mentioned earlier—is that the College Board will not use simple vocabulary for these questions. Rather than "happy," the possible answer choices might include "euphoric" or "enthralled." If a particular paragraph expressed anger, answer choices might include "condemnatory" or "wrathful." In both cases, each answer implies happiness or anger, but each also creates different circumstances and associations. Therefore, it is a good idea to use the tone vocabulary list at the end of this chapter throughout your preparation. Look up any words that are unfamiliar to you. Also, you should practice using more precise words when writing your own analysis of an author's tone, rather than simply saying the author has a "negative tone" or is "dull," "worried," or "ticked off."

TONE VOCABULARY

FEELING GOOD ATTITUDE WORDS

amused	enthusiastic	jocular	proud
boisterous	exuberant	lighthearted	sanguine
cheery	exultant	loving	sentimental
compassionate	fanciful	merry	sympathetic
complimentary	festive	mirthful	tickled
confident	flattering	nostalgic	whimsical
effusive	genial	optimistic	wistful
elated	hopeful	passionate	

FEELING BAD/ANGRY ATTITUDE WORDS

admonitory	exacerbated	inflammatory	outraged
accusing	exasperated	irate	pretentious
arrogant	furious	irritated	resentful
bitter	incendiary	livid	threatening
condemnatory	incensed	manipulative	vexed
disgusted	indignant	offensive	wrathful

FEELING SAD/WORRIED ATTITUDE WORDS

anxious	despairing	hopeless	sober
apprehensive	disconcerted	humorless	solemn
ashamed	disturbed	melancholic	somber
chagrined	fearful	mournful	staid
concerned	foreboding	ominous	urgent
depressed	gloomy	resigned	

FEELING HUMOROUS, IRONIC, AND SARCASTIC ATTITUDE WORDS

amused	derisive	mock-serious	scornful
bantering	disdainful	patronizing	taunting
clever	eccentric	playful	teasing
condescending	facetious	pompous	whimsical
contemptuous	flippant	sardonic	witty
critical	insolent	satiric	
cynical	irreverent	scathing	

FEELING NEUTRAL ATTITUDE WORDS

abrupt	coolheaded	informative	prosaic
ambiguous	cultured	instructive	questioning
apathetic	detached	learned	reflective
authoritative	didactic	lyrical	reminiscent
candid	dramatic	matter-of-fact	restrained
ceremonial	esoteric	objective	scholarly
clinical	factual	official	shocked
colloquial	formal	placid	Spartan
commonplace	incredulous	plain-speaking	tedious

A WORKING VOCABULARY OF FUNDAMENTAL TERMS

ACTIVE VOICE: The opposite of passive voice, the active voice is essentially any sentence with an active verb. *Johnny Appleseed planted his seeds in the garden.* The active verb is "planted." Active voice is usually preferred in writing because it expresses more energy and command of the essay than does the passive voice.

AD HOMINEM: This is an attack on the person rather than the issues at hand—a common fallacy, especially during an election year.

ALLITERATION: The repetition of a phonetic sound at the beginning of several words in a sentence. Students sometimes mention alliteration in rhetorical analysis essays, although it should only be discussed if the alliterative phrase itself is noticeable and the author has a legitimate purpose for using it. Otherwise, it is linguistic window dressing more often used in poetry. Examples are *Simple Simon sat on the straw* and *Peter Piper picked a peck of pickled peppers.*

ALLUSION: A reference that recalls another work, another time in history, another famous person, and so forth. Like metaphor and simile, allusions are always important and begin a literary ripple effect. For example, if you call a piece of real estate "the Promised Land," you are alluding to the Hebrews' forty-year search for the sacred land promised them by God and found in Israel. Similarly, if an author calls a naïve character "Miranda," he or she may be alluding to the adolescent daughter of Prospero in *The Tempest*. The College Board expects you to be well-read and to have adequate knowledge of Greek and Roman mythology, the Judeo-Christian tradition, and Shakespeare, at the very least. Identify the impact of allusions in the same way you would work with a metaphor.

ANADIPLOSIS: This is a wonderful technique of repetition. In anadiplosis, the last word of the clause begins the next clause, creating a connection of ideas important to the author's purpose in some way. *The Furies pursued the men. The men were chased by their nightmares. The nightmares awakened everyone in the room.*

ANALOGY: A term that signifies a relational comparison of or similarity between two objects or ideas. For example, there is an analogy between *the heart* and *a pump* (a heart pushes the flow of blood through the body as a pump pushes air into a tire). You will occasionally see this term combined with another, as in "antithetical analogy" (a relational comparison of two opposing ideas/subjects, such as a news attempt to compare diplomatic negotiations in the Middle East to the NFL playoffs).

ANAPHORA: In rhetoric, this is the deliberate repetition of a word or phrase at the beginning of several successive poetic lines, prose sentences, clauses, or paragraphs. You will see this quite often in political speeches, when politicians make promises to voters: *I will* *fight for medical care for every man, woman, and child. I will fight for social security for our children. I will fight to raise the minimum wage.*

ANASTROPHE: The reversal of the natural order of words in a sentence or line of poetry. It has a nice—if somewhat alarming—effect at times, and it has been known to occasionally cause confusion in inexperienced readers. Shakespeare was a whiz with anastrophe, which is also the reason so many people mistakenly think Shakespeare wrote in Old English. (He didn't! If you can understand the words, it is modern English!) *The poisoned apple she ate <u>to her gave</u> cramps of a serious nature.*

ANTITHESIS: An observation or claim that is in opposition to your claim or an author's claim. If we argue for the *drilling of wells*, the antithesis might be to *divert water from the river*. If we claim that *the electoral college is an outdated anachronism*, the antithesis would be that *like the rest of the Constitution, it has managed to adapt to the changing times.*

APHORISM: A brief statement of an opinion or elemental truth. Aphorisms usually appear only in the multiple-choice section; however, they occasionally show up in rhetorical analysis passages. Ben Franklin specialized in such aphoristic gems as these: *They who can give up essential liberty to obtain a little temporary safety deserve neither liberty nor safety,* and *Glass, China, and Reputation, are easily crack'd, and never well mended.*

APOSTROPHE: Prayer-like, this is a direct address to someone who is not present, to a deity or muse, or to some other power. It rarely appears on the Language exam, but when it does, it is usually significant and nearly always pathos. *O eloquent, just, and mighty Death!*

APPOSITIVE: Also called a noun phrase, an appositive modifies the noun next to it. You will occasionally see one in the multiple-choice section of the test; appositives are relatively easy to spot. *The dragon, a large creature with glittering green scales, looked warily at the approaching wizard.*

ARGUMENT FROM IGNORANCE: An argument stating that something is true because it has never been proven false. Such arguments rely on claims that are impossible to prove conclusively, and they often go both ways: *There are no aliens because we have never identified aliens* or *Aliens exist because we have never proven they don't.* Similarly, *God exists because no one has proven He doesn't* (and vice versa).

ASYNDETON: The deliberate omission of conjunctions from a series of related independent clauses. The effect is to create a tight, concise, and forceful sentence. *All the orcs ate the food, broke the dishes, trashed the hall, beat the dogs to the shower.*

BANDWAGON: Also called *vox populi*. This argument is the "everyone's doing it" fallacy and is especially appreciated, for example, by politicians trying to get voters to agree that everyone agrees that we should all agree to reduce taxes and by teenagers who argue that they should be allowed to go to the concert because all their friends are going.

BEGGING THE QUESTION: This argument occurs when the speaker states a claim that includes a word or phrase that needs to be defined before the argument can proceed. *Because of the extreme conditions before us, we must vote for this tax.* (Uh, what conditions are being called "extreme?")

CAUSE AND EFFECT: Another fallacy, this is also known by another name, *post hoc ergo propter hoc* (Latin for "after this, therefore because of this"). Such an argument falls under the general umbrella of a causality fallacy or false cause. *It seems that every time you turn on the game on television, the team loses. Therefore, you come to believe that you are the cause of the losses.* (It sounds silly, but people do it all the time. Think about superstitions.)

CHIASMUS: This is an ABBA syntactical structure rather than the more common parallel ABAB structure. It is derived from the Greek letter X (*chi*); thus, as you might have guessed, its form is similar to an X. While it is a pleasure to find one (and they are memorable), chiasmus is a rather minor syntactical device. One example everyone recalls is *Ask not what your country can do for you, but what you can do for your country.* The *chi* structure is *country* (A), *you* (B), *you* (B), *country* (A).

COMPLEX SENTENCE: A sentence structure that is a combination of a dependent clause and an independent clause. *If you walk to the top of the tower, you will find a sacred sardine can.*

COMPOUND SENTENCE: A sentence structure made up of two independent clauses joined by a coordinating conjunction. *Don't open the door or a deadly smell will kill you.*

COMPOUND-COMPLEX SENTENCE: A combination of a compound and a complex sentence. *Because the swamp is near your back door, you might expect the Creature from the Black Lagoon to put in an appearance and tear apart Uncle Al's fishin' shack if it is in his way.*

CONNOTATION: The associations or moods that accompany a word. Words generally are negative (*sadistic*), positive (*serendipitous*), or neutral (*instrument*). Pay close attention to the diction choices an author makes and especially take note of any particularly strong connotative words or patterns of connotative words, as this is how you usually determine the author's tone and intention. An example would be the words "trim," "thin," and "skinny." "Trim" carries a positive connotation about a person's physique, whereas "thin" is neutral and "skinny" is negative. For an even stronger negative connotation, you might use "anorexic."

DECLARATIVE SENTENCE: This is a basic statement or an assertion and is the most common type of sentence. *Alternate forms of energy must be found by people who are not capitalists desiring only power and money.*

DEDUCTIVE: A form of logical argumentation that uses claims or premises. The assumption by the author is that you will accept the claims as true and that you will then deduce the correct conclusion from the accepted premises at the outset. Deductive reasoning looks most like geometry proofs. When you encounter a deductive argument, you need to examine the claims. Are they reasonable? Do you accept them? Look for fallacies in the claims. Often a premise will carry an implied premise that is present (and essential) to the argument. Do you accept the implied premise? What appears to be solid reason can manipulate your allegiances more easily than an emotional argument; therefore, be critical when you read. *The infrastructure of American cities was designed and built by human beings. Human beings are fallible. Therefore, one may conclude that there are structural flaws in parts of the infrastructure.*

DENOTATION: This is the opposite of connotation and is quite literally the dictionary meaning of a word. *Denotation: (n.) The most specific or direct meaning of a word, in contrast to its figurative or associated meanings.*

DEPENDENT CLAUSE: This clause contains a noun and a verb but is set up with a subordinate conjunction, which makes the clause an incomplete thought. *Because the magician's rabbit refused to come out of the hat . . .*

DIALECT: A regional speech pattern; the way people talk in different parts of the world. Dialect is a form of regionalism in writing and is often referred to as "colloquial language." When a writer imitates dialect (the speech of a particular area of the country), he or she is relying on language to make a passage feel "homey" and personal. Zora Neale Hurston uses regional dialect in *Their Eyes Were Watching God*: "You mean, you mad 'cause she didn't stop and tell us all her business. . . . The worst thing Ah ever knowed her to do was taking a few years offa her age and dat ain't never harmed nobody."

DICTION: The particular words an author uses in any essay. Diction choices (why one word is used as opposed to another) are the essential building blocks of composition.

DISTRACTOR: A distractor is a *possible answer* that seems to be correct, but is either wrong or is not as good as other answers.

ELLIPSIS: Three dots that indicate words have been left out of a quotation; they also can be used to create suspense. *The dark car appeared at the end of the alley and Herman, the handsome hero (example of alliteration), was trapped against the wall at the opposite end. The engine revved . . .*

EPANALEPSIS: Like chiasmus, this figure repeats the opening word or phrase at the end of the sentence to emphasize a statement or idea, but it is not an ABBA reversal. *The <u>demon</u> descended in a crowd toward a village now afraid of the <u>demon</u>, or <u>common</u> sense is not so <u>common</u>.*

EPISTROPHE: A minor device, epistrophe is the ending of a series of lines, phrases, clauses, or sentences with the same word or words. When it appears in a speech or essay, it is emotionally potent. One of the most famous is Lincoln's *This government <u>of the people, by the people, and for the people</u> shall not perish from this earth.*

ETHOS: One of the fundamental strategies of argumentation identified by Aristotle. Ethos is basically an appeal to credibility. The writer is seeking to convince you that he or she has the background, history, skills, and/or expertise to speak on the issue. Whenever you encounter an ethos argument, always ask yourself if the credibility is substantiated and valid. An essay advocating policy changes on drug rehabilitation programs is more powerful if the person is a former addict or counselor in a current rehab program.

ETYMOLOGY: The study of the origin of words and their historical uses. This is a minor term and rarely appears on the test, but it is nice to know. *The name for the sandwich came from the Earl of Sandwich, an altogether unremarkable peer of the English realm.*

EUPHEMISM: To use a safer or nicer word for something others find inappropriate or unappealing. Euphemism generally appears only in the multiple-choice section. The English language offers many euphemisms for death and bodily functions, such as *Bambi's mother now <u>grazes in the pastures of forever</u>* to mean "died," or *After a long night of partying, the young man spent the morning <u>repenting at the altar of the porcelain god</u>* to mean "vomiting."

EXCLAMATORY SENTENCE: A sentence that conveys excitement or force. *Egads, Wilton, we are being pursued by squirmy, nasty creatures with suckers on their feet!*

FALLACY: A failure of logical reasoning. Fallacies appear to make an argument reasonable, but falsely so. The key, however, is for you to be able to spot when someone is not making sense or is failing to convince. When that happens, you may not remember the right label for the fallacy, but you should be able to identify where the author has messed up. In the chapter on rhetorical analysis, we discuss a variety of common fallacies, and we have included most of them alphabetically in the vocabulary list: ad hominem, begging the question, straw man, slippery slope, etc.

FALSE ANALOGY: An argument using an inappropriate metaphor. To help understand one thing in an argument we compare it to something else that is not at all relevant. *The earth is like a watch and, just as a fine watch was made, so also the earth was made.*

FALSE DILEMMA: Also known as an either/or fallacy. The suggestion is made in the argument that the problem or debate only has two solutions. You can also call it the fallacy of the excluded middle. For example, *There are only two options in gun control: when guns are outlawed, only outlaws will have guns.*

GERUND: A verb ending in "ing" that serves as a noun. *"<u>Stabbing</u> is what I do best," said the thief.*

HYPERBOLE: An exaggeration, fairly common in nonfiction prose arguments, that bolsters an argument. *I know you will all give one thousand percent defending this castle against the onslaught of the murderous mutants.*

IMAGERY: Any time one of the five senses (visual, auditory, tactile, olfactory, gustatory) is evoked by what you have read, you have encountered imagery. It was crucial to the old AP test's style analysis, which asked about mood, tone, or attitude. It is less crucial in the new AP test format, but there may still be important images in an argument. If so, two things are usually happening. The first is that the argument is inductive and relying on examples. The second is that the images will often begin to carry a kind of pathos, or emotional feel, which supports the argument in some way.

IMPERATIVE SENTENCE: A command. *You will rescue the maiden or surrender your sword to the Round Table.*

INDEPENDENT CLAUSE: A clause that can stand alone as a sentence. It must have a noun and a verb (subject and predicate). *The magician's rabbit died.*

INDUCTIVE: A form of logical argumentation that requires the use of examples. Inductive arguments are most like science: You get example after example until you reach a conclusion. These types of argument are fairly easy to spot and very common to argumentative essays. When you encounter an inductive argument, ask yourself two questions: Are there enough examples, and are the examples relevant to the question being addressed? *A writer who argues for the success of a particular diet plan would use testimony from success stories, a scientific study proving its effectiveness, and a few doctors who claim it has safe and natural ingredients.*

INFINITIVE: The word "to" plus a verb, usually functioning as a noun and often as a predicate in a sentence. Infinitives fake out students because they look like prepositional phrases. *To reach the other side of the river* (infinitive phrase and noun and subject) *was the desired goal* (predicate nominative) *of the nearly comatose ogre.*

INTERROGATIVE SENTENCE: A question. *To reach Dracula's castle, do I turn left or right at the crossroads?*

IRONY: The use of words to express something other than and often the opposite of the literal meaning. There are three types of irony: verbal irony, a contrast between what is said and what is meant (sarcasm); situational irony, a contrast between what happens and what was expected; and dramatic irony, a contrast between what the character thinks to be true and what the reader knows to be true. Familiarity with irony is absolutely essential in reading nonfiction prose and especially in doing rhetorical analysis on the exam, as it appears in nearly every piece in one form or another. Irony is often connected to satire or satiric speech. *He bought the ring and brought it back to their apartment. She had left a note, "Gone to find myself in North Dakota."* An example on the linguistic level uses a metaphor:

Your love is a fine cloth—a rag, actually, deteriorating as the elements take their toll.

JARGON: A pattern of speech and vocabulary associated with a particular group of people. It typically appears only in the multiple-choice section and is not significant. Computer analysts have their own vocabulary, as do doctors, astronauts, and plumbers. That is their jargon. To some extent, this glossary and book are an effort to provide you with a new (though we hope not entirely new) jargon.

JUXTAPOSITION: Making one idea more dramatic by placing it next to its opposite. In art it is called chiaroscuro, where a bright white object is placed next to a black object and thus both are made more visible. *My goodness is often chastened by my sense of sin,* or *The gasoline savings from a hybrid car as compared to a standard car seem excellent until one compares the asking prices of the two vehicles.* The juxtaposition of the asking prices shows that the savings are not as significant as they first appear.

LOGOS: An appeal to reason. Logos is one of the fundamental strategies of argumentation identified by Aristotle. It occurs when a writer tries to convince you of the logic of his argument. Writers may use inductive argumentation or deductive argumentation, but they clearly have examples and a generally rational tone to their language. The problem with logos is that it can appear reasonable until you dissect the argument and then find fallacies that defeat the viability of the argument in the reader's eyes. Of course, that presupposes that the reader is able to identify the fallacies.

LOOSE SENTENCE: An independent clause followed by all sorts of debris, usually dependent clauses. It is minor, but might appear in the multiple-choice portion of the test. *She wore a yellow ribbon that matched the shingles of the house, which were painted last year, just before he left for the war.*

MALAPROPISM: A wonderful form of word play in which one word is mistakenly substituted for another that sounds similar. It doesn't appear often, but when it does, it is usually pretty funny. The name comes from the character of Mrs. Malaprop in Richard Sheridan's play *The Rivals*, who said things like "He is the very pineapple of politeness" rather than "He is the very pinnacle of politeness." Another example comes from the Duke in *Huckleberry Finn*, who says "funeral orgy" instead of "funeral eulogy."

METAPHOR: A figure of speech in which what is unknown is compared to something that is known in order to better gauge its importance. Remember the ripple effect and look for patterns in metaphors and similes in any piece of nonfiction prose. *The loose floorboards of his mind rattled as he tried to find his way out of the legal mess he had made.*

METONYMY: A minor figure of speech in which the name of one thing is substituted for another with which it is closely associated. You may find metonymy in multiple-choice questions. *The <u>crown</u> spoke with authority about the gathering crisis over bread and cheese.* "Crown" is not literal, but is associated with a king or queen.

NON SEQUITUR: This literally means "it does not follow." Non sequitur is an argument by misdirection and is logically irrelevant. *"Should we invade Canada, Sire?" "Has anyone seen my wand?*

OBJECT: A noun toward which thought, feeling, or action is directed. Not all sentences have objects, although all must have subjects and predicates. *The entrance to the dark fortress dared the <u>knight</u> to try his hand at entering.*

ONOMATOPOEIA: A minor figure of speech in which a sound imitates the thing or action associated with it. This shows up occasionally in the multiple-choice questions. *Bonks, conks, and calamities whirled through the air from the shifting coconut shells hung on strings.*

OXYMORON: Two words that together create a sense of opposition. Oxymorons often call attention to a particular point in an argument. *The mariner's <u>cultivated vulgarity</u> was alarming to sailors more comfortable with the <u>bubbly heaviness</u> of their captain.*

PARADOX: A major figure of speech in rhetorical analysis that seeks to create a mental discontinuity, which then forces the reader to pause and seek clarity. A paradox is a truth or a group of sentences that defy our intuition. *Be careful how you pace yourself—by walking too quickly you get there more slowly,* or *My silent love grows louder with each passing moment.*

PARALLEL SYNTAX (OR PARALLELISM): A pattern of language that creates a rhythm of repetition often combined with some other language of repetition. Parallel sets of sentences or parallel clauses can exist within a sentence. This is a significant element in syntactical analysis. The College Board loves to ask about parallel syntax and, as its use is a sign of strong, effective writing, you should write this way as well. Parallel syntax may best be likened to a train gaining momentum: It drives through a piece of nonfiction prose, gathering emotional steam as it goes. *We will fight them on the beaches, and fight them in the hills, and fight them in the forests, and in the villages of the dell.* One famous speech filled with parallel syntax is Martin Luther King, Jr.'s "I Have a Dream." Pick a line and it is likely parallel.

PARENTHETICALS: Phrases, sentences, and words inside parentheses ( ). In rhetorical analysis, pay attention to parenthetical statements. Two questions should arise when you see a parenthetical: *Why are these words inside parentheses?* and *Are there other parentheticals that together make a pattern in the essay?* They aren't a big deal, but sometimes they merit a paragraph of analysis. *The Big Bopper (J.P. to his friends) rolled into Chantilly Lace and all the girls went wild.*

PARTICIPLE: A verbal (expressing action or a state of being) that is used as an adjective and most often ends in *-ing* or *-ed*. Participles function as adjectives, modifying nouns or pronouns. *Creating a ruckus* (participle = noun = subject) *confused the robbers and led to an escape. Creating a ruckus* (participle = adjective), *the hero made the really bad guys turn away from the hidden treasure.*

PASSIVE VOICE: The opposite of active voice; in the passive voice something happens *to* someone: *Mordred was bitten by the dog,* rather than the active form *The dog bit Mordred.*

PATHOS: An appeal to emotion. This is one of the fundamental strategies of argumentation identified by Aristotle. Typically, pathos arguments may use loaded words to make you feel guilty, lonely, worried, insecure, or confused. The easiest way to remember what pathos arguments are is to see most advertising as a form of pathos argument.

PERIODIC SENTENCE: A sentence with several dependent clauses that precede the independent clause. An easy way to remember this is to think of the independent clause as appearing immediately before the period (periodic sentence). *While watching the cave and wondering why the rain had not stopped, nor even abated, the hero filed his fingernails and waited.*

PERSONIFICATION: Giving human attributes to non-human things. Although the use of personification in an argument makes something in the issue seem more approachable or potentially agreeable, you will not find too many examples of it in nonfiction prose. *The thunder grumbled all night as rain slapped the windows.*

PHRASE: A grouping of words that define or clarify. The syntactical definition of "phrase" is a group of words that is not a sentence because there is no verb. There are many different forms, but the most common is the prepositional phrase. *The monster jumped into the swamp.*

POINT OF VIEW: The perspective from which the writer chooses to present his or her story (fiction) or essay (nonfiction). This is a fundamental part of any writing. The first element of point of view is the normal fictional element of writing in first, second, or third person (omniscient or limited), which refers to the person telling the story. The second element of point of view dealing with nonfiction refers to the writer's attitude. Is he or she obsessive, neutral, dogmatic, and so forth? What is the nature of the persona who has composed the essay? You will usually have a pretty good sense of this unless the passage contains a shift in point of view. The author may deliberately alter his or her attitude toward the subject in order to give you a different perspective or to convey a better sense of balance toward the topic. You should be alert in your analysis of both multiple-choice passages and essay passages for shifts in point of view. They are always significant.

POISONING THE WELL: A person or character is introduced with language that suggests that he is not at all reliable before the listener/reader knows anything about him. *The next speaker, an alcoholic wife-abuser, will seek to sway us to his view that the Fleur de Lis should become our state flower.*

POLYSYNDETON: The use of consecutive coordinating conjunctions even when they are not needed. The effect is to render the reader somewhat breathless. *He was overwhelmed, as if by a tsunami, and by the fishes, and by the seaweed, and by the salt spray from the heavens.*

PREDICATE: The formal term for the verb that conveys the meaning or carries the action of the sentence. *The fair maiden <u>awakened</u> from a deep sleep to find an ogre at her bedside.*

PREDICATE ADJECTIVE: An adjective that follows a linking verb and modifies the subject of the sentence. *The gigantic whirlpool was <u>inky black</u>, and there was no moon.*

PREDICATE NOMINATIVE: A noun or pronoun that uses a linking verb to unite, describe, or rename the noun in the subject of the sentence. *The silly dwarf is a <u>squirrel</u>.*

PREMISE: Another word for a claim. A premise is a statement of truth, at least to the person making the argument. Premises come in many shapes, sizes, and colors. They can be limited and absolute—*two parallel lines will remain equidistant forever*—or they can be vague and open-ended—*China's trade policy with the United States is unfair.* Every argument has a premise, and most of what you read on the Language AP test is argumentative, so get used to the word and become comfortable identifying claims and deciding whether you agree, disagree, or are waiting to make up your mind.

PROMPT: In essay questions, *prompt* has two definitions: the correct one and the common one. The correct one is that the prompt is the paragraph or language that defines the essay task. It does not include the passage itself. The common definition of *prompt* is one you will hear teachers and consultants (the two of us included) use to refer to any and all parts of an essay question.

PUN: A play on words. In an argument, a pun usually calls humorous attention to a particular point. *He kept <u>waving</u> at the princess. He was a devoted <u>fan</u>.*

RED HERRING: An argument that distracts the reader by raising issues irrelevant to the case. It is like being given too many suspects in a murder mystery.

REPETITION: A fundamental form of rhetorical stress that calls the reader's attention to a particular word, phrase, or image for emphasis of meaning. Repetition is a basic part of all rhetorical analysis. It also reinforces the power of parallel syntax. *She certainly was beautiful, the way a cow is beautiful standing in the beautiful radiance of a moonlit night.*

RHETORICAL QUESTION: A question whose answer is assumed, a rhetorical question is designed to force the reader to respond in a predetermined manner and is a significant tool in the study of rhetoric. One of the most basic purposes for rhetorical questions is cheerleading. Rhetorical questions, therefore, propel an argument emotionally. They often look like extensions of a logical argument, but more often than not, they are setting you up to agree with the writer. As with parallel syntax, rhetorical questions are excellent devices to use in the development of your own essay writing. As graders, we notice when you use them—if you use them to effectively nurture your argument. There are other types of rhetorical questions, but they always follow the same basic pattern: the writer asks herself something and then answers the question in the next sentence or paragraph. Another form is when the question functions as an ironic assault on the writer's adversaries. This kind of rhetorical question can have many uses, and you should notice its function whenever you encounter one in nonfiction prose. *Who's afraid of the big bad wolf? Who's afraid of the Jolly Green Giant? Are we? No!!!*

RHETORICAL SHIFT: This occurs when the author of an essay significantly alters his or her diction, syntax, or both. It isn't exactly a different writer who is writing, but it feels awfully close to it. Rhetorical shifts are important to recognize because they are dramatic and usually occur at critical points in an argument.

SIMILE: A crucial figure of speech in an argument when what is unknown is compared to something that is known using the word "like," "as," or "than" in order to better perceive its importance. Remember the ripple effect and look for patterns in similes and metaphors in any piece of nonfiction prose. *The troll's fishing technique was like a mercenary throwing bombs in the water to catch trout.*

SIMPLE SENTENCE: An independent clause. It has a subject and a verb, and that's pretty much it. *The giant chopped down the bean tree.*

SLIPPERY SLOPE (ALSO CALLED DOMINO THEORY): This fallacy of argumentation argues that one thing inevitably leads to another. Politicians love to use it as a form of exaggeration. *We cannot allow insurgents into the border towns or they will control the entire country by next winter.*

STEM: In the multiple-choice section, this is the question you are asked to complete with the given possible answers. *Which of the following best describes Cyberus's attitude toward the avengers?*

STRAW MAN: This occurs when a person engaging in an argument defines his opponent's position when the opponent is not present and defines it a manner that is easy to attack. It is a fairly easy fallacy to spot and recognizing it has been helpful with rhetorical analysis questions in the past. Politicians use it frequently: *My opponent believes that issuing parking tickets to first-time DUI offenders will reduce the damage they do to our city and our citizens.*

SUBJECT: The formal term for the noun that is the basic focus of the sentence. It is *who* or *what* is doing the action in the sentence. *An anxious <u>gryphon</u> got lost in the queen's maze.*

SUBORDINATE CONJUNCTION: A conjunction that makes an independent clause into a dependent clause. There is a huge list of subordinate conjunctions, but some of the more common are *because, since, which, if, when,* and *although.*

SYLLOGISM: In its basic form, this is a three-part argument construction in which two premises lead to a truth. The term has appeared in the multiple-choice section a few times, but it is also helpful if you can both spot and use a syllogistic argument. In its simplest form, a syllogism looks like this: *All human beings are mortal. Heather is a human being. Therefore, Heather is mortal.* You can also produce really odd ones that are incorrect. *All crows are black. The bird in my backyard is black. The bird in my backyard is a crow.* This is a false argument because an implied premise—all black birds are crows—is false, and thus the logic falls apart. Another is: *Some televisions are black and white. All penguins are black and white. Some televisions are penguins.* There is both misinformation here and false implied premises. Also, despite these simple examples, a syllogistic argument can be set up in three paragraphs: An essential truth is defended. An essential truth is defended. A conclusion is drawn.

SYNECDOCHE: A minor figure of speech in which a part is used for the whole, synecdoche shows up occasionally in multiple-choice questions. Our favorite is *All hands on deck.* (One assumes the rest of the sailors' bodies will follow . . .)

SYNTAX: The study of the rules of grammar that define the formation of sentences. Syntax is critical to the analysis of all the passages on the AP English Language test.

SYNTHESIS: To unite or synthesize a variety of sources to achieve a common end. We use this term almost exclusively to refer to the new synthesis question on the exam. Using your wits and argumentative skill, you combine memory, commentary you've recently read, and a discussion to create a single coherent argument. For example, you may argue and conclude that bicycles would be safer in battle than a Hummer.

THEME: Theme is the basic message or meaning conveyed through elements of character and conflict. The term appears often in literature and is paralleled in nonfiction prose by an argument's thesis.

THESIS: The writer's statement of purpose. Every well-written essay will have one. It is how the reader identifies what the writer is arguing, the position the writer is taking, the action the writer is advocating. Essentially, it is the focal intent of the essay.

TRICOLON: A sentence with three equally distinct and equally long parts (separated by commas rather than colons, despite the name). Such sentences are dramatic and often memorable, but they are used infrequently. The most famous is *I came, I saw, I conquered.* Another might be *The dragon wept, the cow bellowed, and the sheep fleeced.*

UNDERSTATEMENT: This creates exaggeration by showing restraint. It is the opposite of hyperbole. *The knight said to the giant, "Please hand me the barrel of ale if it's not too heavy for you."*

ZEUGMA: A minor device in which two or more elements in a sentence are tied together by the same verb or noun. Zeugmas are especially acute if the noun or verb does not have the exact same meaning in both parts of the sentence. *She dashed his hopes and out of his life when she walked through the door.*

AN IN-DEPTH LOOK AT THE MULTIPLE-CHOICE QUESTIONS

2

The multiple-choice section of the AP exam is made up of four passages of nonfiction prose. The odds are good that one of those passages will be seventeenth- to nineteenth-century British prose; one will be by an American author; and two will be fairly modern and, in some way, political, philosophical, and/or sociological. Although all of the passages will include upper-level vocabulary, you won't have access to a dictionary or a thesaurus. In this test, time is your greatest adversary.

The expectations of the test makers are that you will answer just over 50 percent of the questions correctly. The questions are challenging and often have two or three answers that seem to work, with one of the answers more correct than the others. You must learn to split linguistic hairs, and you must learn to cut yourself some slack if you come away from a question unsure of the right answer, hoping that you chose (or eliminated) correctly.

HOW TO PREPARE?

The best way to prepare is to read nonfiction prose—lots of it! *The Riverside Reader* is always an excellent source and should be seen as an effective companion in preparing for this test. In fact, some of the passages we chose to develop into essay and multiple-choice tests here come from *The Riverside Reader*. You should also read and take practice tests like those in this book. Learn the vocabulary provided in the chapter called "A Working Vocabulary of Fundamental Terms"—but keep in mind that only a handful of questions will test your specific knowledge of that vocabulary. Critical reading, interpretive skills, and inference are most essential to succeeding on the exam.

Other than providing you with sample tests and explanations of the correct answers, the best help we can provide is to tell you to work on your critical reading skills. As you read, you should engage in a dialogue with the passage. That dialogue is evidenced by the notes you make in the margins. Like taking lecture notes in class, making marginal notes in the text is a rather personal but necessary activity. Each reader has his or her own style and will notice and consider different elements, just as two people overhearing the same conversation may interpret it differently. That is why police interviews at the scene of an accident or a crime scene are so complex—people notice different details.

Nevertheless, as the police say, you must have noticed something! Likewise, we say, you *must* notice something. If you do not, you are doomed. The questions will be impenetrable.

WHY ANNOTATE A PASSAGE?

The chief reason to annotate is that it keeps your mind from drifting. If you have read the entire passage and remember nothing, or nearly nothing, you have just wasted valuable time. Annotating helps you keep your concentration. The other reason to annotate is that as you work through the questions, the notes make it easier for your mind and eyes to come back to the passage and find your way around. Besides, who knows? In a moment of pure genius, you may have written the answer to the question in your margin. What a wonderful time saver!

WHAT SHOULD I ANNOTATE?

Annotation styles differ from person to person (we said it was personal). What should you annotate? Certainly not everything and certainly not nothing. (That was a deplorable double negative.) Underline, mark, and write notes that work for you. Take a look at the Introduction to the *Riverside Reader, Alternate Edition,* for one student's example of how to annotate a passage by Virginia Woolf.

Learning the types of questions the College Board asks from books like this will also help you annotate efficiently. In nonfiction prose, identify any clear statement of the argument or thesis. At any and every point, identify the kind of argument being made. Highlight vivid language or particularly vivid metaphors. Mark with an asterisk or checkmark any shifts in point of view or tone. If you find parallel syntax, make a note of it. Underline words outside of your vocabulary; context clues and intelligent guessing will be your ally. Underline any bold claims or obviously false arguments. Don't let the author get away with anything. Remember: You are the one in control. Any time you allow a passage to control, confuse, or dominate you, the odds of getting more than 25 percent of the questions right become very slim indeed. In fact, critical reading and annotating are as much about maintaining an attitude of dominance as they are about getting in touch with the piece and what it is trying to say.

PRACTICE, PRACTICE, PRACTICE!

Before we move on to the questions, let us simply practice critical reading. Read the following passage, but don't look at our annotations. Make your own, spending only about five minutes doing so. Then compare your notes with ours.

Who Are You?

By Nancy Mairs

In her stunning memoir of bicultural girlhood, *The Woman Warrior,* Maxine Hong Kingston writes, "There is a Chinese word for the female *I*—which is 'slave.' Break the women with their own tongues!" English contains no such
5 dramatic instance of the ways in which language shapes women's reality. We can, after all, use the same "I" as men do. We can, but we're not supposed to, at least not often. In myriad ways the rules of polite discourse in this country serve, among other purposes, not to enslave but certainly
10 to silence women and thus to prevent them from uttering the truth about their lives.

Seldom are such rules spoken out loud. Indeed, part of their force arises from their implicitness, which makes them seem natural and essential. They vary in detail, I
15 think, from generation to generation, region to region, class to class, though they stifle communication in similar ways.

Here, roughly put, are a few of the ones I've learned to obey in the company of men. . . . If, in a fit of wishful
20 thinking, you're inclined to dismiss them as passé, spend a few hours in the classrooms and corridors of a coeducational high school or college. We haven't actually come a long way, baby.

Rule 1: Keep quiet. If at all possible, a woman should
25 remain perfectly mute. She should, however, communicate agreement with the men around her eloquently through gestures and demeanor. Think, for instance, of the Presidents' wives. The first First Lady I remember was Mamie Eisenhower, and from then on my head holds a
30 gallery of film clips and still photos of women in the proper polite posture: Jackie and Lady Bird and Pat and Betty and Rosalynn and above all Nancy, eyes widened and glittering, polished lips slightly parted in breathless wonder, heads tilted to gaze upward at the sides of their husband's faces.

35 No one yawns or rolls her eyes (much less speaks unless spoken to). Now, if I were elected President, my husband (who dotes on me, by the way) would fall asleep during my inaugural address. There he'd be in the photos, eyes closed, mouth sagging, head rolled to one side, maybe
40 a bit of spittle trickling into his beard. He wouldn't mean to be rude. . . .

Rule 2: If you must talk at all, talk about something he's interested in. If your feelings are hurt by stifled yawns and retreating backs, dig out this old chestnut. It's still in force. Try not to think of all the women who have used up brain cells memorizing the batting averages of every outfielder in Red Sox history or the difference between the Apollonian and the Dionysian in Nietzsche, depending on their intended target, instead of reflecting on the spiritual dilemma of women denied the priesthood by the Roman Catholic Church or the effect on human reproductive systems of even a "limited" nuclear war or the like.

Rule 3: If you must mention your own concerns, deprecate them prettily. The greatest rudeness in a woman is to appear to take herself seriously. My husband's indictment of feminism, for example—and he's not alone in it—is that feminists "lack a sense of humor." As members of Catholics for Peace and Justice, we both support Sanctuary and Witness for Peace, two nonsectarian groups that work to promote international amity.

In our pained discussions of human-rights issues in Central America I have never heard him criticize Salvadoran and Guatemalan refugees or Sandinista peasants for lacking a sense of humor about their disappeared relatives, their burned infirmaries and bombed buses, their starvation and terror. Nor should he. And he shouldn't expect women to crack jokes when they are enraged by the malnutrition, rape and battering of their sisters and the system that makes such occurrences inevitable.

Actually, in the right places most of the women I know laugh heartily (even though a belly laugh isn't as polite as a giggle). But they weep in the right places, too.

"Lighten up," men tell women who grow passionate about the conditions of their lives. "What *is* all this whining?" one wrote to me. When we are the subjects of our speaking, our voices are too "shrill," "strident"; our tongues are too "sharp"; we are "shrews," "Xanthippes[1]," "termagants," "fishwives." All these words have in common the denigration of women's speech. By ridiculing or trivializing women's utterances, men seek to control what is and is not considered important, weighty, worthwhile in the world.

I, for one, was a well-bred girl who grew into a Yankee lady. From infancy, the language slipped into my mouth was scrubbed as clean as my rattles and teething rings. To this day, I wince at the possibility I might be thought rude. A man's sneer shrivels me. But I guess that's just what I'm going to have to be: rude. Because if women are ever going

---

[1] Wife of the Greek philosopher Socrates (470?–399 B.C.), her name has come to mean shrew.

90   to be really heard, people (including women themselves) are going to have to get used to the sound of their voices and to the subjects they believe worth discussing.

      So I, for one, intend to keep telling the truth about my life as a woman: what I see, whom I love, where I hurt, why I laugh.

95   And you? Tell me, out loud: who are you?

Who Are You?

By Nancy Mairs

In her stunning memoir of bicultural girlhood, *The Woman Warrior,* Maxine Hong Kingston writes, "There is a Chinese word for the female *I*—which is 'slave.' Break the women with their own tongues!" English contains no such

5   dramatic instance of the ways in which language shapes women's reality. We can, after all, use the same "I" as men do. We can, but we're not supposed to, at least not often. In myriad ways the rules of polite discourse in this country serve, among other purposes, not to enslave but certainly

10 to silence women and thus to prevent them from uttering the truth about their lives.

Seldom are such rules spoken out loud. Indeed, part of their force arises from their implicitness, which makes them seem natural and essential. They vary in detail, I

15 think, from generation to generation, region to region, class to class, though they stifle communication in similar ways.

Here, roughly put, are a few of the ones I've learned to obey in the company of men. . . . If, in a fit of wishful

20 thinking, you're inclined to dismiss them as passé, spend a few hours in the classrooms and corridors of a coeducational high school or college. We haven't actually come a long way, baby. *Cigarette ad.*

Rule 1: *Keep quiet.* If at all possible, a woman should

25 remain perfectly mute. She should, however, communicate agreement with the men around her eloquently through gestures and demeanor. Think, for instance, of the Presidents' wives. The first First Lady I remember was Mamie Eisenhower, and from then on my head holds a

30 gallery of film clips and still photos of women in the proper polite posture: Jackie and Lady Bird and Pat and Betty and Rosalynn and above all Nancy, eyes widened and glittering, polished lips slightly parted in breathless wonder, heads tilted to gaze upward at the sides of their husband's faces.

35 No one yawns or rolls her eyes (much less speaks unless spoken to). Now, if I were elected President, my husband (who dotes on me, by the way) would fall asleep during my inaugural address. There he'd be in the photos, eyes closed, mouth sagging, head rolled to one side, maybe

40 a bit of spittle trickling into his beard. He wouldn't mean to be rude. . . . *Just is?*

[Handwritten margin notes:]
speaking creates reality.
myths people believe = tradition never questioned.
girls in school stay quiet to impress boys?
Egos?
in public eyes they are the standard for all women.
Hillary??
conseq's for breaking
after t.v. - Pres. on news

qualifies
Rule 1 Rule 2: *If you must talk at all, talk about something he's* *interested in*. If your feelings are hurt by stifled yawns and retreating backs, dig out this old chestnut. It's still in force.

45 Try not to think of all the women who have used up brain cells memorizing the batting averages of every outfielder in Red Sox history or the difference between the Apollonian and the Dionysian in Nietzsche, depending on their intended target, instead of reflecting on the spiritual

50 dilemma of women denied the priesthood by the Roman Catholic Church or the effect on human reproductive systems of even a "limited" nuclear war or the like.

humor
sports
college boy

hunting; goal.
real issues &
phil. debate
not
"lady-like"
as do all
oppressed
minorities.

qualifies
Rule 2 Rule 3: *If you must mention your own concerns,* deprecate *them prettily*. The greatest rudeness in a woman

55 is to appear to take herself seriously. My husband's indictment of feminism, for example—and he's not alone in it—is that feminists "lack a sense of humor." As members of Catholics for Peace and Justice, we both support Sanctuary and Witness for Peace, two nonsectarian groups that work

60 to promote international amity.

In our pained discussions of human-rights issues in Central America I have never heard him criticize Salvadoran and Guatemalan refugees or Sandinista peasants for lacking a sense of humor about their

65 disappeared relatives, their burned infirmaries and bombed buses, their starvation and terror. Nor should he. And he shouldn't expect women to crack jokes when they are enraged by the malnutrition, rape and battering of their sisters and the system that makes such occurrences

70 inevitable.

What?!
Not even a
valid - or
fair - analogy.

Actually, in the right places most of the women I know laugh heartily (even though a belly laugh isn't as polite as a giggle). But they weep in the right places, too.

"Lighten up," men tell women who grow passionate

75 about the conditions of their lives. "What *is* all this whining?" one wrote to me. When we are the subjects of our speaking, our voices are too "shrill," "strident"; our tongues are too "sharp"; we are "shrews," "Xanthippes[1]," "termagants," "fishwives." All these words have in common

80 the denigration of women's speech. By ridiculing or trivializing women's utterances, men seek to control what is and is not considered important, weighty, worthwhile in the world.

talk about
selves
men control
issues by
silencing
women.

I, for one, was a well-bred girl who grew into a Yankee

85 lady. From infancy, the language slipped into my mouth was scrubbed as clean as my rattles and teething rings. To this day, I wince at the possibility I might be thought rude. A man's sneer shrivels me. But I guess that's just what I'm going to have to be: rude. Because if women are ever going

proper;
clean;
sterile.

---

[1]Wife of the Greek philosopher Socrates (470?–399 B.C.), her name has come to mean shrew.

90 to be really heard, <u>people</u> (including <u>women</u> themselves)
    are going to have to get <u>used to the sound of their voices</u>
    and to the <u>subjects they believe worth discussing</u>.
        So I, for one, intend to keep telling the truth about my
    life as a woman: (<u>what I</u> see, <u>whom I</u> love, <u>where I</u> hurt, <u>why</u> *parallel*
95 <u>I</u> laugh.)   *syatax*
        And you? Tell me, <u>out loud</u>: who are you?

*have we
come very far
in 20 yrs??*

Reagan – '80s.

*Irony: she still isn't speaking – she's
writing about speaking. In a way,
she's still silent & words can be lost
by refusing to read.*

ANSWERING MULTIPLE-CHOICE QUESTIONS

You have just critically read and analyzed a passage in approximately five minutes. Actually, this time around you probably needed longer, but on the actual test five minutes is all you have. That leaves you approximately ten minutes to answer between ten and fourteen questions. What is your best approach?

GENERAL ADVICE FOR ALL THE QUESTIONS

First, please remember that the test makers design the test to be challenging. You can pass the test by getting roughly 50 percent of the questions right. Also, as in the SAT, the AP English Language test graders deduct a point and a quarter for wrong answers (you lose a point for *skipping* an answer and you lose a point and a quarter for giving a *wrong* answer) in order to discourage random guessing. However, you should not take this to mean that skipping a question is better than getting a wrong answer. We always tell our students to answer every question they can because it's usually possible to eliminate two distractors, or even three. Therefore, the mathematics of guessing will be in your favor. For example, if you have reduced the choices to B or D but have absolutely no idea which one is right, guess and go on. *Leave blank only those questions you did not have time to finish*.

Second, unlike the SAT, there is no vocabulary "Hit List" of 250 key words to know. The test writers select nonfiction prose with a strong argumentative bias. They draw from across four centuries and do not adjust choices because of vocabulary. They do expect you to have a working upper-level vocabulary. As you will see, that holds for the essays you write as well. During the school year, our students are allowed to use a dictionary and thesaurus on all passages. We do not want them to be frustrated by vocabulary issues, and we want their working vocabularies to grow. Obviously, you are not allowed these resources on the test. While reading both the passages in this book and those in *The Riverside Reader*, you should always annotate, highlight, and look up unfamiliar vocabulary. The other vocabulary resource is to practice what you have done all your life: improve your skills at finding meaning through context clues. If you have never seen "debilitative" but the sentence it's in includes an image of illness, you can guess that the word is probably negative. If that fails, you may recognize a comparable word that is in your vocabulary, such as "debilitating," and be able to discern meaning from that. Finally, remember that there is a relatively small working list of technical jargon you should know. You have already encountered some of it on the test and you will see more. Keep using the words in the "A Working Vocabulary of Fundamental Terms" chapter in this book to reinforce meaning.

Third, bear in mind that the questions are *not* arranged from easiest to hardest. They are generally arranged sequentially, moving from the beginning of the passage to its end. There are often several questions that deal with the passage as a whole, and they are frequently interspersed within the specific line or paragraph questions. This is important to remember because when you come across a mega-hard question, the one that follows really could be quite easy. Our point? Don't get discouraged or let the test frighten you!

SPECIFIC ADVICE ABOUT CERTAIN TYPES OF QUESTIONS

There is no standard list of question types because the questions are about critical reading and each passage brings its own insights and issues. However, certain basic questions appear fairly often.

The test makers like to ask about pronoun antecedents. For example, they will ask, "'It' refers to which of the following nouns?" They will then give you a list of five nouns from the passage. Put your finger on "it" and plug in each of the nouns. Which one seems to make the most sense?

The test makers also like to ask about difficult vocabulary, but they especially like to do so with words with which we are familiar in another context. For example, in the sample below, the verb "husband" means to conserve, to keep something in storage until it is needed. (In colonial times, it was important to husband the food supply during the winter.) Because you may not be familiar with the verb form and recognize "husband" only as a noun, your normal vocabulary does not work for you and you must intuit meaning entirely based on context clues. Again, plug in the answers and see which one best completes the thought or idea of the sentence.

> "Our future would be better insured if we carefully husband our natural resources." In the context of this sentence, "husband" best means
> (A) to use
> (B) to marry
> (C) to conserve
> (D) to waste
> (E) to join

CORRECT ANSWER: C.

Roman numeral questions are arranged somewhat differently, as you may have noticed in the diagnostic test. The easiest way to handle them is to ignore the A, B, C choices at first. Look only at the Roman numeral answers and decide which one, two, or three are correct. Then look for an answer that corresponds. Another way to handle this type of question is the same as eliminating other answer distractors: Find one that you know with absolute certainty is wrong or right. That will always eliminate two, if not three distractors. *Caution*: Lately, the College Board has not been including Roman numeral questions on the Language and Composition test, but that doesn't mean they won't. Because those kinds of questions are on plenty of other tests, we thought it best to include advice about them.

Another question type evaluates your knowledge of figures of speech, especially similes and metaphors. Such questions generally clarify an unknown with something that is known and add a layer of meaning. You need to recognize that both are occurring. For example, we did not ask a question about "the last quack of a lame duck presidency" in the diagnostic test's "News as Soap Opera." That phrase has so many layers beyond simple metaphor that we couldn't find a way to ask the question. But here, as a metaphor, it clarifies the last days of the Clinton presidency as weak and insignificant, while adding a layer of humor and a lack of sophistication by playing on a common political phrase with added onomatopoeia for humor and wit. It is a metaphoric insult. Another example is below. Learn to read metaphors and similes on both levels and be able to discuss the layers of meaning.

"The new CEO entered the boardroom with the flair of a matador."
This analogy makes all of the following inferences EXCEPT
(A) the new CEO is the center of attention
(B) the new CEO is in a high risk profession
(C) the new CEO faces substantial opposition from others
(D) the new CEO exudes power and strategy
(E) the new CEO is an effective delegator of responsibility

CORRECT ANSWER: E

Main idea stem questions are not complex, but they often appear in the guise of "the author's primary focus," "the intent of the passage," or "the anticipated outcome of the argument." Like any main idea question, they will give you distractors that cover only part of the essay or even suggest an alternative issue altogether; however, the best answer will usually be pretty easy to figure out.

While there are times when the secret underground society of test conspirators seems to feel that tone or mood is important, in the kinds of essays chosen for the test, one tone can't cover the nuances of language and idea. Thus, test makers often ask the question in relation to a specific paragraph or portion of a passage. Tone and mood are best defined by the connotation of the language or the imagery suggested by the language. The greatest problem with tone questions is that their vocabulary is considerably advanced. You would do well to study our short section on tone and then define and make notes on those words that are unfamiliar to you.

A FOOTNOTE ON THE FOOTNOTES

As you noticed in the diagnostic test, one of the passages will have questions about footnotes. There will be three to five such questions and they probably will not be all that difficult. The two key changes on the new AP English Language test involve your ability to cite correctly from several sources in an essay you compose. The test also expects you to be able to recognize and evaluate the information provided in an author's footnotes. The hidden agenda here is to help students avoid the pitfalls of plagiarism. Just as authors must correctly cite sources, students should also be able to correctly cite sources.

Most of the questions will not ask about format but will ask about information. Authors often use footnotes to add information that the casual reader may not need or may wish to gloss over. These footnotes often identify sources, but they can also define terms, add facts or details, clarify confusion around a certain issue, or "set the record straight" if the discussed issue has been controversially argued in other cases.

We include passages with footnotes on all three of the tests in this book. However, for extra practice, let's examine a footnote here. The following is a footnote to a famous speech made by Chief Seattle in 1854:

> [1] In 1854, Governor Isaac Stevens, Commissioner of Indian Affairs for the Washington Territory, proffered a treaty to the Indians providing for the sale of two million acres of their land to the federal government. This address is the reply of Chief Seattle of the Duwampo tribe. The translator was Henry A. Smith.

This is information about the speech and not properly part of the speech. The editor of the book in which it was anthologized wanted readers to have this background information. From it we learn that the federal government wanted to purchase two million acres in 1854 in what is now the state of Washington. We learn who represented the federal government and who represented the Native Americans. We also learn that we are reading a translation and the name of the translator. These are all helpful details that provide a deeper sense of the anguish and the irony inherent in Chief Seattle's speech.

SYNTAX

Most students deal with syntax simply by avoiding it. It seems too much like grammar, which makes you run for cover (this is a metaphor: the study of syntax = war). As in many other aspects of this book, it would be nice if we could write an entire chapter . . . but no one wants to read that! Besides, it is honestly neither feasible nor reasonable, given the small number of syntax questions. Therefore, let us give you a few pieces of quick advice and some examples of a few common syntactical devices.

Parallel syntax is a necessary element in good writing. The purpose of parallel syntax is to provide momentum. It gives drive and energy to an idea. For instance, Martin Luther King, Jr., employed parallel syntax in his "I Have a Dream" speech when he said, "With this faith, we will be able to work together, to pray together, to struggle together, to go to jail together, to stand up for freedom together, knowing that we will be free one day." King's parallel syntax ("to work," "to pray," "to struggle," "to go," "to stand up") creates a passionate energy within the language that nurtures equality and a people's willingness to bring it to fruition.

A second common syntactical device is the rhetorical question. Rhetorical questions may be likened to cheerleading. The reader is manipulated into giving the answer the writer wants. We may ask, for example, "Are rhetorical questions necessary?" We then say, "Yes! And you should help us answer them. Then together, as a nation, we can solve the conundrum created by manipulative rhetorical questions, thereby going to bed at night reassured that our lives will make sense once again." Okay, maybe rhetorical questions don't need to be quite so dramatic, but they can be powerful when used appropriately. In addition, rhetorical questions can also function as transitions from paragraph to paragraph and as organizational techniques from discussion to solution.

A third syntactical element with which you must become familiar is clauses and phrases. Clauses are either independent (IC) or dependent (DC). They all have verbs. The difference between them is that an IC is a complete sentence by itself. You have just read three ICs. You can put a subordinate conjunction in front of an IC and make it a DC, as in "You are reading this book" (IC) as opposed to "Since you are reading this book" (DC). Phrases, on the other hand, do not have verbs. The most common is the prepositional phrase. Clauses and phrases always modify or clarify the nouns and verbs of the sentence. The test makers never ask what a clause or phrase *is,* but they often ask what a clause or phrase *is doing.*

Finally, a quick note on loose and periodic sentences. A loose sentence has an independent clause followed by many dependent clauses: *Congress must address social security issues* (IC) *since many members of the baby boomer generation are reaching the age at which they will be drawing from the very fund to which they have contributed their whole lives.* A periodic sentence is the opposite: It is made up of many dependent clauses preceding the independent clauses. *Because members of the baby boomer generation are coming to the age at which they will be drawing from the social security fund to which they have been contributing their whole lives, Congress must address social security issues* (IC). These two terms—loose and periodic sentences— usually show up once per test.

There is much more to syntax, and we will discuss it in greater detail in the rhetorical analysis chapter. However, the basic terms given here should provide enough support to get you through the few specific questions on the multiple-choice portion of the test.

ATTACKING THE QUESTIONS

The AP exams are a contest of intellect and stamina. Do not let the questions come to you—go after them! Succeeding on this test has a great deal to do with attitude. You cannot be arrogant, but you must feel that you are intellectually capable of handling the test. If you are afraid of the questions, they will steamroll you.

We are about to give you fifteen questions related to Nancy Mairs's essay. Do the same thing with the questions that you did with the passage—read critically and annotate. Read each stem carefully. (The stem is the beginning part of the question, such as "The word 'deprecate' in line 54 means roughly. . ." It is called a stem because it is only part of the full statement; the other part is the answer from the list of five choices.) If you see the words *except, best,* or *primarily,* underline them. Make sure you are clear about what each question is asking. After you have read the stem, try to answer it in your own words first, then read answer A and do one of three things: Put an "X" by it if it is definitely wrong, a "?" if you are unsure of its validity, and a "✓" if you like it as an answer. *Never* go back and reread answers you ruled out. That wastes time. Also, even if you put a check by A, always look at the four other distractors, since C may in fact be a better answer than A. Now look at any question marks you've written. Is there a term, phrase, clause, or word that particularly rules them out? If so, put an "X" or "✓" by the word or phrase. If you see just one check, you just scored. Bubble your answer and move on. If you have written two checks, look once again for a word, phrase, or clause that could rule out one answer or make one of your choices more attractive. Finally, if you just don't see which one is absolutely right, flip your mental coin, bubble in something, and move on. Remember: You will always eliminate two or three distractors, which gives you a 40 to 60 percent better chance of getting the right answer, so go for it!

PRACTICE QUESTIONS

When you are finished, turn the page and compare your annotations of the questions with ours. Then turn the page again and read our discussion of the correct answers. There are two more complete tests at the back of the book for additional practice. Remember that multiple-choice scores improve significantly with practice.

MULTIPLE-CHOICE QUESTIONS ON "WHO ARE YOU?" BY NANCY MAIRS

1) The intended target audience for the essay is
    (A) men
    (B) women
    (C) men and women
    (D) political leaders
    (E) church leaders

2) The purpose of the reference to the work of Maxine Hong Kingston is to
    (A) show how Eastern culture has denigrated women
    (B) demonstrate that women must become warriors to survive in a man's world
    (C) demonstrate the power of language to define reality
    (D) openly establish that all women everywhere are abused
    (E) prove that women are treated like slaves

3) By employing "Rule 1," "Rule 2," and "Rule 3," Mairs is
    (A) suggesting that the conversations between men and women are a game
    (B) suggesting that her argument is logical and deductive
    (C) establishing certainty where there is usually debate and controversy
    (D) organizing her own thoughts so she remains clear
    (E) helping readers keep track of what is most and least important

4) "Rule 1" employs
    (A) a non sequitur
    (B) a straw man argument
    (C) an ad hominem argument
    (D) begging the question

(E) an appeal to authority

5) In the paragraph beginning "In our pained . . ." (61), Mairs's argument now relies primarily on
   (A) an economic fallacy
   (B) a cultural comparison
   (C) a false analogy
   (D) an historic parallel
   (E) a spiritual argument

6) The word "denigration" in line 80 is similar in tone and intent to
   (A) "obey" (19)
   (B) "eloquently" (26)
   (C) "prettily" (54)
   (D) "whining" (76)
   (E) "ridiculing" (80)

7) The most important rhetorical device in the last line of Mairs's essay is
   (A) an adverbial clause
   (B) an apostrophe
   (C) a rhetorical question
   (D) a colon stop
   (E) parallel syntax

8) In context, the word "deprecate" in line 54 means roughly:
   (A) ridicule
   (B) ignore
   (C) de-emphasize
   (D) alleviate
   (E) challenge

9) All of the following suggest a negative perception of women EXCEPT
   (A) "slave" (3)
   (B) "obey" (19)
   (C) "widened and glittering" (32)
   (D) "nonsectarian" (59)
   (E) "Xanthippes" (78)

10) The purpose of using the First Ladies as an example of "Rule 1" is
    (A) they are not in the public eye as much as their husbands
    (B) we make them icons of our culture
    (C) they are as politically influential as their husbands
    (D) they have been recognized for efforts in securing women's rights
    (E) they are well-respected ambassadors

11) Which of the following rhetorical strategies best integrates the next-to-last paragraph?
    (A) passive verbs and rhetorical questions
    (B) strong connotative adjectives and rhetorical questions
    (C) parallel syntax and strong connotative adjectives
    (D) polysyndeton and strong verbs
    (E) parallel syntax and alliteration

12) The "Rules" are syntactically organized according to
(A) absolute, qualification, requalification
(B) thesis, antithesis, synthesis
(C) statement, restatement, synopsis
(D) appositive, restatement, requalification
(E) synthesis, qualification, thesis

13) The types of men identified as "targets" in line 49 are
(A) ministers and businessmen
(B) hunters or fishermen and foreigners
(C) political leaders and businessmen
(D) sports fans and philosophers
(E) sports fans and political leaders

14) The overall tone of this piece is
(A) mournful
(B) apprehensive
(C) indignant
(D) ironic
(E) informative

15) The title of this piece is in the form of a question because
(A) Mairs needs an introduction and sets this up as a pun
(B) it is rhetorical and Mairs expects a particular response
(C) Mairs is asking men and women to take sides in a debate
(D) it builds anticipation to read further
(E) Mairs is trying to find an answer

ANNOTATED QUESTIONS

1) The intended target audience for the essay is
   (A) men
   (B) women
   (C) men and women
   (D) political leaders
   (E) church leaders

2) The purpose of the reference to the work of Maxine Hong
   Kingston is to
   (A) show how Eastern culture has denigrated women
   (B) demonstrate that women must become warriors to survive in a
   man's world
   (C) demonstrate the power of language to define reality
   (D) openly establish that all women everywhere are abused
   (E) prove that women are treated like slaves

3) By employing "Rule 1," "Rule 2," and "Rule 3," Mairs is
   (A) suggesting that the conversations between men and women
   are a game
   (B) suggesting that her argument is logical and deductive
   (C) establishing certainty where there is usually debate and
   controversy
   (D) organizing her own thoughts so she remains clear
   (E) helping readers keep track of what is most and least important

4) "Rule 1" employs
   (A) a non sequitur
   (B) a straw man argument
   (C) an ad hominem argument
   (D) begging the question
   (E) an appeal to authority

5) In the paragraph beginning "In our pained . . ." (61), Mairs's
   argument now relies primarily on
   (A) an economic fallacy
   (B) a cultural comparison
   (C) a false analogy
   (D) an historic parallel
   (E) a spiritual argument

6) The word "denigration" in line 80 is similar in tone and intent to
   (A) "obey" (19)
   (B) "eloquently" (26)
   (C) "prettily" (54)
   (D) "whining" (76)
   (E) "ridiculing" (80)

7) The (most) important rhetorical device in the last line is
   ? (A) an adverbial clause
   ✗ (B) an apostrophe
   ✓ (C) a rhetorical question
   ? (D) a colon stop
   ✗ (E) parallel syntax

8) In context, the word "deprecate" in line 54 means roughly:
   ? (A) ridicule
   ✗ (B) ignore
   ✓ (C) de-emphasize
   ✗ (D) alleviate
   ✗ (E) challenge

9) All of the following suggest a negative perception of women
   EXCEPT
   ✗ (A) "slave" (3) *does*
   ✗ (B) "obey" (19) *does*
   ✗ (C) "widened and glittering" (32) *does*
   ✓ (D) "nonsectarian" (59) *doesn't*
   ✗ (E) "Xanthippes" (78) *does*

10) The purpose of using the First Ladies as an example of "Rule 1" is
   ✗ ? (A) they are not in the public eye as much as their husbands *only b/c of B*
   (B) we make them icons of our culture
   (C) they are as politically influential as their husbands
   (D) they have been recognized for efforts in securing women's rights
   (E) they are well-respected ambassadors

11) Which of the following rhetorical strategies best integrates the next-to-last paragraph?
   ✗ (A) passive verbs and rhetorical questions
   ✗ (B) strong connotative adjectives and rhetorical questions
   ? (C) parallel syntax and strong connotative adjectives
   ? (D) polysyndeton and strong verbs
   ✓ (E) parallel syntax and alliteration *WH's*

12) The "Rules" are syntactically organized according to
   ✓ (A) absolute, qualification, requalification
   ✗ (B) thesis, antithesis, synthesis
   ✗ (C) statement, restatement, synopsis
   ✗ (D) appositive, restatement, requalification
   ? (E) synthesis, qualification, thesis *out of order?*

13) The types of men identified as "targets" in line 49 are
   ✗ (A) ministers and businessmen
   ✗ (B) hunters or fishermen and foreigners *Red Sox & Nietzsche*
   ✗ (C) political leaders and businessmen
   ✓ (D) sports fans and philosophers
   ✗ (E) sports fans and political leaders

14) The overall tone of this piece is
  ✗ (A) mournful
  ✗ (B) apprehensive
  ✓ (C) indignant *she's angry*
  ? (D) ironic
  ✗ (E) informative *not factual!*

15) The title of this piece is in the form of a question because
  ✗ (A) Mairs needs an introduction and sets this up as a pun
  ✓ (B) it is <u>rhetorical</u> and Mairs expects a particular response
  ? (C) Mairs is asking men and women to take sides in a debate
  ✗ (D) it builds anticipation to read further *too simple*
  ✗ (E) Mairs is trying to <u>find an</u> answer *has one*

MULTIPLE-CHOICE ANSWERS AND EXPLANATIONS

1. The intended target audience for the essay is
    (A) men
    (B) women
    (C) men and women
    (D) political leaders
    (E) church leaders

ANSWER: B The repetition of the rhetorical question at the end is clearly directed to women. Mairs mentions all of the other people listed, but she is writing to women about the lack of respect and acknowledgement they receive.

2. The purpose of the reference to the work of Maxine Hong Kingston is to
    (A) show how Eastern culture has denigrated women
    (B) demonstrate that women must become warriors to survive in a man's world
    (C) demonstrate the power of language to define reality
    (D) openly establish that all women everywhere are abused
    (E) prove that women are treated like slaves

ANSWER: C Mairs intends to show how language creates the definition of reality, and she further emphasizes her point by saying "language shapes women's reality." While it is true that Kingston's point seems to be that historically Eastern culture has denigrated women, it is not Mairs's point here. Other answers are not relevant.

3. By employing "Rule 1," "Rule 2," and "Rule 3," Mairs is
    (A) suggesting that the conversations between men and women are a game
    (B) suggesting that her argument is logical and deductive
    (C) establishing certainty where there is usually debate and controversy
    (D) organizing her own thoughts so she remains clear
    (E) helping readers keep track of what is most and least important

ANSWER: B The apparent tone of the piece is logical. Mairs never mentions the concept of a game as a metaphor. It could be implied, but clearly the better answer between A and B is the maintenance of order and the appearance of logic in a rather strident essay.

4. "Rule 1" employs
    (A) a non sequitur
    (B) a straw man argument
    (C) an ad hominem argument
    (D) begging the question
    (E) an appeal to authority

ANSWER: E While it might appear that Mairs is mocking the First Ladies, they are important figures in our national life. None of the other arguments (see vocabulary chapter for definitions) are applicable here. You are expected to know the fundamental fallacies of argument by name. You do not have to use their correct names in the essays, but occasionally a multiple-choice question will offer them.

5. In the paragraph beginning "In our pained . . ." (61), Mairs's argument now relies primarily on
    (A) an economic fallacy
    (B) a cultural comparison
    (C) a false analogy
    (D) an historic parallel
    (E) a spiritual argument

ANSWER: C As in the previous question, you are identifying a failure to reason logically. Here Mairs compares "lacking a sense of humor" about women's roles to the rape, slaughter, and murder in Central American conflicts. To compare one's lack of a sense of humor to such a political and cultural genocide is to commit a false analogy.

6. The word "denigration" in line 80 is similar in tone and intent to
    (A) "obey" (19)
    (B) "eloquently" (26)
    (C) "prettily" (54)
    (D) "whining" (76)
    (E) "ridiculing" (80)

ANSWER: E This one is fairly easy to answer. You can determine from context clues that "denigration" is a negative word. That pretty much narrows it down to D and E and "ridiculing" is at the end of the same paragraph. Also, if using context clues fails you, try substituting the answer choices for the word *denigration* and see which answer best fits the meaning.

7. The most important rhetorical device in the last line is
    (A) an adverbial clause
    (B) an apostrophe
    (C) a rhetorical question
    (D) a colon stop
    (E) parallel syntax

ANSWER: C The last line is a rhetorical question. Mairs is "cheerleading." She wants to hear women roar: "We are important!"

8. In context, the word "deprecate" in line 54 means roughly:
    (A) ridicule
    (B) ignore
    (C) de-emphasize
    (D) alleviate
    (E) challenge

ANSWER: C *Deprecate* means to put down or essentially make light of. Therefore, it means to de-emphasize. The way you solve these fairly common questions is to plug the various answers into the sentence and see if the sentence makes sense with the replacement.

9. All of the following suggest a negative perception of women
    EXCEPT
    (A) "slave" (3)
    (B) "obey" (19)
    (C) "widened and glittering" (32)
    (D) "nonsectarian" (59)
    (E) "Xanthippes" (78)

ANSWER: D This is an easy question if you spotted the "EXCEPT." You needed to do a couple of other things as well. First, you needed to read the footnote on "Xanthippes." Second, you needed to realize that "widened and glittering" is not complimentary in this context. It describes the women as abject believers in male authority.

10. The purpose of using the First Ladies as an example of "Rule 1" is
    (A) they are not in the public eye as much as their husbands
    (B) we make them icons of our culture
    (C) they are as politically influential as their husbands
    (D) they have been recognized for efforts in securing women's rights
    (E) they are well-respected ambassadors

ANSWER: B Although some First Ladies have done C, D, and E, they are recognized for their image. Image equals icon. They are primarily symbols of dutifulness and family loyalty. They are highly publicized, but that is a result of their being icons.

11. Which of the following rhetorical strategies best characterizes the next-to-last paragraph?
    (A) passive verbs and rhetorical questions
    (B) strong connotative adjectives and rhetorical questions
    (C) parallel syntax and strong connotative adjectives
    (D) polysyndeton and strong verbs
    (E) parallel syntax and alliteration

ANSWER: E You are expected to be able to analyze syntactical structure. The brief penultimate paragraph uses strong parallel syntax in conjunction with the alliterative "wh" sound. There are strong verbs and there is a use of asyndeton but not polysyndeton. Adjectives are missing here.

12. The "Rules" are syntactically organized according to
    (A) absolute, qualification, requalification
    (B) thesis, antithesis, synthesis
    (C) statement, restatement, synopsis
    (D) appositive, restatement, requalification
    (E) synthesis, qualification, thesis

ANSWER: A You needed to realize that "Keep quiet" is an absolute command. You could have also arrived at the correct answer by realizing that "Rule 3" is a requalification of "Rule 2." All the other answers sound good but are invalid distractors.

13. The types of men identified as "targets" in line 49 are
    (A) ministers and businessmen
    (B) hunters or fishermen and foreigners

(C) political leaders and businessmen
(D) sports fans and philosophers
(E) sports fans and political leaders

ANSWER: D Mairs facetiously calls men "targets" here for women's choices of verbal partners. Women must adjust to please men. The types of conversation offered here are clearly intended for the sports devotee or the highly educated.

14. The overall tone of this piece is
    (A) mournful
    (B) apprehensive
    (C) indignant
    (D) ironic
    (E) informative

ANSWER: C While there is some humor in this piece, the overall feel is anger. Mairs is upset about the way women are unheard, disregarded, and treated as if they have little importance. You can rule out E easily enough; you can also rule out A because mourning deals specifically with sorrow. While the examples are ironic, Mairs's overall tone is more strident. C comes closest to anger.

15. The title of this piece is in the form of a question because
    (A) Mairs needs an introduction and sets this up as a pun
    (B) it is rhetorical and Mairs expects a particular response
    (C) Mairs is asking men and women to take sides in a debate
    (D) it builds anticipation to read further
    (E) Mairs is trying to find an answer

ANSWER: B As mentioned earlier, this particular question is rhetorical because Mairs already knows the answer. Sometimes two questions on a test can be interlocked and the answer to one may provide help with the answer to the other. Women are people to be heard, appreciated, and respected, and Mairs needs women to realize that truth. D is a nice answer, but only if you want to read the essay as a novel. In a way, this question is eternal. But here, in this essay, Mairs clearly has an answer already and expects women, her intended audience, to respond with force.

3

AN IN-DEPTH LOOK AT THE SYNTHESIS ESSAY QUESTION

After you have completed the multiple-choice section of the test, you will be given a fifteen-minute break. After the break, it is time to settle in for the essays. Before we discuss the specific kinds of essays, there are a couple of elements we need to cover.

INTRODUCTION TO THE ESSAY QUESTIONS

Before you begin, it can be helpful to know how the essay is administered. In the past, you would have received both a green four-page sheet with the prompts for the three essays and a pink lined booklet. You would have made your notes on the green sheet and written your essays in the pink booklet. From the time you received both booklets, you would have been given two hours, which breaks down into forty minutes per essay—five to ten minutes to plan and thirty to thirty-five minutes to write.

Well, that has changed. With the advent of the synthesis question, more time was added—fifteen minutes. At first you will receive only the green booklet, and you will get fifteen minutes to read the material and plan your essays. As you will see later, we recommend focusing on the multi-passage synthesis essay during this time; if you have time left over, use it to plan the rhetorical analysis passage. Spend your fifteen minutes well. At the conclusion of the fifteen minutes, you will be given the pink booklet. You now have two hours to write three essays. Time is precious and reading critically is essential.

The grading of the essays has also been changed. Each grader is given a randomly sorted packet of twenty-five essays. Graders sit at a table with seven other graders, and check with the table leader concerning any odd, unreadable, or incomplete essays. The table leader also reads over some of the essays at the table. The table leader does not reread all the essays—just a portion, to guarantee consistency among the graders and consistency in the scoring scale of 1 to 9. There are other, more sophisticated computer checks and balances, but the reality is that one well-trained grader reads your essay. What are they looking for?

If you are taking an AP English class, your teacher should have shared various rubrics for many of the essays you have written in class. These are the fundamental guides for the graders and cover the key elements for the 1-to-9 scores. So by the time you take the exam, you should be familiar with what the graders are being asked to look for. However, bear in mind that the graders do not have time to ponder or dwell. They read. They form an impression. They assign a score.

To simplify the rubric, the graders are primarily looking for three elements. The first is: "Did the student answer the question?" It's very possible to write an intelligent, clever, witty essay—and believe us when we say we have seen some beautiful ones—that will earn a low score because it does not address the prompt. The second element is: "Did the writer's point remain clear?" There should be no confusion or uncertainty. Your argument should be clear from the first point through the conclusion. Your sentences should not sound like words tossed into a blender and poured out onto the paper in some kind of random confusion. Be clear and concise in your own expression. Some students think that if they throw in a ton of fancy words ("asyndeton," "epanalepsis," "chiasmus," and the like) their score will be higher, but that's not the case. Graders much prefer a good idea that is expressed with the diction most relevant to the essay. The third element is: "Did the student use examples?" You absolutely must include a minimum of three quotations in the synthesis essay. In rhetorical analysis, provide the grader with quoted evidence from the passage for the points you are making. Even in the general argument, if you do not have *specific* examples, your essay will receive no more than a lower-half score.

In addition to those three essential elements, there are two others. The first is grammar. Graders expect your grammar to be fluent, although not necessarily perfect. This is, after all, a hastily conceived rough draft, and graders fully understand that. It is possible for a poor speller to score well on the test. However, if your control of grammar compromises nearly every sentence (see the section on clarity), then your score will suffer.

Last, but not least, is voice. You can write a perfectly acceptable upper-half essay that answers the question, is clear, and gives examples, but is unbelievably dull. As graders, we often find ourselves reading essay after essay that sounds like the same five-paragraph study of diction, syntax, and symbols. When we read one that does not sound like everyone else's, we are immediately drawn to the essay. Be natural; write like yourself. Have your own style, but don't become so fixated on the beauty of your prose that you forget to answer the question or provide examples.

With those thoughts in mind, let us now turn to the new kid on the block: the synthesis essay.

INTRODUCTION TO THE SYNTHESIS ESSAY QUESTION

The synthesis question has a triple purpose. The intent of the general argument question is to ensure that you are able to present and support an argument. The synthesis question further examines your ability to consider and support a rational argument. But unlike the general argument essay, the synthesis essay *also* seeks to evaluate your ability to absorb, understand, and employ several sources on the same topic. Finally, it tests your ability to correctly cite the sources you have quoted or paraphrased in your argument. In completing the synthesis essay question, you need to be able to manage several tasks quickly and thoroughly. This chapter will guide you through the thicket of these responsibilities.

Before beginning, we do want to say that the students in our classes (and in the classes of other AP teachers with whom we have spoken) generally enjoy writing the synthesis essay. Students have more ideas and materials at their disposal and, consequently, have more to say. Even if the prompt is a topic you have never before encountered, you at least have six to eight sources to use in your discussion.

THE PROCESS

Remember that the process for writing the essays has changed from past years. You now have an extra fifteen minutes to examine the essay questions. The fifteen minutes were added specifically for the synthesis question. Therefore, we STRONGLY recommend that you approach the fifteen-minute reading period with that in mind. Look immediately at the synthesis passages. If there is time left over, read and make notes on the rhetorical analysis piece and glance at the general argument question, but spend the majority of your time on the synthesis question.

Read the initial question page carefully. There are three sections. The first is "Directions." In the directions, you will find this crucial sentence: *Your argument should be central; the sources should support this argument. Avoid merely summarizing sources.* As in the general argument, *your* opinion is the most important aspect of this essay. Therefore, it's essential that you form one! The sources you present in your argument are there to support and sustain your own ideas. If you simply repeat what the sources had to say about the issue, you will always earn a lower-half score. This means that bringing your own examples to a synthesis essay, as you are required to do in a general argument essay, is a good idea. It's not essential, but it does help demonstrate to the reader that you are presenting your own argument.

The second section of the first page is the "Introduction," which is unique to this essay question. Its purpose is to get you thinking about the issue by making general statements about the topic. The ideas here are meant to "prime the pump," so to speak. The introduction provides a larger context for the question, but this material is *not* the prompt. Do not get sidetracked by answering any questions that may be asked in the introduction. Likewise, do not address an idea presented in the introductory material if it is not central to the assignment.

After the introductory material you will come to the "Assignment." In this section you are given the prompt, which you must address in a specific manner. The topic is highlighted in bold type. Thus far, you have seen topics that have asked you to take a position that agrees with, disagrees with, or qualifies some claim (we give this the acronym ADQ). However, there are also more open questions that ask students to present recommendations or evaluate current or future effects of a policy. The important thing to remember here is this: DO WHAT THE PROMPT ASKS YOU TO DO! The language of the assignment is very, very important to the task because it *is* the question. Additionally, the prompt will state that you must "synthesize at least three of the sources for support." You cannot have an upper-half score unless you QUOTE OR PARAPHRASE AT LEAST THREE SEPARATE SOURCES IN YOUR ESSAY. To summarize, (1) answer the question, (2) present your own opinion, and (3) use at least three different sources in the essay.

Finally, at the bottom of the first page, there is a brief list of the sources that will follow. It looks something like this:

Source A (Dilby)

Source B (Sollich)

When you cite a source, you do not need to use MLA format. You may simply refer to it as either "Source A" or "Dilby," for example. You may also write, "Dilby makes a startling observation when he suggests . . ." (or "Source A states . . .").

Before turning the page to your sources, you should take a moment to do a couple of things that will help you focus later. At the outset, you should clearly identify the task by either underlining the assignment or restating it in your own words (a task we advocate highly). Also, before you turn the page, write down any opinion you may have about the topic. Then, as with the general argument question, jot down any examples that come to mind. Make a quick list, and then get on with the reading.

DEALING WITH THE PASSAGES AND VISUALS

There is a certain method for reading each of the passages. When you are practicing synthesis questions, it's a good idea to learn this process. On the actual test you won't have sufficient time, as this method really requires you to spend fifteen to twenty minutes looking at each source. However, it is our hope (and the College Board's hope) that practice will indeed make you . . . well, faster. By the time you are ready to take the test, you should have internalized most of these steps so that you will almost automatically identify certain elements right away.

Let's now take a look at the areas you should practice until recognizing them becomes second nature:

1. Is the source biased? You can determine this by looking at the source itself—an article from *Christian Century* might carry a certain inherent bias.

2. Does the source's date of publication have an effect on the relevance of the argument? A passage written in 1975 about advertising is likely to be out of date today, so take this into account if you decide to use this source.

3. What position does the author hold? Determine whether he or she is for, against, or neutral about the topic.

4. For what audience is the author writing? Identify the target audience for the piece, such as businesspeople, political leaders, or university researchers.

Once you have identified these elements, whether you've annotated the passage or just absorbed the ideas the material presents, you are ready to *engage* the authors' arguments or points of view.

In order to engage the text, you must spend some time working with it, which is not a step you simply do in your head. Rather, you should critically mark and annotate the passage by identifying three things:

1. What is the point of view, thesis, or information offered?

2. Are there any "quotables"—particularly succinct or stimulating phrases—you can use?

3. Do you plan to use the piece or a portion of it to support your argument in some way? (You may decide this question after reading all or most of the passages—you are looking for at least three good ones.)

THE VISUAL

There will be at least one visual of some kind among the passages. It may take the form of a chart, table, photograph, political cartoon, painting, or any other image that can be reproduced in black and white. The basic concept behind the use of a visual in this exam is that everything we experience in life conducts an argument in some way. Any visual representation is as much an argument as an essay—think, for example, of print advertising or political cartoons. However, most rhetoricians and probably all first-year composition teachers agree that *everything* we experience can produce a thoughtful encounter.

This means you should study visuals with the same care with which you study written arguments. In fact, you should follow the same steps for analyzing the visual as you do when annotating the passages: look for bias, datedness, position, audience, point of view, and usefulness to your argument. For further instruction and discussion on how to analyze visual representations, take a look at *The Riverside Reader,* which offers several examples for study. But remember, you should make reference to the visual only if it offers specific support or illustration of your argument.

USING ENOUGH PASSAGES

In practicing this type of prompt with our students, we have noticed that several of them did not even read one or two of the final passages in the prompt. That is *not* necessarily an error. We have stressed that time is of the essence. If you have gone over the first five passages and four of them are excellent and you feel ready to go, then write the essay. The specific requirement for this essay is that you must quote or paraphrase and cite at least *three different sources*. You may always use more. If you have sufficient resources after reading five of the passages and feel ready to start writing, go for it.

USING OPPOSING PASSAGES

It is always a good strategy to use passages that disagree with your point of view, especially if you are dealing with an "agree, disagree, or qualify" prompt. If Source C says just the opposite of your point of view, one excellent strategy is to write a paragraph that quotes or paraphrases Source C and then points out what you consider to be the weakness or error in that author's argument. You might note the author's failure to understand the complete picture or point out a biased argument based on the author's background. The ability to recognize an opponent's argument and clarify the weakness in that argument is generally a sign of sophisticated writing and thinking.

COUNTING PASSAGES

You are required to cite at least three different sources. You may use more than three and you may quote more than once from any particular passage. In grading these essays, we have found that students generally used the requisite number of sources and managed to integrate them into their own arguments. However, if there is any doubt, we simply go back and count sources. Just be sure, as you write your argument, that you are including a sufficient number of sources to support it, and check to see that you cite the sources appropriately. Beware: do not put in so many quotes that the grader cannot find *your* argument.

In summary, in answering the synthesis essay question, (1) read the first page carefully and take note of your task; (2) identify your own feelings or opinion before you read the passage; and (3) read, annotate, and comment on each passage, paying close attention to clarity of position and keeping an eye open for any good quotations you might use.

Now read the following practice synthesis question on the electoral college. Read critically and annotate. Write notes all over the page and circle, underline, and cross out words and phrases—any method is fine as long as you understand your annotations. When you are finished, compare your notes with our annotations.

A PRACTICE QUESTION

**English Language and Composition Exam
Section II**

Sample Question 1

**Reading time: 15 minutes
Suggested writing time: 40 minutes**

(This question counts as one-third of the total essay section score.)

Directions: The following prompt is based on the accompanying six sources.

This question requires you to integrate a variety of sources into a coherent, well-written essay. Refer to the sources to support your position; avoid mere paraphrase or summary. Your argument should be central; the sources should support this argument.

Remember to attribute both direct and indirect citations.

INTRODUCTION

The mode of the selection of the president was one of the most difficult and contentious issues in the 1787 Convention. Some delegates advocated presidential election by the national legislature, while other delegates favored direct election by the people. The pressing question facing the delegates was whether the public would have the knowledge of various candidates necessary to make a wise decision. Their final decision was the result of a compromise worked out by a committee comprised of one delegate from each of the states and presented to the Convention on September 4, 1787. However, some analysts and scholars question the validity and purpose of an electoral college in the 21st century when the general public is arguably well-informed about presidential candidates. Would direct popular vote be a more valid process for electing the president in today's society? Should the Electoral College be abolished or is the current system worth keeping?

ASSIGNMENT

Read the following sources (including any introductory information) carefully. Then, in an essay that synthesizes at least three of the sources for support, take a position that defends, challenges, or qualifies the claim that the Electoral College is an outdated institution that should be replaced by direct popular election of the president.

Refer to the sources as Source A, Source B, etc.; titles are included for your convenience.

Source A (National Archives chart)

Source B (Linder)

Source C (Constitutional Convention)

Source D (Levinson)

Source E (McGinnis)

Source F (map)

Source A

Adapted from The U.S. National Archives & Records Administration.
www.archives.gov. May 24, 2007.

Historical Election Results

Electoral College Box Scores 2000

Election	2000		
President	George W. Bush [R]		
Main Opponent	Albert Gore, Jr. [D]		
Electoral Vote	Winner: 271	Main Opponent: 266	Total/Majority: 538/270
Popular Vote	Winner: 50,456,062	Main Opponent: 50,996,582	
Vice President	Richard B. Cheney (271)		
V.P. Opponent:	Joseph Lieberman (266)		
Notes	George W. Bush received fewer popular votes than Albert Gore, Jr., but received a majority of electoral votes. One electoral vote was not cast.		

Source B

Adapted from Doug Linder's "The Electoral College Debate." *Exploring Constitutional Conflicts.* 2001-2007.
http://www.law.umkc.edu/faculty/projects/ftrials/conlaw/home.html. May 23, 2007.

The following passage is excerpted from an online web page that provides a brief summary of the debate concerning the Electoral College.

Arguments for the Electoral College

1. The Electoral College, in recognizing a role for states in the selection of the president, reminds us of their importance in our federal system.

2. The Electoral College encourages more person-to-person campaigning by candidates, as they spend time in both the big cities and smaller cities in battleground states.

3. In close, contested elections, recounts will usually be confined to a state or two, rather than an across-the-country recount that might be required if we had direct election of the president.

4. The Electoral College, with its typical winner-take-all allocation of votes, often turns a small percentage margin of victory into one that appears much larger, thus making the victory seem more conclusive and adding to the winner's perceived legitimacy.

Arguments for Direct Popular Vote

1. Most Americans believe that the person who receives the most votes should become president. Direct election is seen as more consistent with democratic principles than is the Electoral College system.

2. The Electoral College gives disproportionate weight to the votes of citizens of small states. For example, a vote by a resident of Wyoming counts about four times more—electorally—than a vote by a California resident.

3. If presidents were elected by direct popular vote, they would wage a campaign and advertise all across the nation, rather than (as they do in the Electoral College system) concentrating almost all of their time and effort in a handful of battleground states. The Electoral College system encourages candidates to pander to the interests of voters in a few closely contested states.

4. The Electoral College system, especially in a close election, is subject to the mischief that might be caused by disloyal—or even bribed—electors.

Source C

Excerpted from "The Electoral College Debate: The Framers' Debate Concerning Methods for Selecting the President." *Exploring Constitutional Conflicts*. 2001–2007. http://www.law.umkc.edu/faculty/projects/ftrials/conlaw/elector1787.html. May 23, 2007.

The following passage is excerpted from an online source that provides a complete transcription of the debate at the 1787 Constitutional Convention relating to the method of selecting the president, as recorded in the notes of James Madison.

Mr. SHERMAN thought that the sense of the Nation would be better expressed by the Legislature, than by the people at large. The latter will never be sufficiently informed of [the candidates'] characters, and besides will never give a majority of votes to any one man. They will generally vote for some man in their own State, and the largest State will have the best chance for the appointment. If the choice be made by the Legislature a majority of voices may be made necessary to constitute an election.

Mr. GOVERNR. MORRIS was pointedly against his [the president] being so chosen. He will be the mere creature of the Legislature: if appointed & impeachable by that body. He ought to be elected by the people at large, by the freeholders of the Country. That difficulties attend this mode, he admits. But they have been found superable in N[ew] Y[ork] & in Con[necticu]t and would he believed be found so, in the case of an Executive for the U[nited] States. If the people should elect, they will never fail to prefer some man of distinguished character, or services; some man, if he might so speak, of continental reputation. —If the Legislature elect, it will be the work of intrigue, of cabal, and of faction; it will be like the election of a pope by a conclave of cardinals; real merit will rarely be the title to the appointment. He moved to strike out "National Legislature" & insert "citizens of U.S."

Source D

Adapted from "Should We Dispense with the Electoral College?" PENNumbra. 2007 University of Pennsylvania Law Review. http://www.pennumbra.com/debates/debate.php?did=8. May 23, 2007.

The following passage is excerpted from University of Texas Law School Professor Sanford Levinson's examination of the "informal" problems with the Electoral College in the 21st century.

. . . [C]ontemporary presidential campaigns have become perversely structured around the reality of the College and its generation of so-called "battleground states" that have become the obsessive focus of modern campaigns. In 2004, for example, a full 99% of all advertising expenditures by the two major-party candidates were concentrated in only seventeen of the states. Florida and Ohio alone accounted for more than 45% ($111 million) of the $235 million spent in all of these states. Wisconsin, another "battleground," received a total of thirty-one candidate visits, as compared with two visits to California. New York received only one such visit! Other ignored states included Texas and Illinois. This means, among other things, that neither candidate was ever required to prepare serious speeches addressing the needs of the largest states in the Union. As a resident of Texas, I can certainly testify to the fact that it is significantly different from, say, Florida, one of the principal "battlegrounds" in both 2000 and 2004. This undercuts the argument that the Electoral College and the purported benefit given to large states by their ability give the winner of a given state *all* of the state's electoral votes (and thus deprive the losing minorities of any representation at all in the College) undercuts, at least to some extent, the small-state bonus. Only *some* large states are "battlegrounds," and there is no reason at all to believe that the lucky few are necessarily proxies for their ignored sister states.

From a political scientist's perspective, the Electoral College is an outstanding example of the importance (and costs) of "path dependence," whereby decisions made at time X become entrenched and shape future politics, for good and, in this case, decidedly for ill. Perhaps it is correct that there is nothing we can do about the College. But that is completely different from a normative defense of the constitutional iron cage built for us by Framers who were necessarily completely ignorant of the shape the country would take in the ensuing two centuries.

Source E

Adapted from "Should We Dispense with the Electoral College?" PENNumbra. 2007 University of Pennsylvania Law Review.
http://www.pennumbra.com/debates/debate.php?did=8. May 23, 2007.

The following passage is excerpted from Northwestern University School of Law Professor John McGinnis's rebuttal to Levinson on the "informal" problems and an additional benefit of the Electoral College in the 21st century.

Professor Levinson also observes that the Electoral College makes candidates pay attention to swing states rather than the nation as a whole. This tendency does seem to be a defect. But a system of popular vote will also cause candidates to pay more attention to some voters rather than others, most importantly the voters who cast the least per voter turnout. Thus, candidates are likely to campaign more in cities than in rural areas and more in affluent areas than poor ones. This defect of the popular system may be even more substantial than the current focus on swing states, because the voters in swing states are likely to be more heterogeneous than voters chosen by low turnout cost. Both the popular vote and the electoral vote will not actually treat all voters equally in a practical sense, but no system can be devised that will have equal effects, given that voters are only equal as matter of law, but otherwise differently situated.

The Electoral College also performs well, and perhaps better than the popular vote, in the second important goal of an electoral system: bestowing legitimacy on the president. It has been noted that the Electoral College tends to magnify the winner's margin of victory. Particularly among the general public as opposed to the political cognoscenti, this greater margin bestows a greater legitimacy. The sense of legitimacy is especially important for the president because in our system the president is not only the head of government, but the head of state, unifying the nation in times of crisis.

Legitimacy is aided simply by the venerable nature of the system. A large majority understands the basic rules of the game and knows that these rules were not invented with any current election in mind. Given its longevity, even the divergence between the popular vote and the electoral votes does not detract much from the legitimacy of the president. . . . Transitioning to a new system, however, would raise questions about whether its details were structured to aid one or the other of the two great parties. Again, I do not wish to argue that this cost is huge or that in time it would not dissipate, but it is a significant cost not faced by our current system.

Source F

Adapted from *"The Electoral College"* Issues and Controversies. February 15, 2005.
http://www.2facts.com/ICOF/temp/32389tempi0502790.asp. May 23, 2007.

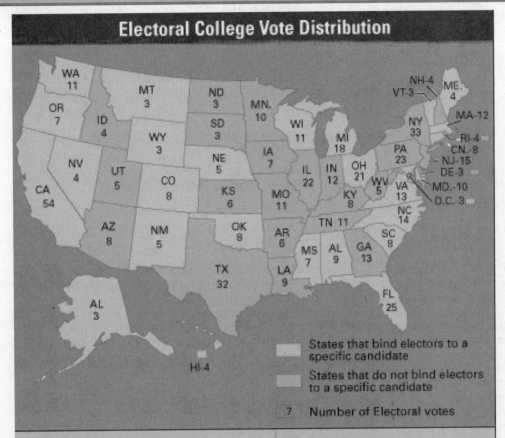

Electoral College Vote Distribution

States that bind electors to a specific candidate

States that do not bind electors to a specific candidate

7 Number of Electoral votes

To be elected president, a candidate must win a majority of votes in the electoral college (at least 270 out of 538). Traditionally, each state gives its electoral votes —which are equal in number to that state's representatives in the Senate and the House of Representatives—to electors who have pledged support to the candidate winning that state's popular vote. Although 26 states and Washington D.C. have laws binding electors to their assigned candidate, the Constitution does not make such requirements. As a result, many critics of the electoral college fear that a "faithless" elector could forgo his or her pledge and alter the outcome of a presidential election. Indeed, over the past 100 years, seven electors have switched their vote to another candidate, though in none of those cases did the changed vote affect the final result.

Source: National Archives and Records Administration

ANNOTATED SYNTHESIS QUESTION

**English
Language and Composition Exam
Section II
Sample Question 1**

**Reading Time: 15 minutes
Suggested Writing Time: 40 minutes**

This question makes up one-third of the total essay section score.

Directions: The following prompt is based on the accompanying six sources.

This question requires you to integrate a variety of sources into a coherent, well-written essay. Refer to the sources to support your position; avoid mere paraphrase or summary. Your argument should be central; the sources should support this argument.

Remember to attribute both direct and indirect citations.

INTRODUCTION

The mode of the selection of the president was one of the most difficult and contentious issues in the 1787 Convention. Some delegates advocated presidential election by the national legislature, while other delegates favored direct election by the people. The pressing question facing the delegates was whether the public would have the knowledge of various candidates necessary to make a wise decision. Their final decision was the result of a compromise worked out by a committee comprised of one delegate from each of the states and presented to the Convention on September 4, 1787. However, some analysts and scholars question the validity and purpose of an electoral college in the 21st century when the general public is arguably well-informed about presidential candidates. Would direct popular vote be a more valid process for electing the president in today's society? Should the Electoral College be abolished or is the current system worth keeping?

ASSIGNMENT

Read the following sources (including any introductory information) carefully. Then, in an essay that synthesizes at least three of the sources for support, take a position that defends, challenges, or qualifies the claim that the Electoral College is an outdated institution that should be replaced by direct popular election of the president. *argue this*

Refer to the sources as Source A, Source B, etc.; titles are included for your convenience.

Source A (National Archives chart)

Source B (Linder)

Source C (Constitutional Convention)   *Electoral College v. Direct election*

Source D (Levinson)

Source E (McGinnis)

Source F (map)

*—Good & bad people can be apathetic
- how many people actually vote?
- Who votes?
- too much media before elections
- good & BAD b/c people can be ill-informed*

Source A

Adapted from The U.S. National Archives & Records Administration.
www.archives.gov. May 24, 2007.

Historical Election Results

Electoral College Box Scores 2000

Election	2000		
President	George W. Bush [R] *271 (1 vote) 50,456,062*		
Main Opponent	Albert Gore, Jr. [D] *266*	*50,996,582 more*	
Electoral Vote	Winner: 271	Main Opponent: 266	Total/Majority: 538/270
Popular Vote	Winner: 50,456,062	Main Opponent: 50,996,582	
Vice President	Richard B. Cheney (271)		
V.P. Opponent:	Joseph Lieberman (266)		
Notes	George W. Bush received fewer popular votes than Albert Gore, Jr., but received a majority of electoral votes. One electoral vote was not cast.		

# of electoral votes per state? Bigger states get more e. votes -

Neutral

Source B

Adapted from Doug Linder's "The Electoral College Debate." *Exploring Constitutional Conflicts.* 2001-2007. http://www.law.umkc.edu/faculty/projects/ftrials/conlaw/home.html. May 23, 2007.

The following passage is excerpted from an online web page that provides a brief summary of the debate concerning the Electoral College.

Arguments for the Electoral College

1. The Electoral College, in recognizing a role for states in the selection of the president, reminds us of their importance in our federal system.

2. The Electoral College encourages more person-to-person campaigning by candidates, as they spend time in both the big cities and smaller cities in battleground states.

3. In close, contested elections, recounts will usually be confined to a state or two, rather than an across-the-country recount that might be required if we had direct election of the president.

4. The Electoral College, with its typical winner-take-all allocation of votes, often turns a small percentage margin of victory into one that appears much larger, thus making the victory seem more conclusive and adding to the winner's perceived legitimacy. *seems weak*

Arguments for Direct Popular Vote

1. Most Americans believe that the person who receives the most votes should become president. Direct election is seen as more consistent with democratic principles than is the Electoral College system.

2. The Electoral College gives disproportionate weight to the votes of citizens of small states. For example, a vote by a resident of Wyoming counts about four times more—electorally—than a vote by a California resident.

3. If presidents were elected by direct popular vote, they would wage a campaign and advertise all across the nation, rather than (as they do in the Electoral College system) concentrating almost all of their time and effort in a handful of battleground states. The Electoral College system encourages candidates to pander to the interests of voters in a few closely contested states. *"I promise to ban soda machines in schools"*

4. The Electoral College system, especially in a close election, is subject to the mischief that might be caused by disloyal—or even bribed—electors.

Both sides of argument.
- heavy positive on side of direct election.
- weak on Elect. Coll.

Source C

Excerpted from "The Electoral College Debate: The Framers' Debate Concerning Methods for Selecting the President." *Exploring Constitutional Conflicts.* 2001–2007. http://www.law.umkc.edu/faculty/projects/ftrials/conlaw/elector1787.html. May 23, 2007.

The following passage is excerpted from an online source that provides a complete transcription of the debate at the 1787 Constitutional Convention relating to the method of selecting the president, as recorded in the notes of James Madison.

Mr. SHERMAN thought that the sense of the Nation would be better expressed by the Legislature, than by the people at large. The latter will <u>never be sufficiently informed</u> of [the candidates'] characters, and besides will <u>never give a majority of votes to any one man</u>. They will generally <u>vote for some man in their own State,</u> and the <u>largest State will have the best chance</u> for the appointment. If the choice be made by the Legislature a majority of voices may be made necessary to constitute an election.

not informed. Too many Chiefs

Check & Balances

Mr. GOVERNR. MORRIS was pointedly against his [the president] being so chosen. He will be the mere <u>creature of the Legislature:</u> if appointed & impeachable by that body. He ought to be <u>elected by the people at large,</u> by the freeholders of the Country. That difficulties attend this mode, he admits. But they have been found superable in N[ew] Y[ork] & in Con[necticu]t and would he believed be found so, in the case of an Executive for the U[nited] States. If the <u>people should elect,</u> they will <u>never fail to prefer some man of distinguished character,</u> or services; some man, if he might so speak, of <u>continental reputation.</u>—If the <u>Legislature elect,</u> it will be the work of <u>intrigue, of cabal, and of faction;</u> it will be like the election of a pope by a conclave of cardinals; real merit will rarely be the title to the appointment. He moved to strike out "National Legislature" & insert "citizens of U.S."

yea, right.

people given credit for choosing good man. Leg. would be, "intrigue, of cabal, & of faction"

- What about primaries - early election to select candidates? (Didn't have parties in 1787)

- Also, $ to campaign so a man w/ "cont. reput." would be rich. That's not representative of most people!

Source D

Adapted from "Should We Dispense with the Electoral College?" PENNumbra. 2007 University of Pennsylvania Law Review. http://www.pennumbra.com/debates/debate.php?did=8. May 23, 2007.

The following passage is excerpted from University of Texas Law School Professor Sanford Levinson's examination of the "informal" problems with the Electoral College in the 21st century.

...[C]ontemporary presidential campaigns have become perversely structured around the reality of the College and its generation of so-called "battleground states" that have become the obsessive focus of modern campaigns. In 2004, for example, a full 99% of all advertising expenditures by the two major-party candidates were concentrated in only seventeen of the states. Florida and Ohio alone accounted for more than 45% ($111 million) of the $235 million spent in all of these states. Wisconsin, another "battleground," received a total of thirty-one candidate visits, as compared with two visits to California. New York received only one such visit! Other ignored states included Texas and Illinois. This means, among other things, that neither candidate was ever required to prepare serious speeches addressing the needs of the largest states in the Union. As a resident of Texas, I can certainly testify to the fact that it is significantly different from, say, Florida, one of the principal "battlegrounds" in both 2000 and 2004. This undercuts the argument that the Electoral College and the purported benefit given to large states by their ability give the winner of a given state *all* of the state's electoral votes (and thus deprive the losing minorities of any representation at all in the College) undercuts, at least to some extent, the small-state bonus. Only *some* large states are "battlegrounds," and there is no reason at all to believe that the lucky few are necessarily proxies for their ignored sister states.

[handwritten margin note: needs?]

From a political scientist's perspective, the Electoral College is an outstanding example of the importance (and costs) of "path dependence," whereby decisions made at time X become entrenched and shape future politics, for good and, in this case, decidedly for ill. Perhaps it is correct that there is nothing we can do about the College. But that is completely different from a normative defense of the constitutional iron cage built for us by Framers who were necessarily completely ignorant of the shape the country would take in the ensuing two centuries.

[handwritten notes: Against E.C.]

[handwritten notes: - Advertising $ - Sister states needs not same.]

Source E

Adapted from "Should We Dispense with the Electoral College?" PENNumbra. 2007 University of Pennsylvania Law Review. http://www.pennumbra.com/debates/debate.php?did=8. May 23, 2007.

The following passage is excerpted from Northwestern University School of Law Professor John McGinnis's rebuttal to Levinson on the "informal" problems and an additional benefit of the Electoral College in the 21st century.

admits problem.

Professor Levinson also observes that the Electoral College makes candidates pay attention to swing states rather than the nation as a whole. This tendency does seem to be a defect. But a system of popular vote will also cause candidates to pay more attention to some voters rather than others, most importantly the voters who cast the least per voter turnout. Thus, candidates are likely to campaign more in cities than in rural areas and more in affluent areas than poor ones. This defect of the popular system may be even more substantial than the current focus on swing states, because the voters in swing states are likely to be more heterogeneous than voters chosen by low turnout cost. Both the popular vote and the electoral vote will not actually treat all voters equally in a practical sense, but no system can be devised that will have equal effects, given that voters are only equal as matter of law, but otherwise differently situated.

b/c these vote

The Electoral College also performs well, and perhaps better than the popular vote, in the second important goal of an electoral system: bestowing legitimacy on the president. It has been noted that the Electoral College tends to magnify the winner's margin of victory. Particularly among the general public as opposed to the political cognoscenti, this greater margin bestows a greater legitimacy. The sense of legitimacy is especially important for the president because in our system the president is not only the head of government, but the head of state, unifying the nation in times of crisis.

kind of weak - ??

Legitimacy is aided simply by the venerable nature of the system. A large majority understands the basic rules of the game and knows that these rules were not invented with any current election in mind. Given its longevity, even the divergence between the popular vote and the electoral votes does not detract much from the legitimacy of the president. . . . Transitioning to a new system, however, would raise questions about whether its details were structured to aid one or the other of the two great parties. Again, I do not wish to argue that this cost is huge or that in time it would not dissipate, but it is a significant cost not faced by our current system.

higher taxes!

"intrigue & cabal"
- everyone bickers too much.
- who to trust to make a new format?

For E.C.
- not treat voters =
- legitimacy] weak
- $

Source F

Adapted from *"The Electoral College"* Issues and Controversies. February 15, 2005.
http://www.2facts.com/ICOF/temp/32389tempi0502790.asp. May 23, 2007.

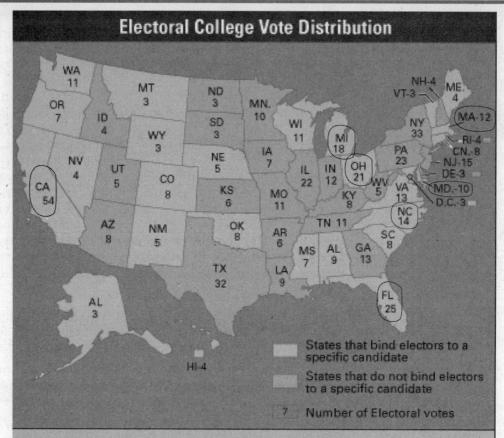

To be elected president, a candidate must win a majority of votes in the electoral college (at least 270 out of 538). Traditionally, each state gives its electoral votes —which are equal in number to that state's representatives in the Senate and the House of Representatives—to electors who have pledged support to the candidate winning that state's popular vote. Although 26 states and Washington D.C. have laws binding electors to their assigned candidate, the Constitution does not make such requirements. As a result, many critics of the electoral college fear that a "faithless" elector could forgo his or her pledge and alter the outcome of a presidential election. Indeed, over the past 100 years, seven electors have switched their vote to another candidate, though in none of those cases did the changed vote affect the final result.

Source: National Archives and Records Administration

Many states with larger number of electoral votes don't bind electors. Possible danger of electing wrong winner b/c of faithlessness.

Scoring Rubric for Synthesis Questions

As much as possible, this scoring guide will follow the concepts and language of those used by the College Board. However, bear in mind that their guides are designed for graders, whereas ours here are designed for you, a student taking the test. This guide should help you determine the quality of your own writing on the College Board's nine-point scale. Keep in mind that a score of 5 or higher will generally produce a final result of at least an overall 3, or what a majority of colleges regard as a passing score. Scores of 4 or below are generally unsuccessful papers.

As you (and others) evaluate your essay, remember that it is composed as a rough draft and is not a finished product. This was not an essay you had all night to write and edit. You should reward yourself for what you did well. Did you answer the question, coherently and thoroughly, and use examples?

There may be mistakes in even the best of papers. Do not kill your score because you misspelled a word or forgot to put a period at the end of a sentence. The grader will largely ignore such errors as well. However, scoring guides always tell graders that any paper with many distracting errors in grammar or mechanics should score no higher than a 2.

A 9 Essay

You will earn this score if the essay meets the criteria for an 8 but is really, really, really good, meaning you have mastery of the language, use relevant examples, write in a sophisticated style, and/or are particularly effective in uniting your own argument with the sources.

An 8 Essay: Effective

Your essay will earn this score if it effectively takes a position on whether changes are needed in the Electoral College in today's political climate. You have supported your position by successfully synthesizing at least three of the sources. Your argument is convincing and the sources integrate with and sustain your argument. Your writing demonstrates an ability to use a broad range of the elements of effective writing. Do not expect your writing to be flawless. Occasional errors are fine.

A 7 Essay

Your paper is a 7 if it fits the description of a 6 but is better. How is it better? Your writing is more mature. Your insight into the political possibilities of change in the electoral process are more developed and your use of the sources is somewhat more thorough.

A 6 Essay: Adequate

Your essay is adequate if it develops a position on whether changes are needed in the Electoral College in today's political climate. You synthesize at least three sources. Your argument is generally convincing and your sources generally sustain that argument. The argument is not as fully developed as an 8, and the sources are not as fully integrated. Your language may contain lapses, but overall, your writing is clear. The key differences between a 6 and an 8 are the thoroughness and thoughtfulness of the argument, and the clarity with which your sources support your position.

A 5 Essay

Papers earning this score develop a position on whether changes are needed in the Electoral College in today's political climate. However, your paper wavers in one of several ways. The sources do not really attach themselves effectively to your argument. Your argument is not thoroughly developed, or your position becomes more unclear as the paper goes along. The writing quality is about the same as in a 6, but there is an overall sense of incompleteness to the argument.

A 4 Essay: Inadequate

Your paper is inadequate and representative of the lower-half score if you did not successfully complete the task on one of three levels: You did not develop a coherent position on whether changes are needed in the Electoral College; you synthesized only two sources; you did cite sufficient sources, but those sources are not very well connected to your own argument. You might receive a score of 4 if you suddenly realize you need to cite some sources and just drop one or two into the paper without tying them effectively to what you were saying at the time. Finally, you may have oversimplified or misunderstood the question. Weakness in any of those areas can produce a 4 or lower.

A 3 Essay

Your paper will be scored a 3 if it meets the criteria for a 4 but your writing is even less successful in developing a position on the Electoral College or sustaining the argument with your sources. There is usually evidence of an immature level of writing.

A 2 Essay: Little Success

Your paper will be a 2 if you have not developed much of an argument on the Electoral College in the current election process. You may allude to the sources without actually citing them or you may cite them but without any relevance to your own argument. Little-success papers often misunderstand the sources, fail at an argument altogether, or simply summarize the sources. Your own writing also demonstrates consistent weaknesses in grammar or organization. Quite often these papers are also brief, indicating a lack of development.

A 1 Essay

Your paper is a 1 when there is almost no development at all. You may well have written a half a page or barely a page. You may have mentioned the Electoral College and that you thought it needed to be changed, but that is pretty much all you had to say.

The College Board also issues scores of **0 and "–."** A 0 is an essay that just repeats the prompt and says nothing else. A dash is a blank page or an essay that is completely off topic. Most often these papers tell us about some recent event in the writer's life or what he or she hopes college will be like, or even why this is a stupid test and the student really didn't want to take it.

SAMPLE STUDENT RESPONSES WITH COMMENTARY

SAMPLE ESSAY 1

In my opinion, the Electoral College should be replaced by direct popular vote because what the people want is what really matters.

As you can see in the chart in Source A, Al Gore should have been president in 2000, but for some reason George Bush won. I think it was a scam and Bush had it rigged. Also, in Source B, it says "direct election is seen as more consistent with democratic principles than is the Electoral College system." Then, in Source F says that faithless electors can switch their votes to whatever they want, which means that they don't have to vote the way the people in their state want them too.

So, in all, the Electoral College is outdated and should be abolished.

COMMENTARY ON SAMPLE ESSAY 1

Essay 1 is a classic example of a **2**. The essay is entirely too brief. The argument is simplistic and demonstrates **little success.** Another key failure is that the center of the essay is summary. While the writer does have an opinion, he or she does not successfully use the sources for argumentative support.

SAMPLE ESSAY 2

I support the claim that the Electoral College is an outdated institution that should be replaced by direct popular election of the president. This is true because of recent elections, it's been two hundred years since the founders.

Source A shows that the election in 2000 did not follow the public's feelings about who should be president. Al Gore had more popular votes than George Bush, but George Bush won the election because of Florida. Also, one elector didn't even vote, so that just shows that there is corruption in the government.

When the founders of our country met, television and radio had not been invented. Since then, presidents have been using television to get people to vote for them. "Mr. SHERMAN thought . . . the people . . . will never be sufficiently informed of [the candidates'] characters, and besides will never give a majority of votes to any one man" (Source C). This is wrong. Like Source D says, "Framers who were necessarily completely ignorant of the shape the country would take in the ensuing two centuries." They didn't know about tv.

Also, there is so much corruption in the government that people can't trust the Electoral College to vote right. Source F says "that a 'faithless elector' could forgo his or her pledge and alter the outcome of a presidential election. Indeed, over the past 100 years, seven electors have switched their vote to another candidate . . ."

In conclusion, as I have shown, the Electoral College should be abolished because people know what they want, the Founders were too long ago, and there is corruption in the government.

COMMENTARY ON SAMPLE ESSAY 2

Essay 2 is a rather ordinary **4.** It lacks argumentative development and several of the ideas offered are not connected to one another. The author shows us a certain level of stream of consciousness that lacks coherence. Three sources are cited, but none of them advance the writer's own argument in any significant way. There is even a structure for a three-part analysis, but none of the analysis progresses to a full argument. This essay is clearly **inadequate.**

SAMPLE ESSAY 3

The question of whether we should keep the Electoral College is not easily answered. They were fighting about it in 1787 and it seems nothing has changed. However, if I must take a position about the Electoral College, I would say it is quite outdated and the current system should reevaluate its methods of electing the President, although I cannot see how this may be accomplished so that both political parties are happy with the outcome.

In a political system where each party strives to be dominant and neither side works with one another, it would be sort of hard to find an unbiased body that would work together to create a system that wouldn't favor either party. However, if we step into this utopian idea, we would see that direct election of the president would be a better overall representation of the people of the United States. One of the main arguments by the Framers was that the people would have no way of knowing who was running for President and would just pick a well-known guy from their own states (source C). At the time, that would have resulted in something like thirteen candidates. Since there was no national advertising, the idea does seem stupid. How could you vote in a situation like that?

Well, things are different today. We have television for advertising and the news can't get enough of scandal so that today's voters are much better informed about the Presidential candidates on everything from what they were like in high school to their college pastimes and even where they get their haircut and how much it costs! While most of this isn't important, we are certainly more informed about our candidates. Direct public election would, therefore, be a better system for a more informed public. This is assuming that the media could grow up, but maybe their current position is a result of the Electoral College: they slander so the swing states will pick up certain electoral college votes. As Source D points out, "a full 99% of all advertising expenditures . . . were concentrated in only seventeen of the states." Media endorsements must count as advertising, even if parties aren't paying for it. As they say, all publicity is good publicity.

In any case, the Electoral College is a bit outdated and should be replaced with direct election, but getting this to happen would require a lot of money and trust on everyone's part. That is not likely to happen.

COMMENTARY ON SAMPLE ESSAY 3

Essay 3, a 4, is truly a tragedy. The student does clearly develop a position and feels the Electoral College should be tossed, while writing with voice and maintaining interest for the reader. This is, quite simply, an interesting and coherent approach to the question. Normally, such an essay would have received a score of 7. However, the writer used and cited only two primary sources; as you can see, that is automatic grounds for a score of 4 or lower.

SAMPLE ESSAY 4

Things are much different in the 21st century than they were in 1787 when we were drafting our Constitution and making laws. Technology has greatly changed the way we view politics mostly because of advertising. As a result, the way we elect the President is a bit outdated and the US should go with direct popular vote.

In 2000, the election clearly showed Al Gore receiving the majority of the popular vote, which one would assume means that more people wanted Al Gore to be president (Source A). But, as we all know, George Bush was given the office after a huge mess in Florida. This of course raises a good question: if we are a democracy built on the idea that the government is "of the people, by the people, and for the people," what people are we representing? The people obviously wanted Al Gore to be president, but George Bush was elected by the Electoral College. So it seems, direct election would be seen as "more consistent with democratic principles" (Source B).

Source C shows us the Framers' real worries were that no one would know who to elect because there was no information on the candidates. Mr Sherman says the people "will never be sufficiently informed of [the candidates'] characters;" while this may be true in 1787, today we see all sorts of information on television and the news about our presidential candidates. We aren't even close to an election yet, but already the news is discussing possible candidates like they were already in office! I know more about Obama's and Hillary Clinton's positions on things than I do about George Bush's and he's still in office and the election is still over a year away! It's crazy! But that just shows that Mr. Sherman's idea that the people wouldn't know who the candidates are is not really valid anymore. Therefore, the people should be allowed to vote for the President and not go through the Electoral College before the President is chosen.

In all, the reasons for having an Electoral College are no longer valid in the 21ˢᵗ century. We know the candidates and what they think, so we should be allowed to chose the President on our own.

COMMENTARY ON SAMPLE ESSAY 4

Essay 4 is a solid **6**. It does the right things: A position is presented. The argument is convincing, although one worries that it is a bit brief and could have been more developed. (In fact, the prior essay is better, but remember that the lack of sources hurt its score.) This writer uses the requisite sources. There is no real flair to the prose, but it is certainly an **adequate** response to the question.

SAMPLE ESSAY 5

Modern sociology tells us that whenever a group of people gather together, they do rather ignorant things they might not otherwise do in their personal lives. We see this in effect at rock concerts, nightclubs, and in gangs. But no where is this more apparent than at the polls. While the majority of Americans watch television and hear what candidates believe, the majority of eligible people do not vote. This was made quite apparent in the last election with Paris Hilton and Snoop Dog's campaign for young voters "Vote or Die!" Ironically, when asked later if they voted, both apparently were going to die because neither went to the polls to register their votes. Why, one may ask? Perhaps they felt their individual votes would not count. And in this case, who would want their votes to count anyway? For this reason, I believe that, in spite of its datedness, election by the Electoral College should be continued in order to offer the greatest representation for the most number of people and an added protection against ignorance and apathy.

One must ask themselves, who exactly goes to the voting polls? It is largely the affluent, suburban, older generation who seeks a voice in government. Thus, as Source E further points out, direct popular election would cause candidates to focus on voting groups that "are likely to be more heterogeneous" than those with low voter turnout. Candidates, therefore, will pander to groups who will vote, thereby making promises for Social Security, medical reform, retirement aids, and lower taxes, all worthy causes, but which alienate the younger and poorer groups of voters. After all, what 18 year old worries about Social Security and medical reform? What poverty-stricken family concerns themselves with retirement in twenty years when it barely makes enough money to survive today? Therefore, allowing the Electoral College to continue ensures that candidates at least focus on broad areas of concern for the entire nation, not a select few.

One may argue quite legitimately that if the people felt their votes counted individually, then more people would go to the polls. The election results of 2000 (Source A) show that approximately 102 million people went to the voting polls, at least for the two major candidates. If one assumes that a third party candidate received at least 20 million votes (I'm being optimistic, here), that leaves us with just over 120 million votes cast in the 2000 election. "Where's the apathy?" some might ask. Well, considering that the current population of the United States is over 300 million, 120 million is a mere third of the population! Accounting for eligible voters and such, one could easily surmise that at least half (if not more) of eligible voters did not vote! Thus, one would have to assume that 1 out of every 2 people seem to believe the democratic process does not work and that we should just chuck the whole system. Yet, talk to anyone on the street, and 9 out of 10 would be quite offended if you suggested that democracy was a sham and that we should overthrow the entire system of government. It isn't that people feel they don't have a voice. It's that people are simply too lazy to take up their civic responsibility. Therefore, until people accept their individual responsibility, it seems best to stick with an Electoral College, which at least provides a unified voice for the people who took the time to vote.

Finally, the same concern the Framers had in 1787 may possibly still exist today, although not in the same form. Mr. Sherman argued two hundred years ago that the people could never be "sufficiently informed" about the candidates, whereas Mr. Morris believed that the people certainly could choose a "man of distinguished character" and "continental" repute, and that if chosen by a Legislature, it would be the work of "intrigue, of cabal, and of faction" (Source C). Certainly, both were correct in their own ways. Without modern media, it would be rather difficult, as Sherman suggests, for the people to find a representative candidate for president, much less learn about his character and his political views. Mr. Morris, however, also makes a valid point that the people would be able to choose a man for the job, and that politicians cannot be trusted to agree on anything. Even before the advent of television, today's two party politics, a condition unforeseen and unknown in 1787, allows the people to whittle down potential office-seekers to a mere handful of candidates. Thus, it seems that Morris' argument for direct election was partially answered. Whether the media plays a helpful role remains trickier. Sherman argued that the people would remain largely uninformed about the candidates, a statement some today would say is untrue. The media often tells us what our potential candidates are doing, what they believe, what they used to do, and how they stab each other in the back.

Every election becomes a media circus fueled by money and presented for our entertainment. We fall for it. The Americans who do vote, vote for an image. I, for one, want to keep the Electoral College, if for no other reason than to protect us from ourselves.

COMMENTARY ON SAMPLE ESSAY 5

Essay 5 is a long-winded but certainly intelligent approach to the question. This writer is well-read and knowledgeable, not only about the use of the sources, but also about political elements that are applicable to the question. The essay has voice and humor. The writer is a bit elitist in the approach, but graders do not expect writers to necessarily favor their own opinions. This student takes a position that most people probably would not endorse after having read these sources and then does an excellent job of fleshing out and defending that position. The long-windedness of the essay would tire some readers, but graders always reward writers for what they do well. This is not only an effective essay, it is an exceptionally effective essay, and thus deserves its score of **9.**

4

AN IN-DEPTH LOOK
AT THE RHETORICAL
ANALYSIS ESSAY QUESTION

Unlike the general argument essay and the synthesis essay, the rhetorical analysis essay does not invite the reader to engage in a debate. This element alone often causes problems for students taking the test because they want to "take the author on." However, if you attempt to do so, you are not answering the question and, consequently, you will receive a lower-half score. Instead, the task of this essay is to *analyze the methods the author employs in his or her writing* to convey the author's attitude, opinion, or conviction about some topic. Nearly every speech, every political cartoon, every ad—even many a conversation—is an argument. To successfully complete this essay, you cannot engage in that argument. Instead, you must talk about how the argument is created. You should dissect the argument and identify the tools the author uses to seek the reader's agreement. The essay you are asked to write will demonstrate your ability to read critically and evaluate effectively the essential elements of a complex piece of prose.

A helpful resource for acquainting yourself with the task of rhetorical analysis can be found in the chapters called "Narration and Description" and "Persuasion and Argument" in *The Riverside Reader, Alternate Edition*. "Narration and Description" will help you understand the author's purpose, audience, and strategies, and will also help you analyze the way the author uses language to conduct his or her argument. "Persuasion and Argument" provides further information on the kinds of persuasive appeals (specifically pathos, ethos, and logos) that often serve as the fundamental strategies for creating an argument. Moreover, this chapter includes some analysis of using visuals in persuasive argument (visuals are a necessary component of the AP test, as we pointed out in the chapter on the synthesis essay). Both chapters also include some brief arguments that have been deconstructed for you, in addition to some longer pieces for you to practice analyzing. For a quick reference and review, see Points to Remember on page 40 and on page 392.

SOME THINGS NOT TO DO

Often students feel like they are being asked to evaluate the essay as if they were writing a movie review: "Twain wrote really well and that held my attention." The test makers wouldn't ask you to evaluate an essay if it were poorly written. Also, whether something held your interest is not an insightful comment, much less an astute analysis.

Do not address the author by his or her first name. In these collegial days of ours, students feel it is acceptable to do just that, as in "Abe made a good point there" or "Jane (Austen) created a great character." This is discourteous and sets a sloppy, unscholarly tone for your essay. Give the author's full name the first time you reference him or her and use only the last name for subsequent mentions.

Avoid using fancy language. In "Politics and the English Language," in the "Division and Classification" chapter of *The Riverside Reader*, George Orwell advocates a style of directness and clarity. This is good advice! Students often think graders will be impressed by a sentence heavily laden with complex words: "The aphoristic asyndeton parallelism of the third sentence provided a syncretistic introduction for his thoughts." The writer learned these words in his English Language and Composition class and felt he had to use them—all at once—before he forgot them. Yet these words are not evidence of good thinking. They are in reality an attempt to obscure the fact that this student does not really understand the essay or the devices the writer is using to convince the reader of his position. It would be far better to say, "The simple and direct diction of the third sentence provided an effective preface to the complex ideas that were to follow." As long as you think and write clearly, the AP graders are happy, and when they are happy, that is reflected in your score.

WHAT TO DO INSTEAD

Let's suppose you have just read an eighteenth-century passage on bear baiting, a fairly common form of sideshow fund-raising during the Renaissance. The prompt on the passage has told you that this is, indeed, a piece about bear baiting, but it didn't mention whether the author considered the practice good or bad. That was left up to you to decide after reading what the author had to say. You then read something like this: "Discuss the author's attitude toward bear baiting and the strategies the author employed to achieve his purpose."

No problem! You read the passage and you know the author finds the "sport" cruel and condemns those who practice it. You're good to go, but wait! There is that little clause about "strategies." You are not asked to simply identify his attitude; you also are asked to identify the techniques he employed to develop his argument. For years we have graded this type of essay, only to find lots of students simply summarizing the author's essay because they have no idea *how* he or she said it. They are lost. Reading the sections that follow will help you identify and describe these strategies.

DETAILED DISCUSSION OF RHETORICAL STRATEGIES

When presenting an argument, a writer has a number of rhetorical techniques he or she can use. Chief among these are diction, syntax, figures of speech, and rhetoric.

DICTION

As you read and annotate critically, notice the author's word choice. Especially take notice of the connotation of words. Identify the key words the author uses. In our previous example of bear baiting, if the author had used words such as "cruel," "inhuman," and "grotesque," these words would help identify a prejudice in his argument. Negative and positive diction are always a key element of any argument. An important note about diction: It is not enough to say "The author uses diction to convey his meaning." Diction is word choice and to say an author uses words would be like saying, "The wind blows wind to make wind."

SYNTAX

As we noted earlier in the multiple-choice chapter, most students do not like to discuss syntax in the analytical essay. They never enjoyed "grammar" and its underappreciated language rules. However, the dissection of sentence structure is a valuable tool in any analysis. There are all sorts of specialized terms for analysis, but here we will cover just the basics. If you want to learn more of the different types of syntactical structures, look in the chapter called "A Working Vocabulary of Fundamental Terms" earlier in this book.

For now, simply recognize that short sentences are almost always abrupt, intense, and confrontational. They force a sudden stop in thinking. Long sentences, on the other hand, are more thoughtful and permit reflection. Parallel syntax always functions like a train gathering steam. When effectively employed, it convinces by nearly overwhelming the reader syntactically. (For examples of parallel syntax, see Chapter 1, "A Working Vocabulary of Fundamental Terms.") Rhetorical questions manipulate you to provide the answer the author wants you to accept. They are never meant as a genuine question, but are always coercive. (Again, for more information and examples, see Chapter 1.) Repetition within a piece is meant to provide emphasis. Repetition provides emphasis. Emphasis.

FIGURES OF SPEECH

The figures of speech to which we refer are no different from those you have been studying in literature all through school. The key list for nonfiction prose includes metaphor, simile, symbol, personification, hyperbole, allusion, imagery, apostrophe, pun, paradox, and oxymoron. Again, as for syntax, there is an expanded list in the "Working Vocabulary" chapter, but these are the basics. You are looking for patterns. Is the passage heavy with metaphors and similes? What kinds of imagery do you find? When an author is creating a rhetorical argument, he or she may use imagery to manipulate the reader's emotions by selecting images that seem attractive or repulsive, depending on the direction of the argument. Are there certain kinds of symbols operating? Particularly powerful metaphors, symbols, or allusions that the author makes can provide enough substance for an entire paragraph of analysis by astute students if they understand the nuances of the allusion itself and the meaning it gives to the passage as a whole. As we said in the answer section to the Diagnostic Test, the College Board expects you to be familiar with Greek mythology, the Judeo-Christian religious tradition, and the main works of Western thought. Key allusions are important in any good analysis of strategies.

RHETORIC

First, allow us a brief rhetorical aside. Most students have never heard the term "rhetoric" and are often confused when they confront it for the first time. It is, as you might imagine, an ancient Greek term coined by Aristotle, who defined it as "the faculty of observing in any given case the available means of persuasion." Aristotle liked to study everything and he especially liked to study the way people argue. That is rhetoric. Rhetoric, therefore, is a thoughtful activity that evaluates communication and, with any luck, leads to an effective and rational exchange of ideas. Rhetoric is *how* we argue, and understanding rhetoric helps *you* argue in return. We use an acronym, PELIDS, to help identify and remember the basic rhetorical strategies that are essential to analysis.

In this acronym, **P stands for pathos.** A pathos argument is a direct appeal to your emotions. It plays upon guilt, insecurity, fear, hope, or worry. All advertising is fundamentally a pathos argument in that most ads go after your emotions. Most political speeches go after your emotions as well, and many a good rhetorical essay will seek to convince you by using words or images that appeal to your emotions. Pathos arguments are not necessarily bad or structurally unsound. Remember that an author is seeking to convince, and emotion is one of the most effective tools of persuasion. However, do not simply say that the author is using pathos. If the author is evoking a feeling, explain why he is doing so. What does the author want you to do—send money, join a cause, vote for someone in particular, write to a member of Congress? Always ask yourself: What is the purpose of the pathos? That answer should be part of your essay.

E stands for ethos. An ethos argument is fundamentally an argument about credibility. When you read an argument, one of the basic questions you have is: Why should I listen? Does the author know what he or she is talking about? Both of us are often asked to speak to or make a presentation to teachers about Advanced Placement English. Our respective credibility to speak and teach on this issue is a given because we both teach AP English Language and Composition and AP English Literature and Composition courses. If a writer is trying to convince you that he or she has the right to speak on that issue, he or she is engaged in ethos. But think, just as in pathos: Why is the author's credibility important for the argument? The key point is that you should not just drop in labels of elements but always identify the purpose of ethos in the piece.

L stands for logos. A logos argument is primarily a rational and reasonable argument. It seeks to convince by persuading you of the fundamental soundness of its point of view. Authors make claims they expect you to accept as true. They will call on authorities who sustain their position or quote from famous sources to support an argument. They will use historical examples to defend a current solution. Identifying a logical argument is not difficult. The most important element is whether the claims are sound or the evidence valid.

I stands for inductive. Inductive arguments work from example and are a type of logos argument. Science is an excellent example of inductive argument. How do scientists define their truths? They conduct studies and look for patterns of repetition to establish whether erosion is increasing, a bird population is declining, or a fruit tree is thriving in certain climates. They provide data and draw conclusions. Rhetoricians do the same thing. You will find many an essay that uses example after example, just as you should in your own general argument question, in order to convince you of the logical validity of the author's point of view.

D stands for deductive. Deductive reasoning is also a type of logos argument. However, this argument does not provide examples but makes claims that it assumes you will accept as true, then builds its argument based on those claims. It is very much like proofs in geometry: if A is true and B is true, then we can deduce that C also must be true. You will encounter many deductive arguments in your reading. In an inductive argument, you must ask whether the examples are relevant and sufficient. In a deductive argument, you ask whether the initial claims are valid, and then ask whether the claims fundamentally result in the conclusions made by the essay. You are essentially analyzing for the soundness of an argument.

S stands for syllogism. Syllogisms are a particular type of deductive argument. A syllogism provides two premises (claims) and then offers a conclusion. The most famous one reads this way: All humans die. Mona is a human. Therefore, Mona will die. Of course, not all syllogisms are this easy to identify—some can be quite tricky, especially if the premises are ideas many people simply accept as truths (God created mankind. All of God's creations are good. Therefore, mankind is good.). Additionally, syllogisms are sometimes used as an answer or as a distractor on the multiple-choice test (as are all of these terms). But you may use it on an essay if you happen to identify the author as someone basing his argument on certain premises and then reaching his conclusion through a three-part structure, as in the above example.

A footnote on logos. You may have heard about fallacies. They are logical arguments that are false in their argumentative structure (some televisions are black and white; all penguins are black and white; therefore, some televisions are penguins). They attempt to engage in the appearance of a rational argument but ultimately fail for some reason.

The AP test uses some of these terms on the multiple-choice test. It is important to learn them; it is even better (and more fun) to practice identifying and dissecting the arguments made by politicians, teachers, or parents. However, for the purpose of the analytical essay, it is not absolutely necessary that you use them and certainly not all at once. Remember what we said about "highfalutin" vocabulary? If you know that the writer is employing a "straw man" argument to convince you of his position, great! You may identify it as such in your essay, but you must also say *how* it creates a flaw in the convictions of the piece. Another student may simply recognize that an argument is one-sided and that the opposing side is not only absent but also defined by the writer to look foolish, and thus that the author's argument is not a good one. That is wonderful! The student did not know the exact term, but he or she was able to recognize a weakness in the logical structure of the piece. We have not given logical fallacies their own section because they really require a book to themselves. If you are interested (or grounded and looking for something to do), several good books and websites are available. Just do a search for "logical fallacies."

SUMMARY

Rhetorical analysis is the kind of essay that is probably the least like anything you have done in most of your English classes up to this point. It is not something that generally comes naturally, even if you sense something is not quite right with an argument presented to you by others. You casually and deliberately engage in arguments all the time with friends, with family, in the classroom, or driving down the highway; often the arguments are one-sided and involve a simple phrase of insult. Even so, you rarely stop to analyze the truth or effectiveness of any given argument. We hope we have given you a set of precepts that you can bring to any passage you have been asked to critically read and analyze. You should use them so frequently that you naturally begin recognizing them as you read different passages.

Therefore, as you read, take note of the author's diction. Look for any strong connotation or a change in the connotative power of the words as you move through the essay. Examine the diction for structures that affect your understanding and appreciation of the work. Are there any rhetorical questions? Why? Where? Is the work heavy with parallel syntax, or does the author like sudden, short sentences? Any time you run into a figure of speech, mark it and determine the meaning it brings to the piece. Are there any others and, if so, do they create a pattern? Is the essay organized fundamentally around pathos, ethos, or logos, and is that the best choice for the argument? Does it conduct the argument convincingly? When you read critically, all of these elements must come to you quickly and naturally—not so much as a part of memorization but as an expression of a skill.

A PRACTICE ESSAY

The following is a nineteenth-century essay written by Nathaniel Hawthorne on Abraham Lincoln. Take ten minutes or so to annotate the essay. Look for all the elements we have described, but most importantly, become clear in your understanding of Hawthorne's feelings for the president. Then mark, identify, and make notes to yourself about the particular elements of writing he uses to define that attitude. Hawthorne would like other Americans to see the president as he does.

Sample Question 2

(Suggested time—40 minutes. This question counts as one-third of the total essay section score.)

The passage below is an observation of Abraham Lincoln made by Nathaniel Hawthorne when he had the opportunity to meet the president in 1862. (Hawthorne was not there by any special invitation but rather was part of a group of Massachusetts manufacturers.) Read the passage carefully. Then write an essay in which you define the attitude Hawthorne takes toward Lincoln and analyze the rhetorical strategies Hawthorne employs to help clarify and define that attitude.

> Of course, there was one other personage, in the class of statesmen, whom I should have been truly mortified to leave Washington without seeing; since (temporarily, at least, and by force of circumstances) he was the man of men. But a private grief had built up a barrier about him, impeding the customary free intercourse of Americans with their chief magistrate; so that I might have come away without a glimpse of his very remarkable physiognomy, save for a semi-official opportunity of which I was glad to take advantage. The fact is, we were invited to annex ourselves, as supernumeraries, to a deputation that was about to wait upon the President, from a Massachusetts whip factory, with a present of a splendid whip. . . .
>
> By and by there was a little stir on the staircase and in the passage-way, and in lounged a tall, loose-jointed figure, of an exaggerated Yankee port and demeanor, whom (as being about the homeliest man I ever saw, yet by no means repulsive or disagreeable) it was impossible not to recognize as Uncle Abe.
>
> Unquestionably, Western man though he be, and Kentuckian by birth, President Lincoln is the essential representative of all Yankees, and the veritable specimen, physically, of what the world seems determined to regard as our characteristic qualities. It is the strangest yet the fittest thing in the jumble of human vicissitudes, that he, out of so many millions, unlooked for, unselected by any intelligible process that could be based upon his genuine qualities, unknown to those who chose him, and unsuspected of what endowments may adapt him for his tremendous responsibility, should have found the way open for him to fling his lank personality into the chair of state,— where, I presume, it was his first impulse to throw his legs on the council-table, and tell the Cabinet Ministers a story. There is no describing his lengthy awkwardness, nor the uncouthness of his movement, and yet it seemed as if I had been in the habit of seeing him daily, and had shaken hands with him a thousand times inn some village street; so true was he to the aspect of the pattern American, though with a certain extravagance which, possibly, I exaggerated still further by the delighted eagerness with which I took it in. If put to guess his calling and livelihood, I should have taken him for a country schoolmaster as soon as anything else.

He was dressed in a rusty black frock-coat and pantaloons, unbrushed, and worn so faithfully that the suit had adapted itself to the curves and angularities of his figure, and had grown to be an outer skin of the man. He had shabby slippers on his feet. His hair was black, still unmixed with gray, stiff, somewhat bushy, and had apparently been acquainted with neither brush nor comb that morning, after the disarrangement of the pillow; and as to a night-cap, Uncle Abe probably knows nothing of such effeminacies. His complexion is dark and sallow, betokening, I fear, an insalubrious atmosphere around the White House; he has thick black eyebrows and an impending brow; his nose is large, and the lines about his mouth are very strongly defined.

The whole physiognomy is as coarse a one as you would meet anywhere in the length and breadth of the States; but, withal, it is redeemed, illuminated, softened, and brightened by a kindly though serious look out of his eyes, and an expression of homely sagacity, that seems weighted with rich results of village experience. A great deal of native sense; no bookish cultivation, no refinement; honest at heart, and thoroughly so, and yet, in some sort, sly,—at least, endowed with a sort of tact and wisdom that are akin to craft, and would impel him, I think, to take an antagonist in flank rather than to make a bull-run at him right in front. But, on the whole, I liked this sallow, queer, sagacious visage, with the homely human sympathies that warmed it; and, for my small share in the matter, would as lief have Uncle Abe for a ruler as any man whom it would have been practicable to put in his place.

ANNOTATED RHETORICAL ANALYSIS QUESTION

Sample Question 2

(Suggested time—40 minutes. This question counts as one-third of the total essay section score.)

The passage below is an observation of Abraham Lincoln made by Nathaniel Hawthorne when he had the opportunity to meet the president in 1862. (Hawthorne was not there by any special invitation, but rather was part of a group of Massachusetts manufacturers.) Read the passage carefully. Then write an essay in which you ①define the attitude Hawthorne takes toward Lincoln and ②analyze the rhetorical strategies Hawthorne employs to help clarify and define the attitude.

—define attitude
—analyze strat's

politician

Of course, there was one other personage, in the class of statesmen, whom I should have been truly mortified to leave Washington without seeing; since (temporarily, at least, and by force of circumstances) he was the man of men. But a private grief had built up a barrier about him, impeding the customary free intercourse of Americans with their chief magistrate; so that I might have come away without a glimpse of his very remarkable physiognomy, save for a semi-official opportunity of which I was glad to take advantage. The fact is, we were invited to annex ourselves, as supernumeraries, to a deputation that was about to wait upon the President, from a Massachusetts whip factory, with a present of a splendid whip. . . .

examples; model for all.

home? war?

By and by there was a little stir on the staircase and in the passage-way, and in lounged a tall, loose-jointed figure, of an exaggerated Yankee port and demeanor, whom (as being about the homeliest man I ever saw, yet by no means repulsive or disagreeable) it was impossible not to recognize as Uncle Abe.

+diction

ugly!

familiar; everyone's Uncle.

opposite

Unquestionably, Western man though he be, and Kentuckian by birth, President Lincoln is the essential representative of all Yankees, and the veritable specimen, physically, of what the world seems determined to regard as our characteristic qualities. It is the strangest yet the fittest thing in the jumble of human vicissitudes, that he, out of so many millions, unlooked for, unselected by any intelligible process that could be based upon his genuine qualities, unknown to those who chose him, and unsuspected of what endowments may adapt him for his tremendous responsibility, should have found the way open for him to fling his lank personality into the chair of state,— where, I presume, it was his first impulse to throw his legs on the council-table, and tell the Cabinet Ministers a story. There is no describing his lengthy awkwardness, nor the uncouthness of his movement, and yet it seemed as if I had been in the habit of seeing him daily, and had shaken hands with him a thousand times inn some village street; so true was he to the aspect of the pattern American, though with a certain extravagance which, possibly, I exaggerated still further by the delighted eagerness with which I took it in. If put to guess his calling and livelihood, I should have taken him for a country schoolmaster as soon as anything else.

(No tv, so easier to be elected!)

imagery

everyday man—common. No airs!

average American

teacher, not President

He was dressed in a rusty black frock-coat and pantaloons, unbrushed, and worn so faithfully that the suit had adapted itself to the curves and angularities of his figure, and had grown to be an outer skin of the man. He had shabby slippers on his feet. His hair was black, still unmixed with gray, stiff, somewhat bushy, and had apparently been acquainted with neither brush nor comb that morning, after the disarrangement of the pillow; and as to a night-cap, Uncle Abe probably knows nothing of such effeminacies. His complexion is dark and sallow, betokening, I fear, an insalubrious atmosphere around the White House; he has thick black eyebrows and an impending brow; his nose is large, and the lines about his mouth are very strongly defined.

The whole physiognomy is as coarse a one as you would meet anywhere in the length and breadth of the States; but, withal, it is redeemed, illuminated, softened, and brightened by a kindly though serious look out of his eyes, and an expression of homely sagacity, that seems weighted with rich results of village experience. A great deal of native sense; no bookish cultivation, no refinement; honest at heart, and thoroughly so, and yet, in some sort, sly—at least, endowed with a sort of tact and wisdom that are akin to craft, and would impel him, I think, to take an antagonist in flank rather than to make a bull-run at him right in front. But, on the whole, I liked this sallow, queer, sagacious visage, with the homely human sympathies that warmed it; and, for my small share in the matter, would as lief have Uncle Abe for a ruler as any man whom it would have been practicable to put in his place.

unworried?

a manly man

+diction

Honest Abe hmm - not so honest. Hunter?

comfort above style

sloppy appearance vs. strong character

commons, not snobbish

pun on Bull-Run

clearly states that he likes & respects the President.

in today's era, Abe never would have been elected. We like "pretty" boys.

SCORING RUBRIC FOR RHETORICAL QUESTIONS

As much as possible, this scoring guide will follow the concepts and language of the scoring guides used by the College Board. However, their guides are designed for graders. Our guides are designed for you as a student taking the test. This guide should help you determine the quality of your own writing on the College Board nine-point rubric. Keep in mind that a score of **5 or higher** will generally produce a final result of an overall 3, or what the majority of colleges regard as a passing score. Scores of **4 or below** are generally unsuccessful papers.

As you and others evaluate your essay, remember that it is composed as a rough draft and is not a finished product. This is not an essay you had all night to write and edit. You should reward yourself for what you did well. Did you answer the question, write coherently and intelligently, and use examples? Always keep that in mind.

You may find mistakes even in the best of papers. Do not take points off because you misspelled a word or forgot to put in a period. The grader will largely ignore such things as well. However, scoring guides always tell graders that any paper with many distracting errors in grammar or mechanics should be scored no higher than a 2.

A 9 ESSAY

You will earn this score if the essay meets the criteria for an 8 but is really, really, really good, which means you have an impressive control of language, use sophisticated examples, and write in a sophisticated style.

AN 8 ESSAY: EFFECTIVE

Your essay earns this score if it effectively develops an analysis of the strategies Hawthorne employs to define and/or clarify the attitude he holds toward Lincoln. Your evidence is appropriate to the question and demonstrates convincing knowledge concerning the impact of the various strategies. You demonstrate an ability to control your style and are able to write well. Don't expect your writing to be flawless; occasional errors are fine.

A 7 ESSAY

Your paper is a 7 if it fits the description of a 6 but is better. How is it better? Your writing is somewhat more mature. Your insight into Hawthorne's ideas about Lincoln is more developed, or your evidence is somewhat more complete.

A 6 ESSAY: ADEQUATE

Your paper is adequate if it develops an analysis of the strategies Hawthorne employed to define and/or clarify the attitude he held toward Lincoln. You offer appropriate evidence and remain fairly clear and organized throughout the essay. Some lapses in the structure of your essay, incompleteness in your analysis, or minor grammatical errors are acceptable, but in general your argument stays properly focused.

A 5 Essay

Essays earning a score of 5 develop an analysis of the strategies. However, such essays may waver in one of several ways. The evidence is not complete or is not quite as connected to the argument as it should be. Evidence is provided but may not explain successfully which rhetorical strategy it illuminates. The writing quality is about the same as in a 6.

A 4 Essay: Inadequate

Your paper is inadequate and representative of the lower-half score if you did not successfully complete the task on any one of three levels. Your evidence may be insufficient or disconnected from the strategies you attempted to analyze. Your writing may lack clarity. The flow of your argument may be uncertain and confusing, or your own syntax made several sentences unclear. The writing is not terrible, but a maturity of writing style is usually not present in these essays.

A 3 Essay

Your paper will receive a 3 if it meets the criteria for a 4 but your writing is even less successful in detailing Hawthorne's rhetorical strategies. Such a paper may have even less evidence and will often end up repeating what Hawthorne seemed to be saying without much analysis at all of his rhetorical strategies.

A 2 Essay: Little Success

Your paper will be scored a 2 if you have written a very poor or a very brief and incomplete essay. Your essay will show little success if you misunderstood Hawthorne or simply summarized what he said but did not analyze how he said it. This score is also given if a paper is particularly poorly written, with consistent weaknesses in grammar. Such papers are often only a single page, fewer than 200 words in development.

A 1 Essay

Your score is a 1 when the essay is hardly developed at all, perhaps only half a page or barely a page in length. You mentioned Hawthorne and may have even mentioned an attitude, but that is pretty much all you had to say.

The College Board also issues scores of **0** and "**—**." A 0 is given to an essay that just repeats the prompt and says nothing else. A dash is given to a blank page or an essay that tells the graders how this is a stupid test and a waste of time or, as was recently the case, an essay stating that the student never really learned rhetorical strategies in class and just watched movies.

Sample Student Responses with Commentary

Sample Essay 1

Hathorne likes Lincoln and even says so at the end, but he does call him ugly and homely "as about the homeliest man I ever saw." But then he calls him "Uncle Abe" and goes on to say he was a "Western man" from Kentucky.

Hathorne was meeting him with a bunch of other men to give him a gift and seemed to enjoy the experience a lot. After all, he did get to meet the President and as you read you get the feeling that Hathorne was glad to have met him and to have been there. He noticed that Lincoln was more like "a country school-master" than a President. But he was really "honest at heart."

So, he must have left with a good impression that even though he was rather ugly, he was still a good president for the country.

COMMENTARY ON SAMPLE ESSAY 1

This paper demonstrates most of the hallmarks of a paper with **little success.** At a very fundamental level, this essay is simply a summary or restatement of what Hawthorne has noticed. There is no analysis. The student is right about Hawthorne's attitude but lacks knowledge of rhetorical strategies or devices. Therefore the essay earns a **2.**

The paper is brief, misspells Hawthorne's name, and is rather disjointed even in the data it does discuss. There is more here than graders usually see in a 1, but this is not a strong 2. However, graders are told, even with a lower-half paper, "Reward the students for what they do well."

SAMPLE ESSAY 2

Nathaniel Hawthorne wrote this essay after meeting President Lincoln. He was part of a group of merchants that met with the President, apparently to give him a whip. Hawthorne, at first, makes it sound like he was against the President. He describes him as ugly and homely, but later he seems to like him and at the end seems to consider him a good president. Hawthorne sounds like a bit of a snob at first, but later he seems OK and nice to Lincoln.

The first part, which is the part where he dislikes Lincoln, is defined by his diction. He calls him "loose-jointed", "homeliest," "exaggerated Yankee." All of these words imply a negative connotation. One suspects that Hawthorne even wonders how he got elected. However, towards the end of the essay, the diction changes and you get really positive words like "redeemed," "brightened," "sagacity," and others which all suggest that when he left he liked the President a lot better.

Another thing you notice is that we learned that Lincoln was called "Honest Abe," but Hawthorne labels him "Uncle Abe" which makes him seem more like a member of the family than a leader of the country. He wants us to see Lincoln in the end as someone who is friendly and easy to get to know, someone good.

Lincoln may have been someone rather ugly to see in person but who was ultimately very nice and as we know he ended up being one of our best presidents.

COMMENTARY ON SAMPLE ESSAY 2

The writer of this essay is making a sincere effort to do the right thing. There is an attempt at diction analysis. It is not wrong, but it is insufficient. The writer turns the diction into a first-half and last-half study, but Hawthorne mixes his positive observations throughout an essay in which he does find it remarkable that a "Westerner," a man of "homely" features and a man without diplomatic fanciness, would find his way to the presidency.

There are many other rhetorical strategies that are employed in the essay and the use of "Uncle Abe" is one of them, but again the author fails to really develop this observation into any astute analysis.

The essay also concludes on a casual note that employs rather empty adjectives—"ugly" and "nice"—and then makes a simplistic truism.

These are all qualities typical of an **inadequate** essay. This is a weak **4**.

SAMPLE ESSAY 3

Hawthorne's attitude toward Abraham Lincoln in his essay is one where he seems to like Lincoln, even if he is ugly. Some of the ways he shows he likes Lincoln is through diction and imagery.

Hawthorne uses diction like "Uncle Abe," "honest," and "I liked this sallow, queer, sagacious visage" to show how he feels about Lincoln. When he says "Uncle Abe" it shows that he thinks of Lincoln as his uncle, a person he probably trusts and likes. To call someone uncle shows you have a relationship with that person that is close and Hawthorne thinks of Lincoln as his family. When Hawthorne calls Lincoln honest, it shows he has great respect for him and he thinks highly of him. He doesn't think Lincoln is hiding anything from people, but he is just a sincere person people can trust. Also, Hawthorne says "I liked... visage", which shows that he likes the way Lincoln looks, even though he is "homely." He talks about the way Lincoln looks when he says that Lincoln is "loose-jointed," his clothes are an "outer skin," his hair is "bushy," and his "nose is large". Taken all together, you can see that Lincoln is not an attractive person and is not someone we would think of as a President.

Another way Hawthorne shows he likes Lincoln is through his imagery. Hawthorne says Lincoln looks like he is just a "country school-master" and not a typical President. He describes Lincoln's "rusty black coat frock" and pants as sort of worn and shabby. His clothes had "adapted itself to... his figure" and he didn't bother to comb his hair. This image seems more like a poor country teacher who doesn't make much money rather than a president of the United States. A president would wear expensive, new clothes and would fix his hair in order to look more powerful in front of people.

In all, Hawthorne shows he likes Honest Abe through his use of regular, every day diction and imagery.

COMMENTARY ON SAMPLE ESSAY 3

This essay achieves a score of **5**. The paper is doing an analysis of diction and imagery. The diction paragraph is fairly successful, but the imagery paragraph needs more development and sounds a bit too simplistic. Keep in mind that a 5 is not a lower-half score. A student can earn a total test score of 3, which is passing for many colleges, by writing three 5 essays.

SAMPLE ESSAY 4

Hawthorne's essay was a little hard to read in parts, but basically it said that despite being rather "homely", Hawthorne found that he rather liked "Uncle Abe" and was rather glad to have him as a president. He was very glad that he got a chance to meet him before he left Washington. Hawthorne describes a rather two-sided point of view using diction, a title, and a rather interesting metaphor at the end.

This passage is all about diction. The negative diction mostly describes how Lincoln appears. He has a "remarkable physiognomy" which makes him about "the homeliest man I ever saw." He later says that he has a "homely sagacity" and his hair had not ever been "acquainted with comb or brush." Despite describing him as an ugly man, Hawthorne turns right around and says it was "by no means repulsive or disagreeable." In an important list towards the end, Hawthorne uses "redeemed, illuminated, softened, and brightened" to give Lincoln a kindly look rather like someone you could talk to.

We were taught in school to call President Lincoln "Honest Abe." Quite suddenly, Hawthorne calls him "Uncle Abe" just like he was a member of the family. Actually, that seems to work, because we always think of presidents as famous and imposing and hard to get to know and by calling Lincoln "Uncle", Hawthorne makes us think of someone who is approachable and easy to get to know and talk to. He is someone you can trust. The president is someone with the right heart.

Finally, Hawthorne uses this military metaphor at the end and describes him as someone "to take an antagonist in flank rather than to make a bull-run at him right in front." I would think that a direct attack would lose and a sneaky side attack would win. Hawthorne implies that Lincoln will win this war and that is a good thing.

COMMENTARY ON SAMPLE ESSAY 4

This essay is certainly **adequate.** It examines three specific analytical elements of the piece (diction, a title, and the military metaphor), although the last one is minor. Unlike the essay receiving a

4, this essay uses diction to make good points about Lincoln's approachability. This same idea is then followed in the discussion of the appellation Hawthorne gives to the president. By noting that Hawthorne refers to Lincoln as "Uncle Abe," the student realizes that Hawthorne appreciated the essential goodness of the man. Lincoln could be trusted to lead the country, and although the analysis of the metaphor is slim, it does suggest that Lincoln could also win the war.

The writing is not particularly strong, but it is certainly capable enough to earn a 6. It is somewhat repetitious and plods along, but succeeds at its task and provides the evidence necessary to support its case.

SAMPLE ESSAY 5

In today's society, television is so important to the way we elect a president. FDR would never have been elected if the people of the country could have seen him in a wheelchair because we think it indicates weakness and impotency. Of course, now we know this would have been a mistake, but we are so caught up in image that we wouldn't have elected him let alone four times. Hawthorne's description of Lincoln as rather "homely" and unattractive causes one to wonder if Lincoln could get elected now. Would we have relied on image or would we have seen past it to the "man of men" Hawthorne so clearly admires?

One of the things that stands out the most is Hawthorne's epithet "Uncle Abe". This familiar title suggests that instead of being a stand offish, arrogant man as most might expect a president to be, Abraham Lincoln is a humble man, one who seems to be the nation's favorite uncle. In fact, Hawthorne seems so surprised by Lincoln's unconventional behavior that he finds it "the strangest...thing" that Lincoln "should have found the way open for him to fling his lank personality into the chair of state." Obviously, Hawthorne sees Lincoln as the real American, the one who sits comfortably at a backyard barbeque rather than at a dignified state dinner with tuxedos and fine wine glasses. Hawthorne's descriptions create a sense of safety and warmth. This was needed in a nation that was terribly divided and in need of reassurance.

Hawthorne's Lincoln is a paradox. He is "tall, loose jointed figure" and "about the homeliest man I ever saw." Hawthorne seems startled by his appearance, like seeing George Bush in his pajamas. But Hawthorne recovers and recognizes behind the messy outward appearance an "honest" man who was wise and who "brightened" a room when he entered.

Indeed, through diction, imagery, and a kind of perception of character, Hawthorne comes away from the White House impressed by this "Westerner", this "country school master" who just happens to be leading the country in a time of crisis.

COMMENTARY ON SAMPLE ESSAY 5

This is an **effective**, strong essay, easily earning a score of 8. The only real issue is solved in the last paragraph. An analysis of Hawthorne's strategies is implied throughout the essay, but the writer only gets around to naming them at the very end.

Had the writer not named them, it still would have been an 8, for it is an extremely effective essay. The writer does understand Hawthorne's appreciation of Lincoln. He realizes that Hawthorne admired him beyond superficial appearance, and found in his encounter with the man an essential spirit of wisdom and home-brewed intelligence that the nation needed. He appreciated Lincoln's simplicity and lack of sophistication. This student recognized the values that Hawthorne truly admired and was able to express them in an essay that demonstrated versatile control of the language and an excellent quality of insight.

The broader appreciation of the media image of the presidency today almost makes this essay a 9, but that ability to connect the then and the now doesn't stay with the essay throughout. It remains an 8, albeit a very good one.

5

AN IN-DEPTH LOOK AT THE GENERAL ARGUMENT ESSAY QUESTION

Regarded by many as the easiest of the three kinds of essay questions, the general argument essay question also has a reputation for creating all sorts of problems. It is designed as a "contemporary issues" question, but actually, it is really a "values" question. What are your values? What do you think our society should value? What should a moral, thoughtful, or reflective society consider its most important strengths? These fundamental issues are inherent to this type of question.

THE BASICS

There are some basic things you should know about how the general argument essay question is asked and how you should go about the process of answering it.

THE PROMPT

The prompt itself is set up by a brief passage from fiction, poetry, or nonfiction. The passage can be as long as half a page or as brief as two lines. It provides you with a spokesperson for an issue—an opinion is offered—and then you are asked to agree, disagree, or qualify that opinion based on your own experiences and/or reading. (We refer to agree, disagree, or qualify as ADQ, which makes it easy to remember.) In recent years students have been asked to consider how blogs and radio talk shows encourage or discourage the democratic process, how the United States' wealth could be better used to foster development in countries just beginning to emerge into the technological age, whether our society pries too much into the lives of its citizens, and whether those with money can purchase justice rather than have it impartially determined. The common thread in all of these questions is that a major economic, social, scientific, or cultural issue is raised, but within the context of larger social norms or values that are being defined. The 2007 AP exam included a question about students involved in a charitable act and the motives behind their actions. Is a charitable act genuine if someone is given an incentive that benefits them? Addressing this question required not only good writing skills, but also a persuasive argument.

IDENTIFY THE CLAIM

When you deal with a general argument prompt, there are essentially three things you must do. First—and this is absolutely vital—you must understand the claim being made by the author. Remember, the College Board is always evaluating your reading skills. For example, a few years ago the test borrowed the following quotation on justice from *King Lear*:

> Through tatter'd clothes small vices do appear;
> Robes and furr'd gowns hide all. Plate sin with gold,
> And the strong lance of justice hurtles breaks;
> Arm it in rags, a pigmy's straw does pierce it.

Because of the inverse order that marks much of Shakespeare's poetry, approximately one-quarter of the students misinterpreted Shakespeare's words. They then argued that Shakespeare is saying poor people are protected and guaranteed justice despite their poverty. Anyone who wrote that argument, even if it was a good essay, could get no higher than a 4. Second, you need to perceive the larger social context and express feelings about it. Do you think justice in our society is fair? Do you feel that certain students are not sent to detention because of who they are or how they are regarded by the vice principal? Finally—and this is also crucial—you are being asked to make your argument using examples from your own experience. Remember the earlier discussion on how the exam is graded. You must provide evidence or examples. If you blather on about justice or simply summarize (paraphrase) what the author said, your essay is doomed.

There is a relatively easy three-step process you should follow before you begin to write your essay. Step one is to critically read the passage and underline anything that clearly defines the author's claim. It can be helpful to go so far as to briefly restate the author's claim in your own words and make a note of anything particular that comes to your mind as you read. Step two is to set forth your immediate reaction to the issue in a few words: are you for it, against it, or ambivalent toward it? You might even create a brief outline. Step three is to make a list of viable, thoughtful examples you can use to help illustrate your argument. When you write the essay, don't just drop the examples into the paragraphs. You must include them with elaboration and commentary, identifying their relevance to and importance in your argument.

CREATING A SAMPLE LIST

One proactive step you can take to ensure success in writing the general argument essay is to create a sample list of works and experiences to draw upon when you are considering your argument. Your list can include books you have read, movies you have seen, television shows you have watched, current events with which you are familiar (including local events), history lessons you have retained, and personal experiences—almost anything related to the topic and prompt can and should be written down during this brainstorming. You may talk about your family, friends, town, or state. However, the family stories must be relevant and must hold a degree of interest for the reader. If your church youth group always takes a trip to Haiti to work in rural areas building homes and churches, this could be an effective narrative to use in an essay considering the value of helping less privileged communities.

Suppose you were given a prompt which suggested that Americans more than any other culture in the world had an obsession for wealth; that Americans, in essence, have made money their highest goal. Before you write the essay, brainstorm! Use all of the categories we have suggested: movies (*The Color of Money, Wall Street*), books (*The Jungle, The Great Gatsby*), current events (savings and loan scandal, gambling addiction), historical periods (America's Golden Age, the lavish courts of Europe in the 19th century, European colonization of Africa for wealth), and personal (a miserly uncle, personal or family poverty). The key here is to have a list sufficient to the task so that the essay provides more than one or two examples, demonstrating your breadth and depth of knowledge.

You can see that there are many different types of evidence you can provide. However, the main problem is that most students are usually tired by the time they get to this essay and they suffer from brain freeze or writer's block. You sit there but NOTHING is coming. You have this prompt and a vague opinion but not ONE SINGLE example comes to your overworked brain. What do you do? We have had many essays come past us with doodles or apologies for their failure to write this prompt. These are considered blank papers and receive no score.

We always tell our students to just start jotting down the most recent events in their lives, movies seen and books and/or articles they have read over the course of the semester. In fact, we practice this the day or two before the test. Without an essay prompt, we simply give the students a starting point from which to begin stream of consciousness listing. We recommend that you practice doing the same. Therefore, when you arrive at this question on the test, you will be able to quickly jot down a few ideas that will make you think of something, perhaps a discussion you had in history class about racial profiling, and that reminds you of a story in the news about how celebrities are treated in prison, which is enough to unlock your brain, causing a list of relevant examples to suddenly appear, and you are off and running with the necessary examples for your essay on the "equal justice" topic we have been discussing.

This Is an Easy Essay to Write

You should start by identifying and restating the fundamental claim and then indicate to the grader whether you intend to agree, disagree, or qualify. A brief word about qualifying: qualifying means simply that you can see some good points and some not so good points about an idea. You might decide that this concept might work well for local government issues but would never be successful for the entire country, or the idea was great one hundred years ago but wouldn't work today. Be clear in your discussion about the positives and negatives you see.

Your subsequent paragraphs should discuss the quality and meaning of your various examples and then close with a summarizing statement. Remember: Formulate your opinion. Explain your evidence. Finish your essay.

A Practice Essay

If you wish to engage in additional argumentation and to learn more about the different categories of arguments, read the chapters and essays on "Persuasion and Argument" in *The Riverside Reader*.

The general argument prompt below was taken from Judith Viorst's essay "The Truth About Lying." As you approach Viorst's prompt, critically read and annotate what she has to say. Then restate the main thesis in your own words. Decide whether you agree with her position, disagree with it, or want to qualify it. Finally, make a list of your evidence. (Hint: this one lends itself well to history, politicians, spies, and personal experience.) When you have completed the task, take a look at both our annotated copy of the prompt and our list of evidence.

Essay Question 3

(Suggested time—40 minutes. This question counts as one-third of the total essay section score.)

The passage below is the final comment by Judith Viorst in a lengthy essay on "The Truth About Lying." In that essay she discusses "Social Lies" ("I like your new hairdo"), "Peace-Keeping Lies" (you're late because of traffic), "Protective Lies" (lying "to the dying about the state of their health"), and "Trust Keeping Lies" (protecting someone by lying about where they were). Read her conclusion to this essay carefully. Then write an essay in which you agree, disagree, or qualify the claim that "the truth's always better" than lying. Be sure to support your view with appropriate evidence.

> For those of us, however, who are good at telling lies, for those of us who lie and don't get caught, the question of whether or not to lie can be a hard and serious moral problem. I liked the remark of a friend of mine who said, "I'm willing to lie. But just as a last resort—the truth's always better."
>
> "Because," he explained, "though others may completely accept the lie I'm telling, I don't."
>
> I tend to feel that way too.
>
> What about you?

Following is a repeat of the prompt on lying with our annotations to give you an example of how to annotate your own prompts.

ANNOTATED GENERAL ARGUMENT QUESTION

Essay Question 3

(Suggested time—40 minutes. This question counts as one-third of the total essay section score.)

The passage below is the final comment by Judith Viorst in a lengthy essay on "The Truth About Lying." In that essay she discusses "Social Lies" ("I like your new hairdo"), "Peace-Keeping Lies" (you're late because of traffic), "Protective Lies" (lying "to the dying about the state of their health"), and "Trust-Keeping Lies" (protecting someone by lying about where they were). Read her conclusion to this essay carefully. Then write an essay in which you agree, disagree, or qualify the claim that "the truth's always better" than lying. Be sure to support your view with appropriate evidence.

sometimes lies cross borders, though— social lies & peacekeeping are not moral or ethical questions Protective & Trust raise moral/ethical ?'s

For those of us, however, who are good at telling lies, for those of us who lie and don't get caught, the question of whether or not to lie can be a hard and serious moral problem. I liked the remark of a friend of mine who said, "I'm willing to lie. But just as a last resort—the truth's always better."

"Because," he explained, "though others may completely accept the lie I'm telling, I don't."

I tend to feel that way too.

What about you?

ADQ:

Truth is always better.

Me: Not always

—Abuse

—Security

—Greater Good!

Depends.
Outline:
I. Bad haircut—don't say anything

II. Protective/Trust:
—Weapons of mass destruction
—false reports
—Iran-Contra Affair
—North takes blame for Reagan
—Vietnam
—media's role?

We spent a considerable amount of time analyzing the prompt and preparing an outline of ideas for the essay. In reality, you must be able to do this in five or ten minutes. Practice helps. Practice writing the essay also helps. DO THAT NOW! Spend about forty-five minutes writing the essay you have outlined and organized. Do it quickly. Write or type it as a rough draft. After you have finished, check your essay against our scoring rubric (see below) and study our scoring samples. You should be able to determine how well you did.

SCORING RUBRIC FOR ARGUMENT QUESTIONS

As much as possible, this scoring guide will follow the concepts and language of the scoring guides used by the College Board. However, their guides are designed for graders. Our guides are designed for you as a student taking the test. This guide should help you determine the quality of your own writing on the College Board's nine-point scale. Keep in mind that a score of **5 or higher** (upper-half essays) will generally produce a final result of at least an overall 3, or what the majority of colleges regard as a passing score. Scores of **4 or below** (lower-half essays) are generally unsuccessful essays.

As you evaluate your essay, remember that it was composed as a rough draft and is not a finished product. This was not an essay you had all night to write and edit. You should reward yourself for what you did well. Did you answer the question, write coherently and intelligently, and use examples? Always keep that in mind.

There will be mistakes even in the best of papers. Don't be too hard on yourself for misspelling a word or forgetting to put in a period or start a new paragraph. The grader will largely ignore that as well. However, scoring guides always tell graders that any paper with many distracting errors in grammar or mechanics should be no higher than a 2.

A 9 ESSAY
You will earn this score if your essay meets the criteria for an 8 but is really, really, really good and, as we say it, if you have an impressive control of language, use sophisticated examples, and write with a sophisticated style.

AN 8 ESSAY: EFFECTIVE
Your essay will earn this score if it effectively develops a position on the ethics of lying. Your evidence is appropriate to the prompt and will be convincing as an argument. You will demonstrate an ability to control your style and be able to write well, but shouldn't expect your writing to be flawless. Occasional errors are fine.

A 7 ESSAY
Your paper is a 7 if it fits the description of a 6 but is better. How is it better? Your writing is somewhat more mature. Your evidence is more complete.

A 6 ESSAY: ADEQUATE

Your paper is adequate if it develops a position on the ethics of lying. You have appropriate evidence and your argument remains fairly clear throughout. You can have lapses in organization, incompleteness in part of your argument, or some occasional errors in grammar, but in general your argument should stay on track throughout.

A 5 ESSAY

Papers earning a score of 5 develop a position on the ethics of lying. However, your paper wavers in one of several ways. Your evidence is not complete or quite as connected as it should be. You may provide evidence but not explain it very well. The writing quality is about the same as a 6.

A 4 ESSAY: INADEQUATE

Your paper earns a lower-half score of 4 if it is inadequate to the task. Your evidence may be insufficient. Your writing may not connect ideas to one another or connect all that well to the primary question that is being asked. Your writing isn't terrible, but a maturity of writing style is usually not present in these essays.

A 3 ESSAY

Papers earning a score of 3 meet the criteria for a 4, but the writing is even less successful in developing a position. Your paper will offer little evidence and will often repeat what the author seemed to be saying without developing an argument.

A 2 ESSAY: LITTLE SUCCESS

Your paper will be a 2 if you have written a very poor or very brief and incomplete essay. Your essay will show little success if you misunderstood what Viorst was saying, or if your own evidence was unrelated to or disconnected from the ideas she was proposing. Essays also earn this score if they are poorly written, with consistent weaknesses in sentences and grammar.

A 1 ESSAY

Your paper is a 1 if it is hardly developed at all. You will have written maybe a half-page to barely a page and you will have mentioned the topic of lying but will not have had much to say about it.

The College Board also issues scores of **0** and "—." A 0 is given to an essay that just repeats the prompt and says nothing else. A dash is given to an unwritten essay or an essay, as was recently the case, that tells us how this is a stupid test and a waste of time. This type of essay receives no points.

Now take a look at these sample essays, read our commentary about whether they are successful, and examine the scores they would most likely earn.

SAMPLE STUDENT RESPONSES WITH COMMENTARY

SAMPLE ESSAY 1

This passages discusses the different reasons people lie. I think lying is bad and can hurt other people like your family or the country. One time my dad lied to me about going fishing because he had to work. I felt bad and wondered why he didn't want to spend time with me. Also, sometimes the government lies to us. Like when they told us they put a man on the moon, when they didn't to keep getting more money. Or they lie to us about Aliens and all the places they try to hide the truth. I know it makes me scepticul about the government, and I don't think I will ever vote because you can't trust them.

In conclusion, lying is bad and it should stop.

COMMENTARY ON SAMPLE ESSAY 1

This essay is a **2** and demonstrates **little success.** The writer does address the prompt by apparently agreeing with the idea that "the truth's always better." However, the argument is brief and undeveloped. The grammar is satisfactory. The first example of the father is not bad, but should have been more thoroughly developed. The governmental lies are the stuff of urban legend. They could have been interesting and acceptable if the writer had gone into more specific detail of what harm comes from them.

SAMPLE ESSAY 2

Judith states that lying should be a last resort because even if other people accept the lie, I don't. I disagree with this statement because lying is sometimes a necessary thing today, especially with threats of terrorism slamming us from every direction.

Judith writes about different kinds of lies like social lies, peace keeping lies, protective lies, and trust keeping lies. Some kinds of lies are not a big deal but important for keeping friends. You can't just tell your best friend that her new hair color is terrible because then she will hate you and not talk to you again, so sometimes lying is better. I really don't care how my friend's hair looks as long as she is loyal to me and isn't a backstabber like some people in school.

Peace keeping lies are also important because they can get you out of trouble like when you are late for work or out after when you were supposed to be home.

Protective lies I think are less about lying to your friend about her talent than about protecting people from themselves. Like, if you watch the news, the terror alert has been high for a long time but it is so common now no one notices it. But we are still afraid of terrorists attacking us. So, shouldn't it be high all the time? But the government lies to us and so we are not out buying batteries and water and guns all the time. No one would do anything right. So, it is good for the government to lie to us.

Judith is not right when she says lying should be a last resort because if people didn't sometimes lie, then we might be saying things that create more problems than the lie would.

COMMENTARY ON SAMPLE ESSAY 2

This essay is a **4** for many reasons. It does answer the question and suggests disagreement with Viorst. However, the argument is not coherent. It demonstrates the danger of just summarizing what Viorst has said. That is a common problem with student essays.

However, the essay then deals with personal relationships, getting out of trouble by lying at work or home, and terrorism. Yet the writer does not successfully connect these arguments to Viorst's passage except indirectly, nor does the writer connect the arguments to one another. They are just tossed in. The writer is "rambling" about the subject rather than making an organized and adequate argument on the topic.

This essay also exhibits a frequent flaw in student writing today. Students may assume that the writer is a "friend" or "pal" and call the author by his or her first name—another weakness that would contribute to a lower-half essay. This is a formal essay and not a phone conversation. Both of the lower-half essays cited above feel more like disorganized casual conversations than proper essays.

GENERAL COMMENTARY ON LOWER-HALF ESSAYS

You may ask, "Do students write this poorly?" They most certainly do. The essay is hastily composed (forty minutes) and often students will sit there stumped for quite some time and then dash off something in ten minutes.

"Do students write as much as they did on sample essay 2 and still get a such a low score?" Yes, and we even have a casual phrase for them. We call them the four-page-4. They just write on and on about the topic without organizing anything into a clearly reasoned argument. REMEMBER: the essay does not have to be polished, but it does need to be argumentative, reasoned, thoughtful, and somewhat interesting.

SAMPLE ESSAY 3

In Judith Viorst's essay "The Truth about Lying," she agrees with a friend who says that "the truth is always better" than lying, since the person telling the lie doesn't always accept his own lie. While the truth may actually be better than lying, *telling* the truth isn't always better than *telling* a lie. Therefore, I qualify the claim that the truth is always better than lying.

Oftentimes, a person has to lie in order to protect themselves or the people around them. For example, my aunt, who lives in another state, was in an abusive marriage and wanted to leave her husband, but she didn't know where she could go that she and her kids would be safe. My parents said she could stay with us until she got on her own feet. She arrived at our house at 6 in the morning and went right to sleep. But less than a day later, my uncle showed up and started banging on the door in the middle of the night. My dad answered the door and told my uncle he had no idea where my aunt and cousins were and that he didn't even know they were gone. My uncle didn't seem like he believed him, but he left anyway. My dad lied to my uncle, but it was important to tell the lie because telling the truth would have caused more harm for my aunt and cousins.

Another example of when it is better to tell a lie than to tell the truth is in the case of Anne Frank. In *The Diary of Anne Frank*, a thirteen year old Jewish girl and her family hide in the attic of her father's office building and his coworkers/friends promise to protect the Franks from the Nazis. For several years, the Franks' hiding place was hidden by a bookcase to the attic. When the Nazis would come to search the office building, they would not find anything. Mr. Frank's coworkers lied to the Nazis, even though it meant they would die a cruel death if the Nazis found out. In the end, the Franks were betrayed by someone else and were discovered in the attic. The Nazis sent them to concentration camps and Mr. Frank was the only one who survived. Even though the Franks were eventually found out by the Nazis, the coworkers and friends did the right thing by lying to the Nazis about their hiding place. At least it gave them a little more time and Anne was able to write in her diary about her experiences.

A last example that shows that telling a lie is not always better than telling the truth is when President Clinton lied about having an affair with Monica Lewinski. He lied on television and was caught. He got in a lot of trouble for lying when he should have just told the truth. Then his wife wouldn't have gotten so famous and would still be with him instead of running for president herself.

As you can see, lying sometimes is good because it saves people, but other times it creates problems for people.

COMMENTARY ON SAMPLE ESSAY 3

This essay is an **adequate 6**. It answers the question and even tells us specifically that the writer is qualifying the claim. The writer fulfills that promise by showing how lies can be helpful and then, in a rather brief and rushed fourth paragraph, how telling the truth can be better. The specific examples are adequate. One is personal and the second is a famous historical one. While the writing is not exceptional, it remains clear and fulfills the requirement of the prompt. As we said, that fourth paragraph is weak, especially compared to the other two examples. One feels that the writer was racing against time. Had he or she pulled off the Clinton paragraph with added fullness, this essay could have been a 7 despite the rather dull writing.

SAMPLE ESSAY 4

Lying, like stealing is something you do if you have to. Both raise moral and ethical questions. Some may seem like an intro to philosophy question: if your wife is dying and you do not have the money to pay for the drug she needs, can you steal it from the pharmacy? Questions like these are as old as the Ten Commandments: "thou shalt not steal" and "thou shalt not lie." Shouldn't some actions override religious and ethical moors? If we use some common sense, sometimes lying, like stealing is OK.

When Viorst says that "lying should be a last resort", one initially agrees with her. We all have had a friend who received a terrible haircut. Do you tell her it's bad or lie and tell her it looks great? I say buy her a hat. It is possible to tell the truth without speaking. Move on with life because in the end, her hair won't matter when there are starving children in the world who are too hungry to even grow hair. The same goes with peace keeping lies. To me, lying to avoid getting into trouble says that you are not responsible and you are really just giving yourself an excuse to lie to your boss the next time. Ultimately, you will get fired.

But what about lies, the lies a person tells to protect himself or others from harm. These are harder to deal with. Should you tell a terminally ill child they are going to die especially if they are not old enough to understand? Or can you lie to the police if a criminal is going to kill your family if you say, "Sure - he's upstairs in the bedroom." I don't know how to answer stuff like this. I do know that it is done all the time, especially by our politicians.

Richard Nixon lied about Watergate and he lied about what was really happening in Vietnam. Thousands of people lost their lives over that one. Or how about "weapons of mass destruction." Americans are still losing their lives over that one. Also, Nixon lied about the tapes and his involvement with breaking into the Democratic Party headquarters in order to avoid impeachment. That doesn't seem like a very protective lie to me. The one I did my research paper on was Ronald Reagan fighting a war in Central America by giving guns and weapons to the Iranians to fight Iraq and using the money to fight an illegal war in Guatemala and Honduras.

In the paragraph before, I looked at people who really had a good reason to lie. However, when I look at all these politicians lying to us, it looks more like they are lying to protect themselves or someone who has given them money, and then Viorst is right and telling the truth is much better.

In the end, I guess I am somewhat agreeing because the "truth" is usually better. It certainly is in our country, but it is not always the best advice in our personal lives.

COMMENTARY ON SAMPLE ESSAY 4

This is a very good essay. It is an **8**, and one could even argue that it is an 8+. There are a few wording errors and some argument flow errors that keep it from being a 9, but this is certainly an effective essay. It answers the question and it does something that we see many writers do: as they write, they figure out their opinion, and only realize their sense of partial agreement in the last paragraph. This person used some vague personal examples, but relied heavily, in the most convincing paragraph, on examples from recent presidential politics. This writer likes history and even told us so. There was a bit of bragging, but remember what we said about voice. This person has a definite personal style that makes the essay interesting to read, including an especially cutting remark about hair and starving children. Lies are only important to this writer when the issue is important. (One lovely and odd P.S.: In the first paragraph, the student spelled "mores" (meaning customs) as "moors" (meaning a group of North Africans in southern Spain). While graders might find this error humorous, they would in no way penalize the student for it. It was a small error in a solid essay.)

GENERAL COMMENTARY ON UPPER-HALF ESSAYS

There are two key differences between essays that receive scores of 6 and 8. First, notice that a 7, 8 or 9 rarely starts by repeating the prompt. Such essays show voice and often begin with a historical analogy, something current in the news, and so forth, and then relate that to the prompt. The 8–9 essay shown above uses more sophisticated examples and explains their relevance. Other than that, both kinds of writers answered the question, remained clear, and used examples. They both avoided serious flaws in grammar. That is what an upper-half paper always does.

You might ask if it is possible for a student to write an 8 of that quality in forty minutes. Well, we said it was an 8+, but yes, we see essays like this all the time. They are written by students who are informed, well-read, and have a good sense of their own values. They write without worrying about what the graders will think. Keep practicing and reading and you will write like this as well.

SUMMARY

Some reading resources that may assist you in generating topics about which to write for the general argument essay include op-ed pages of your newspaper, magazines of opinion such as *Foreign Affairs* or *Criterion*, op-ed sections of reputable news websites, and literary opinion websites such as *Arts and Letters Daily* (aldaily.com), among many others. You should avoid modeling your arguments after radio talk shows and television news shows because they generally rant and engage in simplistic arguments. Ultimately, any collection of essays will include some argumentative pieces and will, therefore, be valuable to you. *The Riverside Reader, Alternate Edition* provides excellent debates on a number of issues such as family structure, political issues, and the environment.

Part III

Practice Tests

PRACTICE TEST 1

ENGLISH LANGUAGE AND COMPOSITION EXAM
SECTION I: Multiple-Choice Questions
Total time: 1 hour
Number of questions: 54

Directions: This part consists of selections from prose works and questions on their content, form, and style. After reading each passage, choose the best answer to each question.

Note: Pay particular attention to the requirement of questions that include the words NOT, LEAST, or EXCEPT.

Questions 1–13 are based on the following passage from "Debtors' Prisons," written by Samuel Johnson in 1758. Read the passage carefully before you choose your answers.

Sir,
As I was passing lately under one of the gates of this city, I was struck with horror by a rueful cry, which summoned me 'to remember the poor debtors'.

5　　The wisdom and justice of the English laws are, by Englishmen at least, loudly celebrated; but scarcely the most zealous admirers of our institutions can think that law wise which, when men are capable of work, obliges them to beg; or just which exposes the liberty of one to the

10　passions of another.
　　The prosperity of a people is proportionate to the number of hands and minds usefully employed. To the community sedition is a fever, corruption is a gangrene, and idleness an atrophy. Whatever body, and whatever

15　society, wastes more than it acquires must gradually decay; and every being that continues to be fed, and ceases to labour, takes away something from the public stock.
　　The confinement, therefore, of any man in the sloth and darkness of a prison is a loss to the nation, and no gain to

20　the creditor. For of the multitudes who are pining in those cells of misery, a very small part is suspected of any fraudulent act by which they retain what belongs to others. The rest are imprisoned by the wantonness of pride, the malignity of revenge, or the acrimony of disappointed

25　expectation.
　　If those who thus rigorously exercise the power which the law has put into their hands be asked why they continue to imprison those whom they know to be unable to pay them, one will answer that his debtor once lived

30　better than himself; another that his wife looked above her neighbours, and his children went in silk clothes to the dancing school; and another, that he pretended to be a joker and a wit. Some will reply that if they were in debt they should meet with the same treatment; some, that they

35 owe no more than they can pay, and need therefore give no account of their actions. Some will confess their resolution that their debtors shall rot in jail; and some will discover that they hope, by cruelty, to wring payment from their friends. . . .

40 Since poverty is punished among us as a crime, it ought at least to be treated with the same lenity as other crimes; the offender ought not to languish at the will of him whom he has offended, but to be allowed some appeal to the justice of his country. There can be no reason why any 45 debtor should be imprisoned, but that he may be compelled to payment; and a term should therefore be fixed in which the creditor should exhibit his accusation of concealed property. If such property can be discovered, let it be given to the creditor; if the charge is not offered, or cannot be 50 proved, let the prisoner be dismissed. . . .

Many of the inhabitants of prisons may justly complain of harder treatment. He that once owes more than he can pay is often obliged to bribe his creditor to patience, by increasing his debt. Worse and worse commodities, at a 55 higher and higher price, are forced upon him; he is impoverished by compulsive traffic, and at last overwhelmed, in the common receptacles of misery, by debts which, without his own consent, were accumulated on his head. To the relief of this distress, no other objection 60 can be made but that by an easy dissolution of debts, fraud will be left without punishment, and imprudence without awe, and that when insolvency shall be no longer punishable, credit will cease.

The motive to credit is the hope of advantage. 65 Commerce can never be at a stop while one man wants what another can supply; and credit will never be denied while it is likely to be repaid with profit. He that trusts one whom he designs to sue is criminal by the act of trust; the cessation of such insidious traffic is to be desired, and no 70 reason can be given why a change of the law should impair any other.

We see nation trade with nation, where no payment can be compelled. Mutual convenience produces mutual confidence, and the merchants continue to satisfy the 75 demands of each other, though they have nothing to dread but the loss of trade.

It is vain to continue an institution which experience shows to be ineffectual. We have now imprisoned one generation of debtors after another, but we do not find that 80 their numbers lessen. We have now learned that rashness and imprudence will not be deterred from taking credit; let us try whether fraud and avarice may be more easily restrained from giving it.

1. Johnson finds a current British law unjust and foolish. In modern
   terms, if that same law were passed today,
   (A) you could make your bank loan you money from your savings
   (B) the government could take your house for taxes
   (C) anything you invented could be used by others to make money
   (D) you could be sent to jail for failure to pay child support
   (E) a credit card company could put you in jail for failure to pay
   your bill

2. Johnson's style demonstrates use of
   (A) parallel syntax
   (B) rhetorical questions
   (C) vivid adjectives and adverbs
   (D) active present tense verbs
   (E) alternating long and short paragraphs

3. In the first four paragraphs, all of the following contribute to the
   central tone EXCEPT
   (A) gangrene (line 13)
   (B) zealous (line 7)
   (C) corruption (line 13)
   (D) malignity (line 24)
   (E) rueful (line 3)

4. Johnson suggests that he was alerted to this problem
   (A) by journalists
   (B) by government officials
   (C) by his tendency to take walks about London
   (D) by a lawyer who accosted him on the street
   (E) by family members who came to see him

5. The word "atrophy" (line 14) most closely evokes which one of the
   seven deadly sins?
   (A) Greed
   (B) Lust
   (C) Pride
   (D) Envy
   (E) Sloth

6. The sentence "The prosperity of a people . . ." (lines 11–12) basically
   says that the debtors' prison commits a double wrong in that it
   (A) deprives the country of its citizens and fails to return assets to
   creditors
   (B) takes away soldiers and encourages idleness
   (C) destroys families while it makes banks rich
   (D) fails to return assets to creditors and encourages emigration
   (E) makes banks rich but the government treasury weak

7. In paragraph 5, Johnson seeks to understand what purpose this law serves. He discovers that people answer with all of the following reasons EXCEPT
   (A) the law quashes the pride of those who lived better than they did
   (B) the law reminds others that they should not commit the crime
   (C) the law punishes the fool
   (D) if the creditor were in the same boat, he would want to be punished
   (E) the law frequently forces payment from others to get family members or friends out of jail

8. In paragraph 6, "Since poverty . . .", Johnson
   (A) offers a retraction to a previous argument
   (B) outlines a solution to the problem of nonpayment
   (C) provides an antithetical argument to his previous arguments
   (D) sustains his argument with an appeal to authority
   (E) provides an inductive reflection on the problem

9. The word "insidious" in line 69 most closely means
   (A) cruel
   (B) dishonest
   (C) wily
   (D) uninvited
   (E) loathsome

10. In the next-to-last paragraph, Johnson essentially compares
    (A) creditors and debtors to trading nations
    (B) creditors to merchants and guildsmen
    (C) traders to debtors
    (D) governments to usurers
    (E) businessmen to conmen or shysters

11. The author's use of "we" in the last two paragraphs is employed to
    (A) invite the reader to avoid debt and family grief
    (B) shift the blame from individuals to the government
    (C) acknowledge his own failure to pay his own debts
    (D) recognize the need for a collective solution
    (E) shift the focus from himself to the debtors he represents

12. Fundamentally, Johnson is seeking legal circumstances that provide for a court hearing where
    (A) the debtor either pays his debts or goes free
    (B) if it is proven the debtor has hidden assets, he is made to relinquish them
    (C) the creditor makes a reasonable claim, which is then paid by the family
    (D) the judge forces a reconciliation and a reasonable payment
    (E) the debtor pays all he can and the British government makes up the difference

13. In a fundamental way, Johnson finds this whole issue paradoxical. Which of the following statements most clearly defines that paradox for him?

(A) "We have now imprisoned one generation of debtors after another, but we do not find that their numbers lessen." (lines 78–79)

(B) "The rest are imprisoned by the wantonness of pride, the malignity of revenge, or the acrimony of disappointed expectation." (lines 23–25)

(C) "He that trusts one whom he designs to sue is criminal by the act of trust." (lines 67–68)

(D) "The confinement, therefore, of any man in the sloth and darkness of a prison is a loss to the nation, and no gain to the creditor." (lines 18–20)

(E) "He that once owes more than he can pay is often obliged to bribe his creditor to patience, by increasing his debt." (lines 52–54)

Questions 14–26 are based on the following passage from "Pain" by Diane Ackerman. Read the passage carefully before you choose your answers.

One of the great riddles of biology is why the experience of pain is so subjective. Being able to withstand pain depends to a considerable extent on culture and tradition. Many soldiers have denied pain despite appalling wounds, not
5   even requesting morphine, although in peacetime they would have demanded it. Most people going into the hospital for an operation focus completely on their pain and suffering, whereas soldiers or saints and other martyrs can think about something nobler and more important to
10   them, and this clouds their sense of pain. Religions have always encouraged their martyrs to experience pain in order to purify the spirit. We come into this world with only the slender word "I," and giving it up in a sacred delirium is the painful ecstasy religions demand. . . .
15   Choose your favorite sport; now imagine seeing all the world's best players on one team. I was interested in the ceremonial violence of sports, the psychology of games, the charmed circle of the field, the breezy rhetoric of the legs, the anthropological spectacle of watching twenty-two
20   barely clad men run on grass in the sunlight, hazing the quarry of a ball toward the net. The fluency and grace of soccer appealed for a number of reasons, and I wanted to absorb some of its atmosphere for a novel I was writing. I was amazed to discover that the players frequently realized
25   only at halftime or after a match that they'd hurt themselves badly and were indeed in wicked pain. During the match, there hadn't been the rumor of pain, but once the match was over and they could afford the luxury of suffering, pain screamed like a noon factory whistle.
30   Often our fear of pain contributes to it. Our culture expects childbirth to be a deeply painful event, and so, for us, it is. Women from other cultures stop their work in the fields to give birth, returning to the fields immediately

35 afterward. Initiation and adolescence rites around the world often involve penetrating pain, which initiates must endure to prove themselves worthy. In the sun dance of the Sioux, for instance, a young warrior would allow the skin of his chest to be pierced by iron rods; then he was hung from a stanchion. When I was in Istanbul in the 1970s, I

40 saw teenage boys dressed in shiny silk fezzes and silk suits decorated with glitter. They were preparing for circumcision, a festive event in the life of a Turk, which occurs at around the age of fifteen. No anesthetic is used; instead, a boy is given a jelly candy to chew. Sir Richard

45 Burton's writings abound with descriptions of tribal mutilation and torture rituals, including one in which a shaman removes an apron of flesh from the front of a boy, cutting all the way from the stomach to the thighs, producing a huge white scar. . . .

50 Pain has plagued us throughout the history of our species. We spend our lives trying to avoid it, and, from one point of view, what we call "happiness" may be just the absence of pain. Yet it is difficult to define pain, which may be sharp, dull, shooting, throbbing, imaginary, or referred.

55 We have many pains that surge from within as cramps and aches. And we also talk about emotional distress as pain. Pains are often combined, the emotional with the physical, and the physical with the physical. When you burn yourself, the skin swells and blisters, and when the blister

60 breaks, the skin hurts in yet another way. A wound may become infected. Then histamine and serotonin are released, which dilate the blood vessels and trigger a pain response. Not all internal injuries can be felt (it's possible to do brain surgery under a local anesthetic), but illnesses that

65 constrict blood flow often are: Angina pectoris, for example, which occurs when the coronary arteries shrink too tight for blood to comfortably pass. Even intense pain often eludes accurate description, as Virginia Woolf reminds us in her essay "On Being Ill": "English, which can

70 express the thoughts of Hamlet and the tragedy of Lear, has no words for the shiver and the headache . . . let a sufferer try to describe a pain in his head to a doctor and language at once runs dry."

14. Taken as a whole, the passage is best described as a
    (A) critique of modern American society
    (B) technical analysis of biological functions
    (C) description that relies on concrete examples
    (D) progressive analysis of the evolution of pain
    (E) discussion of differing cultural attitudes toward pain

15. The author uses the adjective "slender" (line 13) to
    (A) point out how unimportant mankind is
    (B) emphasize the precarious position of human existence
    (C) suggest that life is bitter and short
    (D) produce a painful moment of self-awareness
    (E) show that life will inevitably be incomplete

16. The pronoun "it" in line 13 refers to which of the following?
    (A) "religions" (line 10)
    (B) "pain" (line 11)
    (C) "world" (line 12)
    (D) "I" (line 13)
    (E) "ecstasy" (line 14)

17. The sentence that begins "I was interested . . ." (lines 16–21) draws
    its unity chiefly from the speaker's use of
    (A) parallelism
    (B) alliteration
    (C) irony
    (D) understatement
    (E) hyperbole

18. The statement "pain screamed like a noon factory whistle" (line 29)
    is an example of which of the following?
    (A) Pun
    (B) Metonymy
    (C) Simile
    (D) Onomatopoeia
    (E) Apostrophe

19. All of the following statements are true of the first sentence in
    paragraph 2 (line 30) EXCEPT:
    (A) It alludes to the speaker's knowledge of the subject.
    (B) It states the main thesis of paragraph 2.
    (C) It contradicts the statement at the end of paragraph 1.
    (D) It provides an answer to the riddle introduced at the beginning
        of paragraph 1.
    (E) It offers an approach to the topic with which the passage is
        concerned.

20. The speaker cites Burton's writings (lines 44–46) as
    (A) a contrast to Virginia Woolf
    (B) a bandwagon or *vox populi* appeal
    (C) an inductive argument
    (D) an appeal to tradition
    (E) an appeal to authority

21. "Happiness" has quotation marks in line 52 because the speaker
    believes
    (A) it is relative to the person experiencing it
    (B) it does not exist for anyone
    (C) it is elusive and cannot be achieved
    (D) it is another word for the absence of pain
    (E) it is the only acceptable definition of painlessness

22. Paragraph 3 is critical to the development of the passage primarily because it
    (A) defines the types of pain people feel
    (B) ties the subjectivity of pain to the difficulty of defining pain
    (C) discusses the manner in which people may avoid pain
    (D) analyzes different pains and the tolls they have on the human body
    (E) provides a defense for Virginia Woolf's statement about linguistic failure

23. The tone of the last paragraph is best characterized as
    (A) confident and didactic
    (B) tentative and practical
    (C) detached and ironic
    (D) fervent and agitated
    (E) supportive and reassuring

24. All of the following words in paragraph 3 suggest a negative connotation EXCEPT
    (A) "absence" (line 53)
    (B) "throbbing" (line 54)
    (C) "blister" (line 59)
    (D) "trigger" (line 62)
    (E) "shiver" (line 71)

25. Ackerman concludes by citing Virginia Woolf in order to assert that
    (A) great tragedies help us understand pain
    (B) every person has a different pain threshold
    (C) language is often inadequate when describing pain
    (D) pain is best defined by great writers
    (E) our language screams pain but does not understand it

26. The author's rhetorical strategies in the passage include all of the following EXCEPT
    (A) thesis, antithesis, synthesis
    (B) analogical comparison
    (C) direct comparison
    (D) responses to anticipated criticism
    (E) appeals to authority

Questions 27–39 are based on the following passage, "Two Views of the River" by Mark Twain. Read the passage carefully before you choose your answers.

Now when I had mastered the language of this water, and had come to know every trifling feature that bordered the great river as familiarly as I knew the letters of the alphabet, I had made a valuable acquisition. But I had lost something, too. I had lost something which could never be restored to me while I lived. All the grace, the beauty, the poetry, had gone out of the majestic river! I still keep in mind a certain wonderful sunset which I witnessed when steamboating was new to me. A broad expanse of the river was turned to blood; in the middle distance the red hue brightened into gold, through which a solitary log came floating black and conspicuous; in one place a long, slanting mark lay sparkling upon the water; in another the surface was broken by boiling, tumbling rings that were as many tinted as an opal; where the ruddy flush was faintest, was a smooth spot that was covered with graceful circles and radiating lines, ever so delicately traced; the shore on our left was densely wooded, and the somber shadow that fell from this forest was broken in one place by a long, ruffled trail that shone like silver; and high above the forest wall a clean-stemmed dead tree waved a single leafy bough that glowed like a flame in the unobstructed splendor that was flowing from the sun. There were graceful curves, reflected images, woody heights, soft distances; and over the whole scene, far and near, the dissolving lights drifted steadily, enriching it every passing moment with new marvels of coloring.

I stood like one bewitched. I drank it in, in a speechless rapture. The world was new to me, and I had never seen anything like this at home. But as I have said, a day came when I began to cease from noting the glories and the charms which the moon and the sun and the twilight wrought upon the river's face; another day came when I ceased altogether to note them. Then, if that sunset scene had been repeated, I should have looked upon it without rapture, and should have commented upon it, inwardly, after this fashion: "This sun means that we are going to have wind to-morrow; that floating log means that the river is rising, small thanks to it; that slanting mark on the water refers to a bluff reef which is going to kill somebody's steamboat one of these nights, if it keeps on stretching out like that; those tumbling 'boils' show a dissolving bar and a changing channel there; the lines and circles in the slick water over yonder are a warning that that troublesome place is shoaling up dangerously; that silver streak in the shadow of the forest is the 'break' from a new snag, and he has located himself in the very best place he could have found to fish for steamboats; that tall dead tree, with a single living branch, is not going to last long, and then how is a body ever going to get through this blind place at night without the friendly old landmark?"

No, the romance and beauty were all gone from the river. All the value any feature of it had for me now was the amount of usefulness it could furnish toward compassing the safe piloting of a steamboat. Since those days, I have pitied doctors from my heart. What does the lovely flush in a beauty's cheek mean to a doctor but a "break" that ripples above some deadly disease? Are not all her visible charms sown thick with what are to him the signs and symbols of hidden decay? Does he ever see her beauty at all, or doesn't he simply view her professionally, and comment upon her unwholesome condition all to himself? And doesn't he sometimes wonder whether he has gained most or lost most by learning his trade?

55

60

27. Twain's primary purpose in the passage is to
    (A) discuss the elusiveness of knowledge and the brevity of beauty
    (B) examine the ways in which knowledge destroys one's ability to appreciate beauty
    (C) analyze the changing appearance of nature and life
    (D) empathize with doctors who only see pain and death
    (E) question the usefulness of learning a trade

28. In context, the word "language" (line 1) is best understood to mean
    (A) dialogue
    (B) communication
    (C) character
    (D) vernacular
    (E) poetry

29. The antecedent of "it" (line 26) is
    (A) "river" (line 9)
    (B) "shore" (line 17)
    (C) "sun" (line 23)
    (D) "scene" (line 25)
    (E) "lights" (line 26)

30. In lines 9–26, all of the following phrases contribute to the image of the river and the riverbank as a living organism EXCEPT
    (A) "river was turned to blood" (line 9)
    (B) "solitary log came floating black and conspicuous" (lines 11–12)
    (C) "ruddy flush" (line 15)
    (D) "somber shadow" (line 18)
    (E) "clean-stemmed dead tree waved a single leafy bough" (line 26)

31. The author associates romance and beauty with the river because they both
    (A) link us emotionally rather than rationally with nature
    (B) symbolize the liberation from civilization
    (C) illustrate the metaphorical relationship between man and nature
    (D) require us to rely on experience rather than instinct to appreciate them
    (E) are judged somewhat harshly by most people

32. In the passage, the doctor (lines 55–64) is used primarily as an illustration of
    (A) a tradesman whose knowledge affects his appreciation of beauty
    (B) a trade comparable to a riverboat captain
    (C) the importance of knowledge and power
    (D) the power and utility of a professional trade
    (E) a contradictory viewpoint to balance the necessity of knowledge

33. In the final sentences of the passage (lines 55–64), Twain uses all of the following EXCEPT
    (A) rhetorical questions
    (B) antithetical statements
    (C) argumentative fallacy
    (D) metaphorical comparisons
    (E) an extended analogy

34. The intended audience for this passage is most likely
    (A) riverboat captains
    (B) amateur poets
    (C) young women
    (D) general readers
    (E) Native Americans

35. The second paragraph of the passage serves to
    (A) distinguish between two closely related concepts
    (B) present a contrast to be evaluated
    (C) define an abstract idea for further discussion
    (D) offer a philosophical debate about nature
    (E) cite a common misconception among men

36. The statement "the glories and the charms which the moon and the sun and the twilight wrought upon the river's face" (lines 31–33) is an example of which of the following?
    (A) Metaphor
    (B) Zeugma
    (C) Chiasmus
    (D) Anadiplosis
    (E) Personification

37. The primary effect of the sixth sentence of the first paragraph (lines 9–23) is that
    (A) its length creates an irony inherent to the brevity of the moment
    (B) the parallel syntax creates an energetic momentum
    (C) the use of colons creates a metaphor for a rainbow of hope
    (D) the alliterative elements make it onomatopoetic
    (E) the use of semicolons creates pauses in Twain's reflections

38. Twain's central rhetorical strategy in the passage can best be described as
    (A) contrasting two alternative views to make his case
    (B) developing an argument by using a strong personal appeal
    (C) advancing an extended metaphor that describes the essence of a particular quality
    (D) citing authorities to reinforce the validity of a critical theory
    (E) providing specific examples to illustrate an abstract concept

39. Which of the following aphoristic ideas can be inferred from the last sentence of the passage?
    (A) Change occurs over time.
    (B) Knowledge comes with a price.
    (C) You often take two steps forward and one step back.
    (D) You can paint the surface but the structure remains the same.
    (E) We are alone before the wonder of God.

Questions 40–54 are based on the following passage from "Assimilation in America" by Milton Gordon. Read the passage carefully before you choose your answers.

Probably all the non-English immigrants who came to American shores in any significant numbers from colonial times onward—settling either in the forbidding wilderness, the lonely prairie, or in some accessible urban slum—
5 created ethnic enclaves and looked forward to the preservation of at least some of their native cultural patterns. Such a development, natural as breathing, was supported by the later accretion of friends, relatives, and countrymen seeking out oases of familiarity in a strange
10 land, by the desire of the settlers to rebuild (necessarily in miniature) a society in which they could communicate in the familiar tongue and maintain familiar institutions, and, finally, by the necessity to band together for mutual aid and mutual protection against the uncertainties of a strange
15 and frequently hostile environment. This was as true of the "old" immigrants as of the "new." In fact, some of the liberal intellectuals who fled to America from an inhospitable political climate in Germany in the 1830s, 1840s, and 1850s looked forward to the creation of an all-
20 German state within the union, or, even more hopefully, to the eventual formation of a separate German nation, as soon as the expected dissolution of the union under the impact of the slavery controversy should have taken place.[1] Oscar Handlin,[2] writing of the sons of Erin[3] in mid-
25 nineteenth-century Boston, recent refugees from famine and economic degradation in their homeland, points out: "Unable to participate in the normal associational affairs of the community, the Irish felt obliged to erect a society

---

[1] Nathan Glazer, "Ethnic Groups in America: From National Culture to Ideology," in Morroe Berger, Theodore Abel, and Charles H. Page, eds., *Freedom and Control in Modern Society* (New York, D. Van Nostrand, 1954), p. 161; Marcus Lee Hansen, *The Immigrant in American History* (Cambridge, Harvard University Press, 1940), pp. 129–140; John A. Hawgood, *The Tragedy of German-America* (New York, Putnam's, 1940), *passim*. [Author's note]
[2] *Oscar Handlin:* American historian (b. 1915); winner of the Pulitzer Prize for his work on U.S. immigration.
[3] *Sons of Erin:* Irish immigrants.

30 within a society, to act together in their own way. In every contact therefore the group, acting apart from other sections of the community, became intensely aware of its peculiar exclusive identity."[4] This cultural pluralism was a fact in American society before it became a theory—a

35 theory with explicit relevance for the nation as a whole, and articulated and discussed in the English-speaking circles of American intellectual life.

Early in 1915 there appeared in the pages of *The Nation* two articles under the title "Democracy versus the Melting-Pot." Their author was Horace Kallen, a Harvard-educated

40 philosopher with a concern for the application of philosophy to societal affairs, and, as an American Jew, himself derivative of an ethnic background which was subject to the contemporary pressures for dissolution implicit in the "Americanization," or Anglo-conformity, and

45 the melting-pot theories. In these articles Kallen vigorously rejected the usefulness of these theories as models of what was actually transpiring in American life or as ideals for the future. Rather he was impressed by the way in which the various ethnic groups in America were coincident with

50 particular areas and regions, and with the tendency for each group to preserve its own language, religion, communal institutions, and ancestral culture. All the while, he pointed out, the immigrant has been learning to speak English as the language of general communication, and has

55 participated in the over-all economic and political life of the nation. These developments in which "the United States are in the process of becoming a federal state not merely as a union of geographical and administrative unities, but also as a cooperation of cultural diversities, as a federation or

60 commonwealth of national cultures,"[5] the author argued, far from constituting a violation of historic American political principles, as the "Americanizers" claimed, actually represented the inevitable consequences of democratic ideals, since individuals are implicated in groups, and since

65 democracy for the individual must by extension also mean democracy for his group.

40. This passage primarily seeks to
(A) discount Handlin's theories
(B) explain the organization of German dissident groups prior to the Civil War
(C) clarify two different theories about acculturation of immigrants
(D) defend Americanization as the only acceptable process for immigration reform
(E) explain why cultural pluralism has persisted

---

[4] Oscar Handlin, *Boston's Immigrants* (Cambridge, Harvard University Press, 1959, rev. edn.), p. 176. [Author's note]
[5] Horace M. Kallen, "Democracy *versus* the Melting-Pot," *The Nation,* 18 and 25 February 1915; reprinted in his *Culture and Democracy in the United States,* New York, Boni and Liveright, 1924; the quotation is on p. 116. [Author's note]

41. The phrase "ethnic enclaves" (line 5) is most closely related to which word or phrase?
    (A) "oases" (line 9)
    (B) "familiar institutions" (line 12)
    (C) "exclusive identity" (line 32)
    (D) "cultural pluralism" (line 32)
    (E) "models" (line 46)

42. The sentence beginning "Such a development . . ." (lines 7–15) includes all of the following EXCEPT
    (A) an appositive
    (B) parallel syntax
    (C) two independent clauses
    (D) a parenthetical remark
    (E) loose sentence structure

43. "Cultural pluralism" (line 32) is the antithesis to
    (A) "Americanization" (line 44)
    (B) "federal state" (line 57)
    (C) "cultural diversities" (line 59)
    (D) "American political principles" (lines 61–62)
    (E) "democratic ideals" (lines 63–64)

44. The passage suggests that some Germans in America looked forward to
    (A) the maintenance of the German language in several urban areas
    (B) the promotion of the German language as the language of the educated
    (C) a political alliance between the United States and the Austro-Hungarian Empire
    (D) the creation of a separate German state in the United States following the Civil War
    (E) an accumulation of capital to develop a strong German industrial base

45. Gordon suggests that essential American unity was established
    (A) geographically
    (B) geographically and administratively
    (C) geographically, administratively, and culturally
    (D) geographically, administratively, culturally, and linguistically
    (E) geographically, administratively, culturally, linguistically, and inevitably

46. Horace Kallen's background would seem to imply that he would be someone
    (A) who would be biased against Germans
    (B) who would favor the doctrine of cultural pluralism
    (C) who would be completely nonbiased on the issue of immigration
    (D) who would be biased against the ideas of a westward expansion
    (E) who would be anti-democratic

47. Kallen would argue that cultures merged out of the same general
force that caused
(A) English to predominate
(B) states to merge
(C) acculturation to succeed against individualism
(D) democracy to prevail over autocracy
(E) the common urge to expand westward

48. The use of "federal" (line 57) and "federation" (line 59) in the
sentence beginning "These developments . . ." (lines 56–66) is an
effective example of
(A) paradox
(B) anecdote
(C) metonymy
(D) repetitive emphasis
(E) pun

49. The repetition in the last sentence emphasizes
(A) the lack of equality in immigrant groups
(B) the shifting burden of immigration from ethnic enclaves to the
state
(C) the loss of the American dream of a frontier
(D) the dominance of the English language
(E) the effective acculturation of immigrants

50. What do the three separate sources in footnote 1 have in common?
(A) They all argued that there was a movement within the United
States to create a separate German state.
(B) They were all quoted in *Freedom and Control in Modern
Society*.
(C) They were all published by the same company.
(D) They all advocated the theory of cultural pluralism.
(E) They all had a concern for the unique American experiment in
German and Irish relations.

51. Footnote 1 explains that Nathan Glazer
(A) was a Harvard colleague of Berger, Abel, and Page
(B) agreed with Hansen but disagreed with Hawgood
(C) wrote an article that was reprinted in an anthology compiled in
1954
(D) was published by Harvard University Press, as was Handlin
(E) published *Freedom and Control in Modern Society,* which was
then reprinted by Berger, Abel, and Page

52. According to footnotes 2 through 4, all of the following are true
EXCEPT
(A) Handlin was born in 1915
(B) Handlin originally wrote *Boston's Immigrants* in 1940
(C) Handlin won a Pulitzer Prize for his work on American history
(D) Handlin was interested in the status of Irish immigrants in
Boston
(E) Harvard University Press, which published a Handlin book, is
located in Cambridge

53. Footnote 5 tells us that Horace Kallen's views first appeared in
    (A) a British newspaper
    (B) the collected presentations from a conference on immigrants
    (C) a journal
    (D) an edited collection of several works on the topic of immigration
    (E) a book by Kallen

54. The author included the footnotes in order to
    (A) justify his position
    (B) pose the selective two contrasting debate concerns in a proper context
    (C) suggest that he is not alone in his view of the supremacy of cultural pluralism
    (D) define the extent of the voices engaged in the argument over cultural pluralism and Americanization
    (E) clarify the correct order in which his own ideas proceeded

END OF SECTION I

English Language and Composition Exam
Section II

Reading time: 15 minutes
Writing time: 2 hours
Number of questions: 3

Percentage of total grade: 55

Each question counts as one-third of the total essay section score.

Reading time before receiving booklet.....................................15 minutes

Question 1 Essay..suggested time 40 minutes

Question 2 Essay..suggested time 40 minutes

Question 3 Essay..suggested time 40 minutes

Section II of this examination requires answers in essay form. To help you use your time well, the proctor will announce the time at which each question should be completed. If you finish any question before time is announced, you may go on to the following question. If you finish the examination in less than the time allotted, you may go back and work on any essay question you want.

Each essay will be judged on its clarity and effectiveness in dealing with the requirements of the topic assigned and on the quality of the writing. After completing each question, you should check your essay for accuracy of punctuation, spelling, and diction; you are advised, however, not to attempt many longer corrections. Remember that quality is far more important than quantity.

Write your essays with a pen, preferably in black or dark blue ink. Be sure to write CLEARLY and LEGIBLY. Cross out any errors you make.

The questions for Section II are printed in the green insert. You are encouraged to use the green insert to make notes and to plan your essays, but *be sure to write your answers in the pink booklet.* Number each answer as the question is numbered in the examination. Do not skip lines. Begin each answer on a new page in the pink booklet.

English Language and Composition Exam
Section II

Question 1

(Suggested time: reading time—15 minutes; writing time—40 minutes. This question counts as one-third of the total essay section score.)

Directions: The following prompt is based on the accompanying eight sources.

The question requires you to integrate a variety of sources into a coherent, well-written essay. Refer to the sources to support your position; avoid mere paraphrase or summary. Your argument should be central; the sources should support this argument.

Remember to attribute both direct and indirect citations.

INTRODUCTION

The history of lotteries goes back for centuries. Many believe that lotteries were part of any organized tribal society. We have records of lotteries before recorded history in the Far East. The Romans liked to play the lottery. However, lotteries developed a reputation for scandal and fixing and so were abandoned in the middle of the nineteenth century. States, feeling the economic crunch of services and unwilling to increase taxes, began, in 1964, to organize state-run lotteries. Today it is the rare state that does not have a lottery.

ASSIGNMENT

Read the following sources (including any introductory information) carefully. Then, in an essay that synthesizes at least three of the sources for support, take a position that defends, challenges, or qualifies the claim that lotteries are an ethical and effective way to raise state revenues for education.

Refer to the sources as Source A, Source B, etc.; titles are included for your convenience.

Source A (Steinberg)
Source B (Thompson)
Source C (Fahrenkopf)
Source D (Nelson)
Source E (Campbell)
Source F (Davis)
Source G (Political Cartoon)
Source H (Pie Chart)

Source A

Steinberg, Dr. Marvin. "National Gambling Impact Study Commission."
http://govinfo.library.unt.edu/ngisc/meeting/mar1698/mar16p3.html. 16 March 1998.

The following passage is an excerpt from an online source.

In fact, analogous to alcoholism among bartenders, employees on the gaming floors at casinos and parimutuels are at risk for developing a gambling problem. Buying a hundred or a thousand instant or scratch tickets in the lottery is no different than putting a hundred or a thousand dollars in a slot machine.

In fact, as lotteries expand the variety of gambling options they offer, the boundaries between casino and lottery gambling is becoming blurry. For example, some lotteries offer slot machines under the name video lottery terminals. The lives of those who are vulnerable to a gambling addiction are as damaged by an addiction to lottery games as to any other form of gambling.

I'd like to make four points, five points, relating to the responsibilities of state government and the lottery relating to the issue of problem gambling. Just quickly, because others are going to address this. I think that state governments are compromised in the role of gambling regulator when states directly and indirectly operate the lottery. It is my view that when a state is the operator of a form of gambling such as lottery, the state often loses the ability to adequately regulate the spread of lottery and the way it's promoted.

Third point. An excessive number of minors are gambling in the lottery due to ineffective monitoring by retailers and lottery personnel. Results from state surveys of high school students indicate that between 30 and 35 percent of students report purchasing lottery tickets themselves. This is far more than gambling in any other form of state sanctioned gambling. This problem will only get worse if states continue to install lottery vending machines across communities. I ask the question, haven't we learned from the example of widespread under age access to cigarette vending machines?

Source B

Thompson, William. "Easy Money." <u>Frontline: Easy Money: Pro/Con</u>. www.pbs.org/wgbh/pages/frontline/shows/gamble/procon/ithompson.html. 26 April 2007.

The following passage is an excerpt from an interview from an on-line source.

Poor people playing the lottery in Georgia are shifting money to middle-class kids going to the University of Georgia. Is this the way we tax public services? Take from the poor, give to the middle class and the wealthy people? That everybody that earns a B average gets a free college education at the Universtity of Georgia. Are these poor kids? Or are these middle-class kids?

It's a—it's sort of a tax from—what do we call? Welfare for the middle class and the rich paid for by the poor. The lottery ticket is a bad mechanism for redistributing goods and services in society. . . .

Poor people play more. All sectors of society play the lottery, but there's a disproportionate play among poorer people. Secondly, lotteries just extract money from the local community. There is no influx of outside money for the lotteries. Beyond that, the states extract an extremely high tax.

If you consider that a lottery ticket costs $1, well, you put 50%—you put 50 cents into a pool and redistribute the 50 cents, and it costs you a dollar for the ticket. Well, you bought something that's valued at 50 cents. You just paid a 100% sales tax. That's an extremely high tax. And it's an extremely high take-out for a gambling organization. It's one of the worst bets in our society . . . with a 100% take-out, or a 100% surcharge on the cost of gambling.

So, it's not a good bet, it's extracted from the community. States lose money on the deal because the supply companies are expensive. Usually, oh, 5% or so of the lottery costs go to a supplier. So the State actually loses money on the deal. But, the State government picks up a lot of money.

And—but I don't think they realize what the options are, if people had the money in their pockets and they were spending it on consumer goods. First of all, society would be more wealthy, because at the end of the purchase there would be a consumer good. And the State would also pick up a sales tax on that consumer good.

Source C

Fahrenkopf, Frank. "Responsible Gambling Is Harmless Fun." <u>Gambling: Opposing Viewpoints</u>. Ed. James Torr. San Diego, CA: Greenhaven Press, 2002. 26-30.

The following passage is an excerpt from a series collection.

Gambling is a voluntary activity. Nobody is forced to enter a casino or pick up a playing card. If you disapprove, don't do it. . . .

But the [National Gambling Impact Study Commission] took a poke at state lotteries, on the grounds that government services should not be financed largely on the backs of the low-income minorities and other poor people who are the heaviest players. The commission urged states and communities to consider a moratorium on new lotteries until the social consequences can be further evaluated.

Fiddlesticks. That is bleeding-heart liberalism at its bloodiest. Lotteries are a clean way to get people to do voluntarily what they resent doing through mandatory taxes, which is to pay for education and other public necessities. If lotteries offer impossible hope against insurmountable odds, so be it. A buck is a cheap price to pay for a dream, however temporary.

Source D

Nelson, Michael. "State Lotteries Are an Unethical Source of Government Revenue." Gambling: Opposing Viewpoints. Ed. James Torr. San Diego, CA: Greenhaven Press, 2002. 31–36.

The following passage is an excerpt from a series collection.

What a deal with the devil Carlin and his fellow governors struck. To begin with, lotteries are a wildly regressive way of raising revenue. Although members of nearly every demographic group bet the lottery in roughly equal numbers, some bet much more frequently than others did. "The heaviest players," Duke University economists Charles Clotfelter and Philip Cook have found, are "blacks, high-school dropouts, and people in the lowest income category." Yet state lotteries depend on the participation of these frequent players. "If all players spent the same as the median player, $75 a year," report Clotfelter and Cook, "[lottery ticket] sales would fall by 76 percent." Eighty-two percent of lottery bets are made by just 20 percent of players—and this group is disproportionately poor, black, and uneducated.

Despite laws to the contrary, minors bet the lottery, too. The presence of lottery tickets alongside candy, chips, and crackers in neighborhood convenience stores places children directly in contact with gambling. In lottery states, three-fourths of high school seniors report having bet in a lottery, according to the 1999 report of the National Gambling Impact Study Commission. In Massachusetts the attorney general found that children as young as age nine were able to buy lottery tickets in 80 percent of their attempts.

An additional problem with lotteries is that the money that states make from them seldom goes where the law says it should. Eighteen states earmark their lottery revenues for education; others, for transportation or programs for seniors. But economists have discovered that in most states little if any net increase in spending for the earmarked purpose actually occurs. Instead these states substitute lottery revenues for money they otherwise would have spent from their general funds.

Source E

Campbell, Felicia. "The Future of Gambling." <u>Frontline: Easy Money: Pro/Con</u>. www.pbs.org/wgbh/pages/frontline/shows/gamble/procon/future.html. 26 April 2007.

The following passage is an excerpt from an on-line source.

We all take chances; we all gamble to some extent. Yet it is the person who bets in the formal sense who is criticized. His actions are termed masochistic, sexually sublimative, and aberrant—harsh descriptions for behavior that has been ubiquitous in human history and that has often served people well.

The gambling impulse is part of what has been called "the adventurer within us"—that part of ourselves which lusts for change, the wooing of all the unknown, chance, danger, all that is new. The gambling impulse sends us both to the gaming tables and to the moon, to the laboratory and to the numbers man. It is part of what makes us human.

Contrary to popular belief, I have found gambling to be largely beneficial to the gambler, increasing rather than decreasing his efficiency. Gambling stimulates, offers hope, and allows decision-making. In many cases, it provides the gambler with a "peak experience," that godlike feeling that occurs when all of one's physical and emotional senses are "go."

Source F

Davis, Bertha. <u>Gambling in America</u>. New York: Franklin Watts (An Impact Book), 1992. 43–44.

The following passage is an excerpt from a book.

Despite the widespread acceptance of lotteries, they are still controversial. Some people question the wisdom of using lotteries as revenue raisers. Those who defend such use rightfully claim that lotteries do raise large sums for good purposes. But, say critics, there is another side to this picture.

Public belief that lottery proceeds serve worthwhile ends—education is by far the most important beneficiary—has produced mixed results. Certainly that belief increases participation in the lottery. It makes purchase of a ticket seem a commendable act rather than just plain gambling. However, general awareness of the good purposes served by lotteries seems to foster a misconception: some believe that with lottery money flowing to education, the schools must have ample funds at their disposal. In Florida, for example, during the 1990–91 school year, the lottery contributed $691.2 million to elementary and secondary schools. But that sum was only about 8.4 percent of a $7.9 billion public education budget.

Defeat of school bond issues is sometimes attributed to misunderstanding of lotteries' actual impact on the financial condition of a state's schools. Even more unfortunate, some state legislatures have used lottery receipts as an excuse to cut normal budget allotments to education.

Supporters of lotteries-as-revenue-raisers argue that buying a lottery ticket is actually payment of a voluntary tax. (States retain about half the sums raised through lotteries.) Think how much better voluntary taxes are, they argue, in a time when "no new taxes" is such a rallying cry. The voluntary taxation argument loses some of its potency, however, when the regressive nature of that taxation is made clear. One survey by a respected research center found that households with incomes under $10,000 earned 11.49 percent of the total household income of the survey population, but those households bought 24.68 percent of all the non-winning tickets purchased. In other words, poor people's purchase of lottery tickets means they make a larger contribution to states' treasuries than their incomes warrant.

Source G

"State Gambling Addiction Clinic." Political cartoon. http://www.caglecartoons. com/images/preview/%7Ba15d6bd1-6697-4f9f-8d49-3f0470835. 26 April 2007.

Source H

Freeney, Don. "Is Gambling Immoral?" <u>Beyond the Odds</u>, June 1999.
www.miph.org/gambling/bto/jun99/1.html.

The following is an excerpt from an on-line quarterly newsletter.

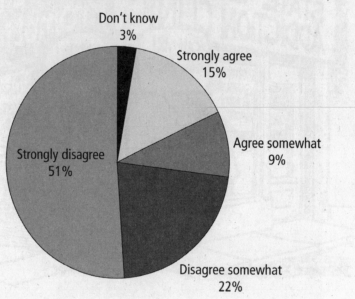

**"I am opposed to gambling for moral
or religious reasons."**

Don't know 3%
Strongly agree 15%
Agree somewhat 9%
Disagree somewhat 22%
Strongly disagree 51%

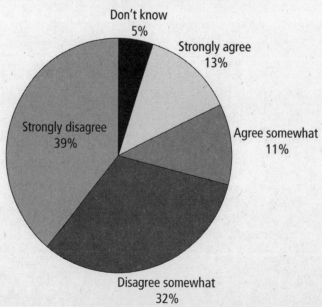

"All gambling should be outlawed."

Don't know 5%
Strongly agree 13%
Agree somewhat 11%
Disagree somewhat 32%
Strongly disagree 39%

Question 2

(Suggested time—40 minutes. This question counts as one-third of the total essay section score.)

The passage below is an excerpt from a speech Daniel Webster made in 1825 at the site of the Bunker Hill Monument, a monument to an important battle for the American Revolutionary forces against the British. Read the speech carefully. Then, in a well-written essay, analyze the rhetorical devices Webster uses to define how his listeners should feel about this monument and what it means for the fledgling republic.

This uncounted multitude before me and around me proves the feeling which the occasion has excited. These thousands of human faces, glowing with sympathy and joy, and from the impulses of a common gratitude turned reverently to heaven in this spacious temple of the firmament, proclaim that the day, the place, and the purpose of our assembling have made a deep impression on our hearts.

If, indeed, there be any thing in local association fit to affect the mind of man, we need not strive to repress the emotions which agitate us here. We are among the sepulchres of our fathers. We are on ground, distinguished by their valor, their constancy, and the shedding of their blood. We are here, not to fix an uncertain date in our annals, nor to draw into notice an obscure and unknown spot. If our humble purpose had never been conceived, if we ourselves had never been born, the 17th of June 1775 would have been a day on which all subsequent history would have poured its light, and the eminence where we stand a point of attraction to the eyes of successive generations. But we are Americans. We live in what may be called the early age of this great continent; and we know that our posterity, through all time, are here to enjoy and suffer the allotments of humanity. We see before us a probable train of great events; we know that our own fortunes have been happily cast; and it is natural, therefore, that we should be moved by the contemplation of occurrences which have guided our destiny before many of us were born, and settled the condition in which we should pass that portion of our existence which God allows to men on earth.

We do not read even of the discovery of this continent, without feeling something of a personal interest in the event; without being reminded how much it has affected our own fortunes and our own existence. It would be still more unnatural for us, therefore, that for others, to contemplate with unaffected minds that interesting, I may say that most touching and pathetic scene, when the great discoverer of America stood on the deck of his shattered bark, the shades of night falling on the sea, yet no man sleeping; tossed on the billows of an unknown ocean, yet the stronger billows of alternate hope and despair tossing his own troubled thoughts; extending forward his harassed frame, straining westward his anxious and eager eyes, till Heaven at last granted him a moment of rapture and ecstacy, in blessing his vision with the sight of the unknown world.

Question 3

(Suggested time—40 minutes. This question counts as one-third of the total essay section score.)

The passage below is an excerpt from "Women and the Future of Fatherhood" by Barbara Dafoe Whitehead. Her article begins with a discussion of the Million Man March and Promise Keepers as efforts to reinvest men in the important role of fatherhood. She argues that this is not possible unless women support men as fathers. Read the passage carefully. Then write an essay in which you take a position on the value of fathers in the raising of children, supporting your view with appropriate evidence.

> But what has not yet been acknowledged is that the success of any effort to renew fatherhood as a social fact and a cultural norm also hinges on the attitudes and behavior of women. Men can't be fathers unless the mothers of their children allow it.
> Women can be good mothers without being married. But especially with weakened communities that provide little support, children need levels of parental investment that cannot be supplied solely by a good mother, even if she has the best resources at her disposal. These needs are more likely to be met if the child has a father as well as a mother under the same roof. Simply put, even the best mothers cannot be good fathers.

STOP

END OF EXAM

ANSWERS AND EXPLANATIONS FOR PRACTICE TEST 1

Using the answer key below, score your test and determine how many questions you answered correctly and incorrectly. Then look over the answer explanations.

ANSWER KEY FOR MULTIPLE-CHOICE QUESTIONS

1. E	10. A	19. C	28. C	37. E	46. B
2. A	11. D	20. E	29. D	38. A	47. B
3. B	12. B	21. D	30. B	39. B	48. D
4. C	13. C	22. B	31. A	40. C	49. E
5. E	14. E	23. A	32. A	41. A	50. A
6. A	15. B	24. A	33. C	42. C	51. C
7. B	16. D	25. C	34. D	43. A	52. B
8. B	17. A	26. D	35. B	44. D	53. C
9. E	18. C	27. B	36. E	45. E	54. D

ANSWERS AND EXPLANATIONS FOR MULTIPLE-CHOICE QUESTIONS

1. ANSWER: E Debtors' prisons were used to incarcerate people for the failure to pay a debt. If this law were in force today, there would be a lot of people in jail.

2. ANSWER: A Johnson is a master of parallel syntax. He does use vivid language, and here and there is anger in his description, but neither is as dominant as his parallelism.

3. ANSWER: B The initial tone of the piece describing his encounter with the outside walls of the prison is very negative, nearly heartrending. Every word here carries a negative connotation except "zealous."

4. ANSWER: C Johnson clearly states that this encounter with sorrow was occasioned by a stroll through the streets of London.

5. ANSWER: E "Atrophy" means essentially to waste away from disuse. More specifically, it is the loss of muscle through a complete lack of exercise, which is what happens within the prison walls. The sin is not the fault of the debtors but the fault of the system.

6. **ANSWER: A** The sentence essentially condemns the practice because it takes hard-working people off the street and incarcerates them. Later, remember, Johnson does an entire mathematical calculation of the cost to the country as a whole. The creditors do not get their money and the country loses potential employees.

7. **ANSWER: B** All answers except deterrence are found in this paragraph.

8. **ANSWER: B** This is the paragraph where Johnson suggests an altering of the legal system. His suggestion is that the creditor must prove that the debtor is holding out on him with hidden assets. Otherwise, the debtor would be back out on the streets.

9. **ANSWER: E** All the indicators suggest not only a negative connotation, but a strong one. In the list of possible answers there are three negatives, but "loathsome" is by far the most negative.

10. **ANSWER: A** Johnson is making a clear financial analogy comparing the way countries conduct trade and the current local situation of lending money. One country cannot put another in jail, so if creditors did not put debtors in jail the promotion of commerce would improve.

11. **ANSWER: D** By using "we," Johnson encompasses the entire community: himself, creditors, debtors, government. In so doing, he makes it a community problem that society must address together or suffer the consequences.

12. **ANSWER: B** This was discussed earlier. Johnson's best solution—at least the one he offers here—is that a trial determines whether the debtor is holding out. If that can be demonstrated, then he is required by the court to pay the debt. Otherwise, he should be freed.

13. **ANSWER: C** The entire article is fundamentally ironic and angry. Johnson finds it utterly paradoxical that if one is engaged in the business of making money, that person would then lock up people who could potentially give him that money. Johnson sees nothing in a debtors' prison but cruelty and meanness. There are several potential paradoxical statements in the answer, but the one that comes closest to the focus of the essay is C. Trust is the very opposite of criminality, and yet here it is found in union. Johnson considers that deplorable.

14. **ANSWER: E** The passage offers a discussion of several cultural attitudes toward pain not only in modern society, but throughout history. Although there are concrete examples, answer choice C is too vague to be a solid answer. E is the best choice.

15. **ANSWER: B** "Slender" is commonly used as a description of body type. However, here Ackerman employs the term metaphorically. She implies that our entire existence on this earth is brief and perpetually threatened. Pain is a physical reminder of threats to that existence. Hence, B is the best answer.

16. **Answer: D** In this line "it" refers to the "I" in the phrase "the slender word 'I'". One must sacrifice oneself, one's entire being, to pain to be considered a martyr.

17. **Answer: A** The sentence is cohesive due to parallelism: "the ceremonial violence," "the psychology," "the charmed circle," "the breezy rhetoric," "the anthropological spectacle." None of the other answer choices applies to this sentence.

18. **Answer: C** The phrase is a simile that uses the requisite "like" to compare screaming pain to a factory whistle.

19. **Answer: C** The best way to approach these questions is to look at all the answer choices and eliminate those that *are* true, since the question says "EXCEPT." The sentence "Often our fear of pain contributes to it" does allude to the speaker's knowledge about pain, it is the main idea of the second paragraph, it does offer an answer of sorts to the biological riddle of why pain is subjective, and it is one approach to the topic of pain. It does not contradict the final statement of the first paragraph, that soccer players feel pain only after the match is over.

20. **Answer: E** The answer that makes sense is that the author is referring to Burton's writing as authoritative. According to this passage, Burton has written about pain and the historical conceptions of pain in other cultures, an idea that the author is also discussing.

21. **Answer: D** The sentence specifically states "what we call 'happiness' may be just the absence of pain." The author is offering a definition of the word.

22. **Answer: B** The last paragraph provides a connection to the author's first statement that pain is subjective and the last statement that it is difficult to define pain. The idea is that something so subjective is difficult to define.

23. **Answer: A** The last paragraph is quite scientific, offering descriptions of the kinds of pain people may experience (throbbing, etc.), as well the body's reaction to pain (histamine and serotonin).

24. **Answer: A** Every answer choice here is tied to pain (a negative experience) except "absence," which is used to define "happiness" as an "absence of pain."

25. **Answer: C** Woolf's statement tells us that language cannot express such a unique experience as pain. Her references to Hamlet and Lear are merely literary references to characters who are great commentators about human psychology and the human experience, but even they cannot describe pain. In fact, Lear's inability to express his pain resulted in his madness and subsequent death.

26. **Answer: D** Ackerman employs every strategy except D. Nowhere in the piece does she give a hint of what others might argue. She is making her own definition, about which she sees no real critical response. She definitely appeals to authority and both types of

comparison are made. It is more difficult to perceive, but she does make a thesis statement, which she follows with a counterproposal that then results in a finished statement that synthesizes her perspective on pain and the human condition.

27. **ANSWER: B** Twain begins his essay by commenting that once he had learned everything there was to know about the river, he felt he lost something. The end of the essay questions whether the doctor's knowledge keeps him from appreciating a young woman's beauty. Thus, one may infer that the purpose is to examine the ways in which knowledge destroys one's ability to appreciate beauty.

28. **ANSWER: C** Plug in the various answer choices and you will find that the word "character" best suits the meaning of the word "language" in this context. His point is not literally linguistic, but more emotional.

29. **ANSWER: D** Again, put your finger on the word "it" and plug in the answer choices to see which best fits the context of the sentence and paragraph. Here, "scene" is the antecedent to the pronoun "it."

30. **ANSWER: B** In each of the answer choices, the river and riverbank are personified (it is "bloody," it has a flush, it carries a shadow, and it waves), except in answer B. A floating log does not contribute to the environment's humanity.

31. **ANSWER: A** As most will attest, romance and beauty are acutely personal and emotional connections. The speaker capitalizes on the emotional connection with the river as something lost, and it is his sense of nostalgia for that loss that keeps the piece from becoming too rational and logical.

32. **ANSWER: A** This is a tricky question mainly because of today's notions of doctors as professionals rather than tradespeople. However, the end of the piece specifically asks, "And doesn't he [the doctor] sometimes wonder whether he has gained most or lost most by learning his trade?" Since the speaker refers to the doctor as a tradesperson whose knowledge also affects his ability to appreciate beauty, A is the correct answer.

33. **ANSWER: C** You can arrive at the correct answer through the process of elimination. The last sentences include rhetorical questions (looking for question marks is a good place to begin), antithetical statements (his comparison of his view of the river as a novice to his view of that same river, that same moment, as a captain), metaphorical comparisons ("lovely flush" to "a 'break' that ripples"), and an extended analogy (a doctor's knowledge of biology compared to a riverboat captain's knowledge of the river).

34. **ANSWER: D** One of Twain's most endearing features is his ability to relate to the general reader. That aside, however, one can see that his essay appeals to more than just riverboat captains and young women. While his essay is also quite poetic, the purpose of the essay is to convey the beauty of the river and the loss of that beauty through the poetry of language for *all* readers.

35. ANSWER: B The second paragraph describes a technical view of the river, which is the antithesis to the first paragraph's description of the beauty of it.

36. ANSWER: E Here, the river is personified as having a face.

37. ANSWER: E Once again, the process of elimination should remove at least C and D as viable choices. Although the sentence is parallel, it doesn't necessarily give the river energy so much as mimic the slowness of the its movement. A is not possible because Twain's purpose and description carry no irony. Thus, we are left with the illustrious semicolon, which, when used appropriately, serves as a connector between ideas, giving pause to each idea separately.

38. ANSWER: A The speaker contrasts his two views of the river—one as beautiful, one as ominous and threatening—to show that sometimes knowledge can ruin one's outlook and complicate the ability to see beauty.

39. ANSWER: B The text clearly states that learning a trade, gaining extensive knowledge of something, is beneficial, but is also a loss of innocence. Thus, knowledge comes with a price.

40. ANSWER: C The passage clearly discusses two theories about how immigrants integrated into American culture.

41. ANSWER: A The phrase "ethnic enclaves" is most closely related to the word "oases," as both inspire a sense of refuge or sanctuary. Although "familiar institutions" is a good distractor, it is not the correct answer because the context of the word is not in line with "enclaves," which is a kind of community or closed society.

42. ANSWER: C This is the process of elimination again. The sentence includes an appositive ("natural as breathing"), is parallel ("by the later accretion," "by the desire," "by the necessity"), has a parenthetical remark (the phrase "necessarily in miniature" in parentheses), and has loose sentence structure (an independent clause—"Such as development . . . was supported"—followed by several parallel dependent clauses). The only choice left is C, and when you look, you'll see there is only one independent clause followed by several dependent clauses.

43. ANSWER: A The speaker defines "Americanization" as "Anglo-conformity," the opposite of cultural pluralism, which allows many cultures to coexist in one society without conforming to any particular culture.

44. ANSWER: D Look to the text and you will see that it clearly states that some immigrants who fled Germany "looked forward to the creation of an all-German state within the union, or, even more hopefully, to the eventual formation of a separate German nation, as soon as the expected dissolution of the union under the impact of the slavery controversy should have taken place." Of course, knowing a bit of history helps here as well, since you would have to know that the

"expected dissolution of the union under the impact of the slavery controversy" is a direct reference to the Civil War.

45. ANSWER: E As you read through the paragraphs, notice that Gordon progressively identifies the ways in which disparate groups have unified. Being located in the same place, living under the same government, and speaking a common language of commerce ultimately created a common culture.

46. ANSWER: B Kallen would see the maintenance of the Jewish identity as positive; hence, he would see the positive in cultural pluralism. However, he also saw that groups did not remain distinct and hostile but rather successfully integrated into an American culture that happened naturally rather than by coercion (Americanization). If you force groups to become "American," they resist. If you allow them their own space in the larger culture, they will integrate.

47. ANSWER: B Do you remember the big fight over the Articles of Confederation and the new Constitution? Americans were afraid of a centralized government even though they needed one. The states maintained their separate identities, and yet they have, over time, created networks of interstate cooperation. The exact same forces that brought states together also coerced separate immigrant groups to seek out fiscal and governmental and, finally, cultural unity.

48. ANSWER: D The only possible answer is "repetitive emphasis." None of the other choices apply at all.

49. ANSWER: E The implication of this sentence is that immigrants are effectively adapting to American democracy while still maintaining their own cultural identities.

50. ANSWER: A One may infer from the sentence preceding the footnote that each source separately discussed a movement in the United States to create a German state after the Civil War.

51. ANSWER: C All of the answer choices are untrue or cannot be inferred except that C. Glazer's article is reprinted and appears in Berger, Abel, and Page's book, *Freedom and Control in Modern Society*, which was published in 1954.

52. ANSWER: B Footnote 4 states that *Boston's Immigrants* was published in a revised edition in 1959. The first printed edition is unknown and unstated. Referring to the text will show the other statements as true.

53. ANSWER: C Knowing the documentation style of a journal will help, but you are given a specific date of publication in the journal *The Nation*. The author's views were reprinted in his book *Culture and Democracy in the United States* in 1924.

54. ANSWER: D To some extent, the author included the footnotes to appeal to scholarly authorities in the field. He wanted them to know that he was aware of the extent of the debate and was familiar with all sides of it. He wanted to appear dispassionate and firmly aware of the issues involved.

Explanations and Rubrics for Essay Questions

Essay Question 1: Upper-Half Papers: Scores of 5–9

Synthesis papers require you to make *your own argument*. The sources assist and help sustain that argument, but it is crucial that you offer your own point of view on the topic. Upper-half paper writers clearly sustain their own argument. They integrate quotations from the sources provided and cite them correctly in a coherent essay. Upper-half papers may include some citations that do not quite fit the argument, but for the most part, the quotations are part of a fairly seamless whole. The writing is not necessarily flawless, but the paper is clear and well-argued. In this prompt, writers can take a variety of positions on lotteries: everything from "Lotteries are absolutely unethical" to "Lotteries are completely ethical," as well as any opinion in between. The crucial element, as always, is that the opinion be sustained and supported by the citations.

Essay Question 1: Lower-Half Papers: Scores of 1–4

Remember: Yours will be a lower-half essay if you do not quote and correctly cite at least three sources. We have provided one example in the synthesis chapter of a good paper that scored in the lower half because the writer made such an error. However, most lower-half papers will have used the requisite number of sources, but the quotations used will often have little to do with the writer's argument about lotteries. Lower-half paper writers seem to drop in quotations without fitting them to the essay in any cohesive way. They also often find themselves summarizing all the sources without attempting to make any kind of argument on their own. Finally, such essays are often too brief and/or are grammatically weak.

Essay Question 2: Upper-Half Papers: Scores of 5–9

These papers will clearly demonstrate an understanding of Webster's eloquent prose. Their writers will appreciate his sense of history and the emphasis he places on this monument, dedicated in this fledgling republic. The writers of upper-half papers will also discuss specific strategies employed by Webster and the possible effects they might have had upon his audience. Such writers will also use specific quotations to illustrate these strategies. They may note but are not limited to his diction, syntactical structure, and appeals to the Divine and especially that tradition of the original colonists. These papers are not necessarily flawless but generally remain coherent throughout.

Essay Question 2: Lower-Half Papers: Scores of 1–4

There are many ways an analytical paper can go wrong. The first is if the student misread the passage and misunderstood Webster's purpose. The second and more common failure is to summarize and restate what Webster said without analyzing his methods of oratorical flair. Sometimes writers of these essays will merely identify strategies without discussing their impact on the reader. If the essays are either too brief or grammatically unsound, they will also land in the lower half.

ESSAY QUESTION 3: UPPER-HALF PAPERS: SCORES OF 5–9

Upper-half essays clearly understand the argument Barbara Whitehead makes. Writers of these essays will argue coherently and provide examples that help sustain the argument. Any position may be taken: fathers are essential to the raising of children; mothers are essential but fathers are not; both mothers and fathers are equally important in raising successful and healthy children. The crucial element in the upper-half paper is not the argument, but that the writer provides concrete examples from personal experience, current events, current trends, books, and movies to support that position. Upper-half papers are not always without grammatical error, but they are generally clearly written, and the relationship between the examples and the argument is well-defined.

ESSAY QUESTION 3: LOWER-HALF PAPERS: SCORES OF 1–4

Lower-half paper writers may have misunderstood Whitehead's claim and argue that she sees fathers as unnecessary and/or that she thinks marriage is a hopeless institution. However, most of the weaker papers earn low scores because their writers fail to provide evidence. They generalize about the topic and give little support to their arguments. Lower-half papers are often unacceptably brief and/or have grammatical and mechanical errors throughout.

COMPUTING YOUR SCORE ON THE PRACTICE TEST

Please keep in mind that these numbers are subjective. Two variables affect the computation every year: the number of the multiple-choice questions and the difficulty level of the essays. There is a slight curve created every year in terms of the numbers. Having said that, remember that earning fifteen points on the essays and getting 50 percent right on the multiple-choice questions will generally produce a score of 3.

SCORING THE MULTIPLE-CHOICE SECTION

$$\underline{\hspace{2cm}} - (1/4 \times \underline{\hspace{2cm}}) = \underline{\hspace{4cm}}$$
number   number   multiple-choice score
correct   incorrect

SCORING THE FREE-RESPONSE SECTION

$$\underline{\hspace{2cm}} + \underline{\hspace{2cm}} + \underline{\hspace{2cm}} = \underline{\hspace{2cm}}$$
Question 1 Question 2 Question 3   total essay
(0–9 score) (0–9 score) (0–9 score)   score

COMPOSITE SCORE

$$1.29 \times \underline{\hspace{3cm}} = \underline{\hspace{3cm}}$$
        multiple-choice   weighted section I
          score   score

$$3.05 \times \underline{\hspace{3cm}} = \underline{\hspace{3cm}}$$
        free response   weighted section II
          score   score

$$\underline{\hspace{3cm}} + \underline{\hspace{3cm}} = \underline{\hspace{3cm}}$$
weighted section I weighted section II composite score

You now have a number between 0 and about 150. Each year that scale is adjusted. Generally it goes like this:

0–49 = 1   50–75 = 2   76–94 = 3   95–110 = 4   112–150 = 5

PRACTICE TEST 2

ENGLISH LANGUAGE AND COMPOSITION EXAM
SECTION I: Multiple-Choice Questions
Total time: 1 hour
Number of questions: 54

Directions: This part consists of selections from prose works and questions on their content, form, and style. After reading each passage, choose the best answer to each question.

Note: Pay particular attention to the requirement of questions that include the words NOT, LEAST, or EXCEPT.

Questions 1–15 are based on the following passage from "A Meditation upon a Broomstick, according to the Style and Manner of the Honourable Robert Boyle's Meditations" by Jonathan Swift. Read the passage carefully before you choose your answers.

THIS single stick, which you now behold ingloriously lying in that neglected corner, I once knew in a flourishing state in a forest; it was full of sap, full of leaves, and full of boughs; but now in vain does the busy art of man pretend

5 to vie with nature, by tying that withered bundle of twigs to its sapless trunk; 'tis now at best but the reverse of what it was, a tree turned upside down, the branches on the earth, and the root in the air; 'tis now handled by every dirty wench, condemned to do her drudgery, and, by a

10 capricious kind of fate, destined to make other things clean, and be nasty itself: at length, worn to the stumps in the service of the maids, 'tis either thrown out of doors, or condemned to its last use, of kindling a fire. When I beheld this I sighed, and said within myself, *Surely mortal man is a*

15 *Broomstick!* Nature sent him into the world strong and lusty, in a thriving condition, wearing his own hair on his head, the proper branches of this reasoning vegetable, till the axe of intemperance has lopped off his green boughs, and left him a withered trunk: he then flies to art, and puts

20 on a periwig, valuing himself upon an unnatural bundle of hairs, all covered with powder, that never grew on his head; but now should this our broomstick pretend to enter the scene, proud of those birchen spoils it never bore, and all covered with dust, through the sweepings of the finest

25 lady's chamber, we should be apt to ridicule and despise its vanity. Partial judges that we are of our own excellencies, and other men's defaults!

But a broomstick, perhaps you will say, is an emblem of a tree standing on its head; and pray what is a man, but a

30 topsyturvy creature, his animal faculties perpetually mounted on his rational, his head where his heels should be, grovelling on the earth! And yet with all his faults, he

35

40

sets up to be an universal reformer and corrector of abuses, a remover of grievances, rakes into every slut's corner of Nature, bringing hidden corruptions to the light, and raises a mighty dust where there was none before; sharing deeply all the while in the very same pollutions he pretends to sweep away. His last days are spent in slavery to women, and generally the least deserving, till, worn to the stumps, like his brother besom, he is either kicked out of doors, or made use of to kindle flames for others to warm themselves by.

1. The first sentence (lines 1–13) contains how many independent clauses?
   (A) 2
   (B) 3
   (C) 4
   (D) 5
   (E) 6

2. The item being described in the first sentence is a broom, which apparently resembles
   (A) a dirty mop
   (B) a bat or kind of weapon
   (C) a dirty wench
   (D) kindling
   (E) an upside-down tree

3. The diction in the first sentence is largely
   (A) furious
   (B) irreverent
   (C) sympathetic
   (D) detached
   (E) sober

4. The italics in lines 14–15 serve to
   (A) alert the reader to a change in direction for the argument
   (B) seek the reader's approval for the fundamental premise
   (C) switch tenses to assert the power of history
   (D) emphasize the humor of the analogy
   (E) seek a rhetorical response to a developing question

5. The word "capricious" (line 10), in this context, can be taken to mean
   (A) unpredictable
   (B) careless
   (C) systematic
   (D) unequal
   (E) unreliable

6. Swift finds man to be essentially
   (A) a book of wisdom left on a dusty shelf
   (B) a fool goaded by vanity
   (C) a religious saint seeking to rid the world of evil
   (D) an unappreciated provider, husband, and father
   (E) a basic resource like air that is underutilized and polluted

7. All of the following are metaphors for man and man's actions
EXCEPT
(A) "proper branches" (line 17)
(B) "puts on a periwig" (lines 19–20)
(C) "raises a mighty dust" (line 36)
(D) "worn to the stumps" (lines 39–40)
(E) "a topsyturvy creature" (line 30)

8. The sentence "Partial judges that we are . . . " (line 26) basically
implies that men are
(A) creatures prone to judge favorably the faults of others
(B) persons of merit who find it easy to discover weaknesses in
others
(C) religious creatures sent to live a life worthy of God
(D) persons of sentiment and compassion
(E) beings who favor their own opinions and easily find faults in
others

9. What basically brings the most harm to man?
(A) Age
(B) Bad habits
(C) Women
(D) Honor
(E) Hypocrisy

10. Swift relies heavily on the exclamation point because he
(A) is deeply worried about our collective future
(B) is so angry that he feels like screaming
(C) wants to emphasize the ludicrous nature of man
(D) is trying to make important what he knows is not
(E) wants to emphasize how significant it is for man to quit
following others

11. All of the following are participial phrases EXCEPT
(A) "condemned to do her drudgery" (line 9)
(B) "and left him with a withered trunk" (line 19)
(C) "grovelling on the earth" (line 32)
(D) "a remover of grievances" (line 34)
(E) "bringing hidden corruptions to the light" (line 35)

12. The phrase "generally the least deserving" (line 39) suggests that
(A) difficult and intemperate women have men to care for them
(B) poor and impoverished women rarely have husbands
(C) stupid men usually are married
(D) drunken and unkind men abuse women but rarely
(E) the ones we least suspect will go to heaven

13. The most important metaphoric aspects of brooms are that they
are
(A) nonrational and last a long time
(B) easy to store somewhere and last a long time
(C) good for cleaning and they can burn
(D) easy to store and they can burn
(E) good for cleaning and are nonrational

14. "A mighty dust" (line 36) is
    (A) a man slowly deteriorating
    (B) God's wrath attacking human error
    (C) all different ways people gossip about one another
    (D) a man attacking the wickedness of others
    (E) the arguments occurring at this moment in the homes of Dublin

15. Based on the title of the piece and the tone of Swift's essay, what might he think of Robert Boyle's work?
    (A) Sadness
    (B) Discontent
    (C) Admiration
    (D) Antipathy
    (E) Neutrality

Questions 16–28 are based on the following passage from "Shades of Black" by Mary Mebane. Read the passage carefully before you choose your answers.

I don't know whether African men recently transported to the New World considered themselves handsome or, more important, whether they considered African women beautiful in comparison with Native American Indian
5   women or immigrant European women. It is a question that I have never heard raised or seen research on. If African men considered African women beautiful, just when their shift in interest away from black black women occurred might prove to be an interesting topic for
10 researchers. But one thing I know for sure: by the twentieth century, really black skin on a woman was considered ugly in this country. This was particularly true among those who were exposed to college.
      Hazel, who was light brown, used to say to me, "You
15 are *dark*, but not *too* dark." The saved commiserating with the damned. I had the feeling that if nature had painted one more brushstroke on me, I'd have had to kill myself.
      Black skin was to be disguised at all costs. Since a black face is rather hard to disguise, many women took refuge in
20 ludicrous makeup. Mrs. Burry, one of my teachers in elementary school, used white face powder. But she neglected to powder her neck and arms, and even the black on her face gleamed through the white, giving her an eerie appearance. But she did the best she could.
25   I observed all through elementary and high school that for various entertainments the girls were placed on the stage in order of color. And very black ones didn't get into the front row. If they were past caramel-brown, to the back row they would go. And nobody questioned the justice of
30 these decisions—neither the students nor the teachers.
      One of the teachers at Wildwood School, who was from the Deep South and was just as black as she could be, had been a strict enforcer of these standards. That was another irony—that someone who had been judged outside the
35 realm of beauty herself because of her skin tones should

have adopted them so wholeheartedly and applied them herself without question.

40

One girl stymied that teacher, though. Ruby, a black cherry of a girl, not only got off the back row but off the front row as well, to stand alone at stage center. She could outsing, outdance, and outdeclaim everyone else, and talent proved triumphant over pigmentation. But the May Queen and her Court (and in high school, Miss Wildwood) were always chosen from among the lighter ones.

45

When I was a freshman in high school, it became clear that a light-skinned sophomore girl named Rose was going to get the "best girl scholar" prize for the next three years, and there was nothing I could do about it, even though I knew I was the better. Rose was caramel-colored and had

50

shoulder-length hair. She was highly favored by the science and math teacher, who figured the averages. I wasn't. There was only one prize. Therefore, Rose would get it until she graduated. I was one year behind her, and I would not get it until after she graduated.

55

To be held in such low esteem was painful. It was difficult not to feel that I had been cheated out of the medal, which I felt that, in a fair competition, I perhaps would have won. Being unable to protest or do anything about it was a traumatic experience for me. From then on I instinctively

60

tended to avoid the college-exposed, dark-skinned male, knowing that when he looked at me he saw himself and, most of the time, his mother and sister as well, and since he had rejected his blackness, he had rejected theirs and mine.

16. The passage focuses primarily on the
   (A) difficulties the author faces as a dark-skinned woman
   (B) advisability of women considering careers in teaching
   (C) author's analysis of how her own writing style developed
   (D) author's pride in being a black black woman
   (E) inspiration that enabled the author to overcome societal biases

17. In line 15, "saved" refers to
   (A) people who are Christians
   (B) people who are light-skinned
   (C) people who have escaped death
   (D) people who have attended college
   (E) people who find beauty in nature

18. The sentence in lines 15–16 ("The saved . . . damned") is an example of
   (A) personification
   (B) metaphor
   (C) rhetorical statement
   (D) pun
   (E) chiasmus

19. Mebane's point in the last sentence of the fifth paragraph (lines 33–37) is that
    (A) women can change their outward appearance to fit society's ideal standards
    (B) people are too easily fooled into accepting social norms
    (C) society's standards are unquestioned even by those who are hurt by them
    (D) life is more ironic than natural
    (E) she finds it easy to understand why people judge others based on appearance

20. In line 48, "it" refers to
    (A) "the justice of these decisions" (lines 29–30)
    (B) "standards" (line 33)
    (C) "high school" (line 43)
    (D) "light-skinned sophomore girl" (line 46)
    (E) "one prize" (line 52)

21. The "May Queen and her Court" (lines 42–43) is presented as an illustration of
    (A) discreet models of royal behavior
    (B) the unjustifiable torment of darker-skinned students by teachers
    (C) the popular, light-skinned students who are favored by others
    (D) admirable behavior that is rewarded with recognition
    (E) the honor awarded to those who triumph over prejudices

22. In repeating the word "rejected" (line 63), the author specifically emphasizes
    (A) the redundancy of cultural stereotypes
    (B) the abandonment of one's culture and family for social standards
    (C) one's escape from the prejudices of society
    (D) the perpetual circumstances that shape the values of several generations
    (E) the depth of self-loathing created by racial prejudice

23. In the first paragraph, Mebane contrasts early African men with twentieth-century African men to
    (A) surprise the reader with an unspoken question
    (B) provoke an argument with the audience
    (C) present a scholarly topic for research
    (D) show how time changes one's perception of beauty
    (E) introduce a point of contention for the remainder of the passage

24. As used in line 38, "stymied" most nearly means
    (A) succeeded
    (B) hindered
    (C) annoyed
    (D) satisfied
    (E) frustrated

25. The most probable reason Mebane says "But she did the best she could" (line 24) is to
    (A) ridicule the woman's attempts to disguise her skin tone
    (B) deemphasize the author's criticism of the teacher
    (C) emphasize the importance of concealing one's appearance
    (D) underscore "eerie appearance" by following it with an abrupt sentence structure
    (E) provide evidence that the woman was an inept teacher

26. The antecedent of "them" (line 36) is
    (A) "decisions" (line 30)
    (B) "students" (line 30)
    (C) "teachers" (line 30)
    (D) "standards" (line 33)
    (E) "skin tones" (line 35)

27. The fundamental irony in the last paragraph (lines 55–63) is that
    (A) Mebane's avoidance of dark-skinned men perpetuates the social standards she criticizes
    (B) Mebane's words belie the pain of being stereotyped by those of her own race
    (C) the images explain why Mebane does not date college men
    (D) Mebane's actions are the effect of generations of low self-esteem
    (E) Mebane's anger is rationalized by her recollection of an unjust society

28. The author's rhetorical strategies in the passage include all of the following EXCEPT
    (A) analogical comparison
    (B) personal reflection
    (C) specific examples
    (D) repetition
    (E) pathos argument

Questions 29–41 are based on the following passage from "The Paradox of Individualism" by Robert N. Bellah, et al. Read the passage carefully before you choose your answers.

Both the cowboy and the hard-boiled detective tell us something important about American individualism. The cowboy, like the detective, can be valuable to society only because he is a completely autonomous individual who
5 stands outside it. To serve society, one must be able to stand alone, not needing others, not depending on their judgement, and not submitting to their wishes. Yet this individualism is not selfishness. Indeed, it is a kind of heroic selflessness. One accepts the necessity of remaining alone
10 in order to serve the values of the group. And this obligation to aloneness is an important key to the American moral imagination. Yet it [sic] is part of the profound ambiguity of the mythology of American individualism that its moral heroism is always just a step away from despair.
15 For an Ahab, and occasionally for a cowboy or a detective, there is no return to society, no moral redemption. The

hero's lonely quest for moral excellence ends in absolute nihilism.[1]

If we may turn from the mythical heroes of fiction to a mythic, but historically real, hero, Abraham Lincoln, we may begin to see what is necessary if the nihilistic alternative is to be avoided. In many respects, Lincoln conforms perfectly to the archetype of the lonely, individualistic hero. He was a self-made man, never comfortable with the eastern upper classes. His dual moral commitment to the preservation of the Union and the belief that "all men are created equal" roused the hostility of abolitionists and southern sympathizers alike. In the war years, he was more and more isolated, misunderstood by Congress and cabinet, and unhappy at home. In the face of almost universal mistrust, he nonetheless completed his self-appointed task of bringing the nation through its most devastating war, preaching reconciliation as he did so, only to be brought down by an assassin's bullet. What saved Lincoln from nihilism was the larger whole for which he felt it was important to live and worthwhile to die. No one understood better the meaning of the Republic and of the freedom and equality that it only very imperfectly embodies. But it was not only civic republicanism that gave his life value. Reinhold Niebuhr[2] has said that Lincoln's biblical understanding of the Civil War was deeper than that of any contemporary theologian. The great symbols of death and rebirth that Lincoln invoked to give meaning to the sacrifice of those who died at Gettysburg, in a war he knew to be senseless and evil, came to redeem his own senseless death at the hand of an assassin. It is through his identification with a community and a tradition that Lincoln became the deeply and typically American individual that he was.[3]

29. Throughout the passage, the authors use the word "nihilism" to mean
    (A) a philosophical school that celebrates the individual over the group
    (B) an attitude that rejects hope and ends in despair
    (C) a point of view that defends freedom of choice over fate
    (D) the surrender of goods for friendship
    (E) a willingness to sacrifice self for the good of others

---

[1] On the hero's avoidance of women and society see Leslie Fiedler, *Love and Death in the American Novel* (New York: Stein and Day, 1966), and Ann Swidler, "Love and Adulthood in American Culture," in *Themes of Work and Love in Adulthood*, ed. Neil J. Smelser and Erik H. Erikson (Cambridge, Mass.: Harvard University Press, 1980), pp. 120-47. [Author's note]
[2] *Reinhold Niebuhr*: American theologian (1892-1971), best known for a series of books on Christianity, politics, and history.
[3] The best book on Lincoln's meaning for American public life is Harry V. Jaffa, *Crisis of the House Divided: An Interpretation of the Lincoln-Douglas Debates* (Garden City, N.Y.: Doubleday, 1959). Reinhold Niebuhr's remarks appear in his essay "The Religion of Abraham Lincoln," in *Lincoln and the Gettysburg Address*, ed. Allan Nevins (Urbana, Ill.: University of Illinois Press, 1964), p. 72.[Author's note]

30. Based on this passage, what does American individualism favor?
    (A) Selfishness
    (B) Selflessness
    (C) Culture
    (D) Understanding
    (E) Republicanism

31. The authors use the word "mythic" (line 20) in describing Lincoln
    to mean
    (A) a person who is so famous as to sustain a magical aura
    (B) a man whose greatness makes people lie about him
    (C) a person who is so integral to cultural identity as to seem
        unreal
    (D) a leader more significant after his death than during his life
    (E) a man whose historical impact is greater than critics believed it
        would be

32. The cowboy and the detective are similar in all of the following
    ways EXCEPT
    (A) they combat evil without the assistance of others
    (B) they are never co-opted by the violence inherent in a mob
        mentality
    (C) they both faced a frontier with uncertain moral clarity
    (D) they serve not for monetary reward but for principle
    (E) they further the cause of social compassion

33. Lines 15–18 provide an example of
    (A) begging the question
    (B) a straw man argument
    (C) an inductive argument
    (D) allusion
    (E) personification

34. The shift from paragraph 1 to paragraph 2 is from
    (A) a primary claim to a secondary qualifier
    (B) the thesis to the antithesis
    (C) the main theme to a specific problem
    (D) an abstract ideal to a more specific quality of that ideal
    (E) a general description to a specific example

35. Lincoln was a "lonely, individualistic hero" (lines 23–24) for all of
    the following reasons EXCEPT
    (A) he was a westerner
    (B) he was self-made
    (C) he did not follow prescribed dogma
    (D) he was mistrusted by congressional leadership
    (E) he was not integrated into his family life

36. Lincoln was "biblical" (line 41) in his sense of the Civil War because
    he understood
    (A) death and rebirth
    (B) pain and suffering
    (C) righteousness and sin
    (D) sin and atonement
    (E) divine retribution and divine forgiveness

37. Individualism as perceived in this context most likely leads to despair because
    (A) individual heroism creates alienation from others
    (B) individualism leads to loneliness
    (C) individuals are regarded with suspicion
    (D) other people suspect individuals of being self-righteous
    (E) individuals are misunderstood because they cannot return to society

38. The reader may infer from footnote 1 that
    (A) heroic isolation has been previously discussed in a book by Fiedler published in 1980
    (B) Ann Swidler wrote a book titled *Themes of Work and Love in Adulthood*
    (C) according to Fiedler, the discussion of individualism and social isolation has always been prominent in American fiction
    (D) heroism and the denial of marriage have long been common in the American workplace
    (E) Smelser and Erikson edited several works on love as a theme in American literature

39. According to footnote 2, which would most likely be a title of a book written by Reinhold Niebuhr?
    (A) *Moral Man, Immoral Society*
    (B) *Increasing Church Attendance*
    (C) *The Doctrine of God: The Election of God*
    (D) *Missionaries: Spreading God's Word in the Middle East*
    (E) *Unconsciousness and an Awareness of the Divine*

40. Footnote 3 informs us that
    (A) Allan Nevins edited essays published on Lincoln and the Gettysburg Address
    (B) Harry Jaffa edited a book on the Lincoln-Douglas debates
    (C) Allan Nevins and Harry Jaffa collaborated on several books about Lincoln
    (D) Doubleday was the publisher of Niebuhr's original remarks about Lincoln
    (E) Niebuhr's remarks appeared in an anthology of politics and religion

41. According to the passage and footnotes, which of the following is true?
    (A) Reinhold Niebuhr is the most thorough interpreter of the Gettysburg Address.
    (B) Allan Nevins has produced the most authoritative collection of Lincoln's speeches.
    (C) Leslie Fiedler wrote the only book successfully discussing lonesome women in history.
    (D) Erik Erikson is the foremost authority on love in American adult life.
    (E) Henry Jaffa is the person to read to better understand Lincoln's mythic meaning.

Questions 42–54 are based on the following passage from "Why Boys Don't Play with Dolls" by Katha Pollitt. Read the passage carefully before you choose your answers.

Theories of innate differences in behavior are appealing. They let parents off the hook—no small recommendation in a culture that holds moms, and sometimes even dads, responsible for their children's every
5　misstep on the road to bliss and success.

They allow grown-ups to take the path of least resistance to the dominant culture, which always requires less psychic effort, even if it means more actual work: just ask the working mother who comes home exhausted and
10　nonetheless finds it easier to pick up her son's socks than make him do it himself. They let families buy for their children, without too much guilt, the unbelievably sexist junk that the kids, who have been watching commercials since birth, understandably crave.

15　But the thing the theories do most of all is tell adults that the *adult* world—in which moms and dads still play by many of the old rules even as they question and fidget and chafe against them—is the way it's supposed to be. A girl with a doll and a boy with a truck "explain" why men are
20　from Mars and women are from Venus, why wives do housework and husbands just don't understand.

The paradox is that the world of rigid and hierarchal sex roles evoked by determinist theories is already passing away. Three-year-olds may indeed insist that doctors are
25　male and nurses female, even if their own mother is a physician. Six-year-olds know better. These days, something like half of all medical students are female, and male applications to nursing school are inching upward. When tomorrow's 3-year-olds play doctor, who's to say
30　how they'll assign roles?

With sex roles, as in every area of life, people aspire to what is possible and conform to what is necessary. But these are not fixed, especially today. Biological determinism may reassure some adults about their present, but it is
35　feminism, the ideology of flexible and converging sex roles, that fits our children's future. And the kids, somehow, know this.

That's why, if you look carefully, you'll find that for every kid who fits a stereotype, there's another who's
40　breaking one down. Sometimes it's the same kid—the boy who skateboards *and* takes cooking in his after-school program; the girl who collects stuffed animals *and* A-pluses in science.

Feminists are often accused of imposing their "agenda"
45　on children. Isn't that what adults always do, consciously and unconsciously? Kids aren't born religious, or polite, or kind, or able to remember where they put their sneakers. Inculcating these behaviors, and the values behind them, is a tremendous amount of work, involving many adults. We
50　don't have a choice, really, about *whether* we should give our children messages about what it means to be male and

female—they're bombarded with them from morning till night.

The question, as always, is what do we want those messages to be?

42. Pollitt suggests that the primary purpose of the passage is to
    (A) analyze sex roles among adults and find correlations to children
    (B) describe biological determinism and its effects on children
    (C) question the dominant theories of sex roles and the messages they send children
    (D) compare the ideologies of previous generations with those of the current generation
    (E) explore the influences of the dominant culture on parents' interactions with their children

43. Which of the following best describes the tone of the passage?
    (A) Incensed
    (B) Logical
    (C) Pedantic
    (D) Condescending
    (E) Moralistic

44. What is the author's attitude toward gender theories in general?
    (A) They are useful in allowing adults to rationalize their own behaviors.
    (B) They are important for integrating children into the adult world.
    (C) They serve no purpose and burden children with too many worries.
    (D) They are ridiculous notions created by scientists for grant money.
    (E) They are permanently ingrained in society's collective behavior and beliefs.

45. The function of the opening sentence might best be described as
    (A) rebutting previous theories
    (B) dismissing current theories
    (C) qualifying succeeding statements
    (D) generating interest in the issue
    (E) establishing a position in order to make a claim

46. In line 8, "psychic" most directly refers to
    (A) a supernatural experience
    (B) an intuitive feeling
    (C) a cognitive ability
    (D) a spiritual understanding
    (E) a psychological insight

47. The primary effect of the discussion in the second and third paragraphs (lines 6–21) is one of
    (A) exaggerated urgency because of the domestic imagery
    (B) calm reflection on an issue of great concern to modern parents
    (C) subtle humor through the planetary allusion
    (D) confusion because of the convoluted messages
    (E) emotional turmoil because of the author's inconsistent position

48. In the third paragraph, Pollitt develops the metaphor "men are from Mars and women are from Venus" (lines 19–20) by describing
    (A) adults' abilities to live in relative harmony
    (B) the unique needs and desires of men and women
    (C) the relative likes and dislikes of the genders
    (D) children's preferences for certain toys
    (E) culturally accepted adult roles

49. In the context of the sentence in line 33, "fixed" evokes which of the following meaning(s)?
    I. Repaired
    II. Secured
    III. Made permanent
    (A) I only
    (B) II only
    (C) I and II only
    (D) II and III only
    (E) I, II, and III

50. The author most likely includes the example of three-year-olds and six-year-olds (lines 24–30) for all the following reasons EXCEPT
    (A) to identify how gender-role stereotypes are changing
    (B) to demonstrate how rapidly images of adult role changes are perceived
    (C) to suggest that cultural stereotypes are rapidly falling away
    (D) to show that children mature faster in today's society than they did in previous generations
    (E) to imply that changing roles are not temporary

51. The rhetorical strategy of the sixth paragraph (lines 38–43) can best be described as
    (A) inductive
    (B) cause-and-effect fallacy
    (C) deductive
    (D) syllogistic
    (E) aphoristic

52. The sentence in lines 49–53 ("We don't have a choice . . . morning till night") contributes to the development of the passage primarily by
    (A) maintaining that political solutions pale in comparison to the media
    (B) reminding all of us that gender stereotypes evolve naturally
    (C) suggesting that parental pressure is minor
    (D) offering an opposing point of view
    (E) sustaining a deductive claim through parallel syntax

53. Which of the following strategies is most often used by Pollitt to propel the argument?
    (A) Metaphor
    (B) Periodic sentences
    (C) Rhetorical questions
    (D) Parenthetical remarks
    (E) Appeals to authority

54. How does the contrast in sentence structure between "Biological determinism . . . children's future" (lines 33–36) and "And the kids . . . know this" (lines 36–37) reflect the ideas being expressed?
(A) It creates a parallel structure that mimics gender roles.
(B) It recognizes a past reality and acknowledges a force for change.
(C) It maintains a strategy of broad claims and cause-and-effect solutions.
(D) It challenges previous claims.
(E) It opens up the possibility of change without closing the door on permanence.

END OF SECTION I

English Language and Composition Exam
Section II

Reading time: 15 minutes
Writing time: 2 hours
Number of questions: 3

Percentage of total grade: 55

Each question counts as one-third of the total essay section score.

Reading time before receiving booklet....................................15 minutes

Question 1 Essay..suggested time 40 minutes

Question 2 Essay..suggested time 40 minutes

Question 3 Essay..suggested time 40 minutes

Section II of this examination requires answers in essay form. To help you use your time well, the proctor will announce the time at which each question should be completed. If you finish any question before time is announced, you may go on to the following question. If you finish the examination in less than the time allotted, you may go back and work on any essay question you want.

Each essay will be judged on its clarity and effectiveness in dealing with the requirements of the topic assigned and on the quality of the writing. After completing each question, you should check your essay for accuracy of punctuation, spelling, and diction; you are advised, however, not to attempt many longer corrections. Remember that quality is far more important than quantity.

Write your essays with a pen, preferably in black or dark blue ink. Be sure to write CLEARLY and LEGIBLY. Cross out any errors you make.

The questions for Section II are printed in the green insert. You are encouraged to use the green insert to make notes and to plan your essays, but *be sure to write your answers in the pink booklet.* Number each answer as the question is numbered in the examination. Do not skip lines. Begin each answer on a new page in the pink booklet.

English Language and Composition Exam
Section II

Question 1

(Suggested time: reading time—15 minutes; writing time—40 minutes. This question counts as one-third of the total essay section score.)

Directions: The following prompt is based on the accompanying seven sources.

The question requires you to integrate a variety of sources into a coherent, well-written essay. Refer to the sources to support your position; avoid mere paraphrase or summary. Your argument should be central; the sources should support this argument.

Remember to attribute both direct and indirect citations.

INTRODUCTION

An individual's right to a jury trial is guaranteed in the Sixth Amendment to the Constitution and has been a fundamental aspect of our legal system for more than two hundred years. However, there is significant disaffection with the current jury system, and many proposals have been presented for discussion; smaller juries, allowing juries to ask questions, jury note-taking, and a non-unanimous verdict are a few of the key ones. Since 1934, Oregon has had a 10–2 verdict system for juries. That non-unanimous law was reaffirmed by the Supreme Court in Apodaca *v.* Oregon in 1972.

ASSIGNMENT

Read the following sources (including any introductory information) carefully. Then, in an essay that synthesizes at least three of the sources for support, take a position that defends, challenges, or qualifies the proposal that other states should adopt the Oregon model for jury verdicts.

Refer to the sources as Source A, Source B, etc.; titles are included for your convenience.

    Source A (Jury Duty)
    Source B (Tanzer)
    Source C (Abramson)
    Source D (Sullivan)
    Source E (Campos)
    Source F (Leib)
    Source G (Conrad)

Source A

"Jury Duty: A Handbook for Trial Jurors." Prepared by the Supreme Court of Appeals of West Virginia. 2007.

The following is an excerpt from an official handbook.

The first duty upon retiring to the jury room is to select someone to preside over the deliberations and act as a spokesperson in the courtroom. It is the duty of this juror, usually called the "foreperson," to see that discussion is carried on in a sensible and orderly fashion, that the issues submitted for decisions are fully and fairly addressed, and that every juror has a chance to say what he or she thinks upon every question. The foreperson conducts voting and also signs any written verdicts required and any written requests made by the judge. While the foreperson should express his or her opinions during the deliberations, these opinions are entitled to no more or less weight than those of the other jurors.

Differences of opinion often arise between jurors during deliberations. When this happens, each juror should say what he or she thinks and why. By reasoning the matter out, it is usually possible for jurors to agree. Jurors should not hesitate to change their minds if they decide their first opinion was not right, but they should not change their decision unless their reason and judgment is truly changed. Jurors should vote according to their own honest judgment of the evidence. If a jury cannot agree within a reasonable time, it may result in a new trial, which may be a great expense to the parties and the state. Jurors are expected to be fair, reasonable and courteous to each other, and try to reach an agreement which is a "fair and true verdict."

Source B

Tanzer, Jacob. "The Majority Verdict Should Be Adopted." <u>The Jury System</u>. Ed. Mary E. Williams. San Diego, CA: Greenhaven Press, 1997. 25–27.

The following passage is an excerpt from a book about the legal system and juries.

The historic reason for juries was to allow the people, rather than kings or even judges, to decide guilt or innocence. Juries began as gatherings of witnesses. For the people rather than the king to decide, however, it was not necessary for a particular number of jurors to agree. A super-majority of one's peers is a sturdy bulwark against oppression by the state.

Non-unanimous verdicts should not be considered a "get tough on crime" strategy. Jurors are not necessarily the prosecutor's friends. The question is whether super-majority verdicts improve the justice system. The answer is that they allow more accurate and more efficient decision-making by jurors, whether for convictions or acquittals. A study by the University of Chicago Law School showed that the ratio of convictions and acquittals was about the same under either system, but that the number of hung juries was reduced by more than 40% where 10 or 11 jurors could decide.

The problem with unanimous verdicts

The strategy of many defense lawyers, particularly when the prosecution's case is strong, is often not to seek an acquittal, but to hang the jury by choosing at least one juror with the temperament to hold out against the others and to convince this juror to do so. Such lawyers try their cases to one juror instead of to 12. I do not criticize defense lawyers for using every legal advantage for their clients, but there is something fundamentally wrong with a system of justice that makes indecision a victory. The purpose of a trial is to produce a decision. A hung jury is not a success for the jury system. To the contrary, a hung jury represents a failure of the justice system to produce a decision.

Perfect unanimity is simply not consistent with human nature. Seldom do 12 people hold the same opinion, particularly on grave matters. In ancient times, juries were starved into unanimity; often they were denied food and sleep until they reached a verdict. Today, jurors are sequestered together until they reach a unanimous verdict. Too often, they reach compromise verdicts instead of verdicts that truly reflect the convictions of the individual jurors. That is why armed robbers and rapists are sometimes convicted merely of assault. When the majority must compromise with an unreasonable, biased or screwball juror in order to reach a verdict, justice suffers. When jurors can vote their minds without the need to compromise, the verdict better reflects the truth.

Source C

Abramson, Jeffrey. <u>We, the Jury: The Jury System and the Ideal of Democracy</u>. New York: BasicBooks, HarperCollins, 1995. Epilogue.

The following passage is an excerpt from the epilogue of a book about the legal system and juries.

Many people argue that the jury system would be improved if the unanimous-verdict requirement were replaced by a majority-verdict requirement. However, studies reveal that when jurors must reach a unanimous verdict, they spend more time in deliberation and engage in higher-quality discussions of the case. Furthermore, in a significant number of cases, a minority of jury members turns around an initial majority vote through the process of deliberation. Unanimous verdicts require jurors to actively reason with, learn from, and persuade one another as they work toward a final decision. Because this characteristic of the unanimous-verdict system ensures that most jury decisions are carefully considered, both jurors and the general public feel more confident about the validity of unanimous verdicts.

Source D

Sullivan, Eugene R., and Akhil Reed Amar. "Jury Reform in America—A Return to the Old Country." <u>American Criminal Law Review</u>. Volume 33, 1996.

The following passage is an excerpt from a legal journal.

REFORM 1: EMPOWER THE JURY BY CHANGING THE JURY VERDICT TO A TEN-TO-TWO VOTE.

The requirement of unanimous jury verdicts has been widespread in America's state and federal jury system since the eighteenth century. The unanimous jury verdict may have been necessary to ensure a fair trial for a defendant in those times when a defendant had few rights. But in modern times, a defendant enjoys many trial safeguards which ensure that a fair trial is given to all defendants. Now is the time to rethink whether a unanimous verdict is necessary for America's modern trial process. The Supreme Court has ruled that the Sixth Amendment's guarantee of a jury trial does not require a unanimous jury verdict.

In England, the criminal code was changed in 1967 to allow a ten-to-two verdict after the jury has deliberated at least two hours. The English experiment in this area has proved successful.

Since the ten-to-two jury verdict is not outlawed by the Constitution and is not necessary to protect a defendant's right to a fair trial, why not move to it in America? The United States Senate has recently introduced a bill which would change the Federal Rules of Criminal and Civil Procedures to allow the ten-to-two jury vote in criminal trials in federal courts.

Adoption of the ten-to-two (super-majority) jury vote would strengthen the power of the jury by eliminating the occurrences of hung juries as well as reducing the danger of a single juror corrupting the jury process. It is not reasonable that one or two jurors should thwart the will of a strong super-majority of the serving jurors. Note finally, ten-to-two verdicts would protect some defendants who are unprotected by unanimity rules. If the jury votes ten-to-two in the defendant's favor, this vote would count as an acquittal instead of a mistrial and thus, under the double jeopardy protection rules, would [prevent] the prosecutor from retrying the case.

Source E

Campos, Carlos. "Legislature 2007: House says allow death penalty even if 2 jurors oppose." <u>Atlanta Journal-Constitution</u>. Metro News, D1. 21 March 2007.

The following passage is an excerpt from a newspaper.

Imposing the death penalty in Georgia will take only 10 of 12 jurors under a House bill passed Tuesday that produced the most lengthy and heated debate yet of an otherwise sedate legislative session.

House Bill 185, sponsored by House Majority Whip Barry Fleming (R-Harlem), would allow a judge to impose a death sentence on a defendant even if two jurors vote against it.

Current Georgia law requires that juries vote unanimously when imposing capital punishment.

If the bill passes the Senate and is approved by the governor, Georgia would be one of only five states in the nation with the death penalty that does not require a unanimous jury verdict for a death sentence, according to the Death Penalty Information Center. The other four are Alabama, Delaware, Florida, and Montana. A judge decides sentences in Delaware and Montana, while juries only make recommendations to judges in Alabama and Florida.

Georgia's HB 185 would still give judges discretion to impose life, with or without parole, instead of death on an 11-1 or 10-2 verdict. A unanimous jury verdict would automatically lead to a death sentence.

The bill only addresses the sentencing stage of a trial and does not change the guilt or innocence phase of a verdict. Unanimity is still required for a judgment of guilt.

Source F

Leib, Ethan J. "The Problem of Hung Juries—and How to Solve It." <u>Find Law</u>. http://writ.news.findlaw.com/commentary/20060512_leib.html. 21 May 2007.

The following passage is an excerpt from an on-line source.

Another story of jury "deadlock" has made the papers. The defendant is Osama Awadallah, accused of lying to a grand jury investigating the 9/11 attacks. The jury charged with adjudicating whether Mr. Awadallah in fact lied failed to reach agreement on a verdict—because, according to press reports, a lone holdout refused to convict. Now the government faces the choice of dropping the case against Awadallah, or using considerable resources on a retrial.

We need to stop giving holdouts the power to prevent convictions. We don't require unanimity for any other important decision in our pluralistic polity, so why this one? No other modern country (save Canada and a few jurisdictions in Australia) has such stringent jury decision rules.

My point isn't that we should make it easier to convict: It's that we should make the process of reaching a decision fairer to all parties concerned and more democratic. Accordingly, I believe that just as we must relax the unanimity decision rule for conviction, we must also render it much easier for juries to acquit.

Currently, both acquittals and convictions must be unanimous—in federal court and in forty-eight states. That's not fair to the defendant: He fails to get the benefit of a clear outcome that would allow repose, and he faces the risk of retrial, even if eleven jurors thought either that he was innocent, or that the government had failed to prove its case.

I recommend that a supermajority be required to convict, and a mere majority be required to acquit. These reforms would effectively abolish the hung jury.

Source G

Conrad. <u>The Legal System</u>. Ed. Laura Egendorg. Opposing Viewpoints Series. Farmington Hills, MI: Greenhaven Press, 2003. 70.

The following is a cartoon from a series collection.

Conrad. © 1994 by Los Angeles Times Syndicate. Reprinted with permission.

Question 2

(Suggested time—40 minutes. This question counts as one-third of the total essay section score.)

The passage below is an excerpt from an essay, "On the Pleasure of Hating," written by nineteenth-century author William Hazlitt. The essay begins with a description of a spider that Hazlitt does not kill but allows to leave his house. From this momentary encounter, Hazlitt begins his examination of human hatred. Read the passage carefully. Then, in a well-written essay, analyze the rhetorical devices Hazlitt uses to sustain his argument about the nature of hatred in human life.

> . . . Nature seems made up of antipathies: without something to hate, we should lose the very spring of thought and action. Life would turn to a stagnant pool, were it not ruffled by the jarring interests, the unruly passions, of men. The white streak in our own fortunes is brightened by making all around it as dark as possible; so the rainbow paints its form upon the cloud. Is it pride? Is it envy? Is it the force of contrast? Is it weakness or malice? But so it is, that there is a secret affinity, a hankering after, evil in the human mind, and that it takes a perverse, but a fortunate delight in mischief, since it is a never-failing source of satisfaction. Pure good soon grows insipid, wants variety and spirit. Pain is a bittersweet, wants variety and spirit. Love turns, with a little indulgence, to indifference or disgust: hatred alone is immortal. Do we not see this principle at work everywhere? Animals torment and worry one another without mercy: children kill flies for sport: everyone reads the accidents and offences in a newspaper as the cream of the jest: a whole town runs to be present at a fire, and the spectator by no means exults to see it extinguished. It is better to have it so, but it diminishes the interest, and our feelings take part with our passions rather than with our understandings. . . .
>
> The pleasure of hating, like a poisonous mineral, eats into the heart of religion, and turns it to rankling spleen and bigotry; it makes patriotism an excuse for carrying fire, pestilence, and famine into other lands: it leaves to virtue nothing but the spirit of censoriousness, and a narrow, jealous, inquisitorial watchfulness over the actions and motives of others. What have the different sects, creeds, doctrines in religion been but so many pretexts to set up for men to wrangle, to quarrel, to tear one another in pieces about, like a target as a mark to shoot at? Does any one suppose that the love of country in an Englishman implies any friendly feeling or disposition to serve another bearing the same name? No, it means only hatred to the French or the inhabitants of any other country that we happen to be at war with for the time. Does the love of virtue denote any wish to discover or amend our own faults? No, but it atones for an obstinate adherence to our own vices by the most virulent intolerance to human

frailties. This principle is of a most universal application. It extends to good as well as evil: if it makes us hate folly, it makes us no less dissatisfied with distinguished merit. If it inclines us to resent the wrongs of others, it impels us to be as impatient of their prosperity. We revenge injuries: we repay benefits with ingratitude. Even our strongest partialities and likings soon take this turn. "That which was luscious as locusts, anon becomes bitter as coloquintida;" and love and friendship melt in their own fires. We hate old friends: we hate old books: we hate old opinions; and at last we come to hate ourselves.

Question 3

(Suggested time—40 minutes. This question counts as one-third of the total essay section score.)

In the April 2000 issue of the journal *Wired,* Bill Joy wrote the article "Why the Future Doesn't Need Us." In the article, Joy imagines the following future:

> As society and the problems that face it become more and more complex and machines become more and more intelligent, people will let machines make more of their decisions for them, simply because machine-made decisions will bring better results than man-made ones. Eventually a stage may be reached at which the decisions necessary to keep the system running will be so complex that human beings will be incapable of making them intelligently. At that stage the machines will be in effective control.

From *The Matrix* to *2001* to *I, Robot,* images of a machine-controlled world dominate the imagery of the future. In a well-written essay, develop a position that agrees, disagrees, or qualifies the argument offered by Bill Joy that human beings could become irrelevant in an increasingly complex world. Support your position with evidence from your own reading, observation, and/or experience.

STOP

END OF EXAM

ANSWERS AND EXPLANATIONS FOR PRACTICE TEST 2

Using the answer key below, score your test and determine how many questions you answered correctly and incorrectly. Then look over the answer explanations.

ANSWER KEY FOR MULTIPLE-CHOICE QUESTIONS

1. D	10. C	19. C	28. D	37. B	46. C
2. E	11. B	20. A	29. B	38. C	47. B
3. B	12. C	21. C	30. B	39. A	48. E
4. D	13. C	22. E	31. C	40. A	49. D
5. A	14. D	23. E	32. C	41. E	50. B
6. B	15. D	24. E	33. D	42. C	51. A
7. B	16. A	25. B	34. E	43. B	52. C
8. E	17. B	26. D	35. A	44. A	53. C
9. B	18. B	27. A	36. A	45. E	54. B

ANSWERS AND EXPLANATIONS FOR MULTIPLE-CHOICE QUESTIONS

1. **ANSWER: D** Most likely you will not see a question quite like this one on the actual test. However, you are expected to know the difference between independent (stand-alone sentences) and dependent clauses. The style of essay writers, especially from the seventeenth and eighteenth centuries, was complex, with parallel syntax created by many different types of clauses and phrases. Here Swift uses several connected independent clauses to create his parallel syntax. The simplest approach here is to count the number of semicolons.

2. **ANSWER: E** This one is rather easy, unlike the last one. He even says it is a "tree turned upside down."

3. **ANSWER: B** What a nobility is man! "No!" yells Swift. Man is a fool and will proceed to demonstrate that he is nothing more than a broom. Therefore, Swift's tone is irreverent.

4. **ANSWER: D** The essay is all about ridicule, and if this were a "roast," Swift would be roasting man. Therefore, his italics are there for emphasis, to make it clear that man is nothing much, nothing much at all.

5. ANSWER: A Plugging the various words into the sentence results in A or B, but A is the better answer as you have the definite feeling that man never knows what will happen to him next.

6. ANSWER: B The "periwig" is but one of the elements by which man tries to make something better of a bad situation. Being human is bad enough; getting older just makes it worse. We are fooled into believing we can change our appearance and our aging. What fools us? Why, vanity, of course. Swift was a minister. He was aware of the opening to the Book of Ecclesiastes.

7. ANSWER: B A, C, and D are all easy-to-spot metaphors. E is more difficult but suggests a children's game or toy. B is simply describing an action that could be interpreted as a symbol of man trying to hide his ugly nature or a bad hair day, but it is not metaphoric.

8. ANSWER: E B and E look similar, but the essential irony of the passage suggests that Swift would never see persons as having merit. We are corrupt beings who spend most of our time finding and criticizing the faults of others; hence, we go about raising a great deal of dust without accomplishing much of anything.

9. ANSWER: B Swift would not have a problem with E and basically uses the dust metaphor as a critique of hypocrisy. The sense of the entire essay is that man is done in by his proclivity to do all sorts of things badly. He is hypocritical, but he is also vain, greedy, and self-indulgent, and he eats badly. For Swift there was not much that man did that could be called commendable.

10. ANSWER: C This basic theme runs throughout the Swift piece: man is not a pretty piece of work. In fact man is a broom, a tree upside down, and useful for cleaning up some messes for a while. Finally, when man no longer has any value, he is best burned up in a good fire.

11. ANSWER: B B is part of a compound sentence and is not a participial modifier.

12. ANSWER: C The participial is connected to marriage and clearly suggests that men we would perceive as "jerks" would be the ones most likely to have a woman to look after them or abuse them, whichever the case may be.

13. ANSWER: C One metaphor that Swift loves is that men go around stirring up dirt because they love to accuse and abuse others. Another of his favorite metaphors is that all brooms, when finally worn out and no longer valuable, are tossed in the fire as kindling. The fire reference would be just fine to the preacher in Swift.

14. ANSWER: D Question 13 is somewhat related to question 14. There are two possible answers here, C and D. However, given the tone of the essay, one doubts that it would be "merely" gossip that is being condemned here.

15. ANSWER: D The entire force and tone of the essay ridicule man. Swift uses a style that imitates Robert Boyle (see the title of the essay), but

rather than advocating the noble, Swift focuses on the base. Hence, his ridicule is not just aimed at man in general, but at Boyle in particular, most likely for being such an optimist and a hopeful guy. Therefore, you need a negative word; you are offered three. Again, you want the strongest possible, and that would be "antipathy."

16. ANSWER: A Look to the text. The author states "one thing I know for sure" and "I had the feeling that if nature had painted one more brushstroke on me, I'd have had to kill myself." From this one may infer that the author is intimately familiar with her topic and that she is a dark-skinned woman.

17. ANSWER: B Contextually, "saved" refers to people who are light-skinned, since the author is discussing the hardships of being "damned" as a dark-skinned person.

18. ANSWER: B This statement is a metaphor that invokes the idea of Christianity and the opposing elements of salvation and damnation.

19. ANSWER: C The text plainly supports this answer choice, as the author's point is that it is ironic that "someone who had been judged outside the realm of beauty herself . . . should have adopted them so wholeheartedly and . . . without question." No other answer choices are viable.

20. ANSWER: A Go to the old standby: Put your finger on "it" and plug in answer choices. Answer A is the one that logically and contextually makes sense.

21. ANSWER: C Like the homecoming and prom queens, this group is likely made up of the popular, well-known students. Based on the speaker's comments, this group is also light-skinned. The other answer choices are just plain silly.

22. ANSWER: E The repetition of "rejected" reinforces the self-loathing that the young, dark-skinned man must feel to reject his own identity and, by association, others who are like him.

23. ANSWER: E Process of elimination rules out A, B, and C. D may be possible, but it isn't the speaker's point. Given the discussion of the rest of the passage, the contrast between early and twentieth-century tastes among African men for women is meant to introduce a point with which the author argues throughout the passage.

24. ANSWER: E Context clues are your best friend in this question. You may not know what "stymied" means, but you do know the differences in meaning among the other words. Plug them in. Which makes the most sense? Although the girl may have annoyed the teacher with her excellent abilities, she mostly frustrated that teacher's conception of what certain students in the front row (both figuratively and literally) should look like.

25. ANSWER: B You can immediately eliminate C, D, and E as wrong answers. Of the two that are left, it is likely that the author does not

mean to ridicule the teacher, but instead means to soften her criticism that the teacher attempted to hide her appearance with makeup.

26. ANSWER: D Again, put your finger on "them" and, plugging in answer choices, you find that "them" refers to "standards."

27. ANSWER: A Inherent to Mebane's argument is the idea that many people discriminate against dark-skinned people. The irony is that by avoiding dark-skinned men, she, too, is discriminating against dark-skinned people. She is merely doing the same as the teacher earlier in the passage: accepting society's standards, even though by doing so she is hurting herself as well.

28. ANSWER: D The only place the author uses repetition is in the last sentence. One can't count that as a strategy for the passage overall. The speaker uses analogy, personal reflection, specific examples from her own life, and an argument that appeals to one's emotions.

29. ANSWER: B The definition of *nihilism* is an extreme form of skepticism that holds that all values are baseless. But even without knowing the dictionary meaning, you can contextually guess the meaning of the word by the author's use of it. For example, lines 14–18 state that "moral heroism is always just a step away from despair. For an Ahab, and occasionally for a cowboy or a detective, there is no return to society, no moral redemption. The hero's lonely quest for moral excellence ends in absolute nihilism," which is to say that the hero will be lonely, hopeless, and despairing. The author then offers, in lines 34–36, another use of the word in relation to Abraham Lincoln as an example of what a hero must do to avoid hopelessness and despair: "What saved Lincoln from nihilism was the larger whole for which he felt it was important to live and worthwhile to die." That is, Lincoln felt there was hope for a nation divided and felt it was important to fight for it, which is the opposite of hopelessness and despair.

30. ANSWER: B The text states that American individualism is "a kind of heroic selflessness" that accepts isolation "in order to serve the values of the group."

31. ANSWER: C By using "mythic," the author intends to show that Lincoln was a real-life example of the truly heroic American, that "Lincoln conforms perfectly to the archetype of the lonely, individualistic hero."

32. ANSWER: C In no way does the passage intimate that either the cowboy or the detective faced his peculiar frontier (the West and the city, respectively) with *uncertain moral clarity*. They both were quite clear in their moral outlooks.

33. ANSWER: D The literary allusion is to Ahab in *Moby-Dick*. The other answer choices simply do not apply.

34. ANSWER: E The author moves from a general discussion of the general American hero of cowboy or detective to a specific example of an American hero, Abraham Lincoln.

35. ANSWER: A The text states that Lincoln conforms to the archetype of the lonely, individualistic hero because he "was a self-made man," his "belief that 'all men are created equal' roused the hostility of abolitionists and southern sympathizers alike," and he was "isolated, misunderstood by Congress and cabinet, and unhappy at home." The passage mentions nothing about Lincoln being a westerner.

36. ANSWER: A The passage states, in lines 40–44, that "Lincoln's biblical understanding of the Civil War" found expression in the "great symbols of death and rebirth that Lincoln invoked to give meaning to the sacrifice of those who died at Gettysburg."

37. ANSWER: B The first paragraph states that to serve society, individualists "must be able to stand alone, not needing others, not depending on their judgment, and not submitting to their wishes." As such, it is "part of the profound ambiguity of the mythology of American individualism that its moral heroism is always just a step away from despair."

38. ANSWER: C The footnote tells us that Leslie Fiedler wrote about the hero's avoidance of women and society in a book titled *Love and Death in the American Novel.*

39. ANSWER: A Niebuhr is a theologian who wrote books about "Christianity, politics, and history," so one may deduce that he writes books that integrate these three concepts. Thus, a book about church attendance, the doctrine of the elect, missionaries in the Middle East, and the awareness of the divine are too specific (and silly) to be considered as viable works by Niebuhr. According to the footnote, Niebuhr would write about ethics and politics in society; the title *Moral Man, Immoral Society* seems best to fit this description.

40. ANSWER: A The footnote tells us that Allan Nevins is the editor of *Lincoln and the Gettysburg Address.* None of the other answer choices may be chosen with any degree of certainty from the footnote.

41. ANSWER: E The only answer choice that makes sense is that Jaffa is considered an authority on Lincoln's mythic meaning. None of the other answer choices may be inferred from the text or footnotes.

42. ANSWER: C The author's primary purpose is understood when she begins the passage with the statement that "[t]heories of innate differences in behavior are appealing" and ends the passage with the comment that children receive messages about sex roles and that the "question, as always, is what do we want those messages to be?"

43. ANSWER: B The overall tone of the passage is understood to be logical as Pollitt provides points and counterpoints to the discussion. She is not angry, scholarly, condescending, or moralistic.

44. ANSWER: A The text states that gender theories not only "allow grown-ups to take the path of least resistance to the dominant culture," but also (and more important) "tell adults that the *adult* world—in which moms and dads still play by many of the old rules

even as they question and fidget and chafe against them—is the way it's supposed to be."

45. **Answer: E** The opening sentence "Theories of innate differences in behavior are appealing" offers the reader a topic and a position from which the author will make her case about gender theories and sex roles in society.

46. **Answer: C** There really is only one answer choice that makes sense in context. "Taking the path of least resistance" means that something is always done a certain way and requires no real thought, planning, or cognitive effort.

47. **Answer: B** This is one of those questions for which you can eliminate answer choices before deciding which is *most* correct. You can eliminate A because there is no urgency in Pollitt's tone, and D and E because she is quite clear in her explanation and position. This leaves B and C. Although the author's reference to the "men are from Mars, women are from Venus" metaphor is humorous, it is NOT the *primary effect* of the discussion. Therefore, B is the correct answer—it describes *both* paragraphs.

48. **Answer: E** It is obvious the author is not being literal, so her qualifying clause "why wives do housework and husbands just don't understand" explains what she means by the Mars/Venus metaphor.

49. **Answer: D** The word appears in context as "sex roles are not fixed." The word "fixed" means both secure and permanent. Plug in all three words to see which best fit the meaning of the sentence. In a Roman numeral question, be sure to try all the answers listed by the Roman numerals before looking to the answer choices.

50. **Answer: B** Pollitt recognizes throughout the essay that images are rapidly altering, especially due to the impact of the media on our changing cultural life. A six-year-old, in the space of three short years, has become much more media-savvy and has quickly learned to apply to all women images that she had only seen in a mother. In the media, women have a strong cultural and economic impact and are visualized in every conceivable occupation. That change in our society is reflected in the rapid change from three to six.

51. **Answer: A** This brief paragraph is inductive because the author uses two examples. They are generic, but they are examples, and thus her argument fulfills the inductive requirement. Remember that when you analyze an inductive argument, you should ask two questions: One, is there a sufficient number of examples? Two, are the examples relevant to the issue? For Pollitt, the answer to the first is no and the answer to the second is yes. However, here you are asked only to recognize that the argument is inductive.

52. **Answer: C** The sentence itself describes a rather passive pressure on parents: their children will receive these messages whether or not the parent teaches them. It isn't until the next sentence (paragraph) that we recognize the actual pressure on parents to teach and differentiate among the messages children receive from media.

53. **ANSWER: C** Pollitt's most effective tool for moving her argument is the rhetorical question. You may arrive at this answer through the process of elimination: she doesn't use metaphors, and she makes her statements quite clear up front (she doesn't have an abundance of periodic sentences—dependent clauses preceding independent clauses). Although she does give a parenthetical remark in lines 16–18 (even though it is set off by dashes) and she does discuss theories as an appeal to authority, we don't know where she found her theories. Therefore, we can only accept what *she* says the theories are as authoritative, which doesn't "propel" her argument so much as support it. Thus, the speaker moves her argument *forward* with the use of rhetorical questions as a method of bringing up additional points to consider.

54. **ANSWER: B** Although answer A is tempting, Pollitt's syntax and her ideas do not mimic gender roles. She is summing up and, in an important way, trying not to appear strident about the issue. She recognizes what has been the reality of the past and also that the world is changing. C, D, and E are not relevant to what was discussed in this essay.

EXPLANATIONS AND RUBRICS FOR ESSAY QUESTIONS

ESSAY QUESTION 1: UPPER-HALF PAPERS: SCORES OF 5–9

Synthesis papers require you to make *your own argument*. The sources can be used to help sustain that argument, but it is crucial that you share your own point of view on the topic. Upper-half papers will integrate quotations and references to the sources and cite them correctly in order to maintain and make their own case (a nice pun, given the topic). For example: You might begin the paper with a mention that this idea of a non-unanimous jury had never occurred to you before. However, now that you think about it, it sounds like a fairly rational approach to an increasing problem in our courts. Using sources B, D and F, you sustain your own argument that such an approach to justice seems reasonable. Remember: You must use three sources. It is often a good idea to use an opposing source, like C, and then counter what that source says in your argument to make your ideas and your command of the issue stronger. The writing in an upper-half paper is not necessarily flawless, but the paper is clear and well-argued and focused on the topic. Most students will take a position that advocates majority or unanimous verdicts. However, there is middle ground allowing states to make their own decision.

ESSAY QUESTION 1: LOWER-HALF PAPERS: SCORES OF 1–4

A paper can be scored in the lower half, even with good writing, if its author does not quote or correctly cite at least three sources. We have provided one example in the synthesis chapter of a good paper that scored in the lower half because of such an error. However, writers of most lower-half papers will quote the requisite number of sources, but those quotations often have little to do with the argument at that point. The quotations often feel dropped into the paper rather than related to the paper. Lower-half papers can also be identified by their tendency to summarize what the various sources said, repeating and nearly completely quoting source D, for example. Finally, lower-half papers can be identified by their brevity (an insufficient argument) or are grammatically weak.

ESSAY QUESTION 2: UPPER-HALF PAPERS: SCORES OF 5–9

While Hazlitt can be a challenging essayist, with complex ideas couched in complex syntax, this is not one of those essays. It uses an upper-level vocabulary and fairly complex syntax, but his ideas are clear: Hate drives human motivation. It is a bold and cynical claim. Upper-half-paper writers will have no difficulty understanding his purpose. These papers will also recognize that their task *is not* to continue the argument. Instead, their task is to analyze Hazlitt's methods of argumentation and clarify the force of his argument. Upper-half papers will also integrate quotes from the passage to illustrate the types of methods he used in seeking to convince. Possible devices include but are not limited to: diction, parallel syntax, metaphors and similes, and rhetorical questions. Upper-half papers are not necessarily flawless, but are generally clear in their delineation of methodology.

ESSAY QUESTION 2: LOWER-HALF PAPERS: SCORES OF 1–4

Writers of these essays will demonstrate that they struggled with Hazlitt and never fully comprehended his thesis. They will also state what Hazlitt said (or what they thought he said) without really analyzing his methods. They will end up summarizing and paraphrasing. These papers will not understand their task, or they will simply see that task as applying labels without understanding how they functioned in the essay. Papers scored in the lower half are often brief and undeveloped. They often also exhibit weak grammar.

ESSAY QUESTION 3: UPPER-HALF PAPERS: SCORES OF 5–9

The Bill Joy quotation is not difficult to manage, given the media focus on this issue for the last few years. Films and novels covering the issues of robotics, artificial intelligence, and computer control are numerous. However, Joy offers a reasonable hypothesis rather than generate a future of hysteria. He suggests that the change will just happen. Upper-half paper writers will recognize the calmness and potency of his position and clearly indicate their agreement, disagreement, or qualification of it. These writers will employ a variety of specific examples from *The Matrix; I, Robot; Wargames; 2001; Necromancer;* and the like. These writers will also share what they know of current events in artificial intelligence (current robot experiments in Japan, for example) and trends, such as the complex systems we use to monitor our own homes or travel. These examples will be integrated within the argument. The writing will not necessarily be flawless, but it generally will be smooth, and the argument will be convincing.

ESSAY QUESTION 3: LOWER-HALF PAPERS: SCORES OF 1–4

Most students will have an opinion about this issue. The difficult part will be keeping that opinion focused—that is where the examples come in. Weaker papers will turn the quotation into a rant. Students will engage in all sorts of diatribes against modern society, human ignorance in the face of increasing technology, or the failure of their own expensive iPhone. Their examples will be tangential to the argument, and overall, these lower-half essays will lack coherency. These papers may also be unacceptably brief or grammatically confusing.

COMPUTING YOUR SCORE ON THE PRACTICE TEST

Please keep in mind that these numbers are subjective. Two variables affect the computation every year: the number of the multiple-choice questions and the difficulty level of the essays. There is a slight curve created every year in terms of the numbers. Having said that, remember that earning fifteen points on the essays and getting 50 percent right on the multiple-choice questions will generally produce a score of 3.

SCORING THE MULTIPLE-CHOICE SECTION

$$\underline{\hspace{2cm}} - (1/4 \times \underline{\hspace{2cm}}) = \underline{\hspace{3cm}}$$

number correct   number incorrect   multiple-choice score

SCORING THE FREE-RESPONSE SECTION

$$\underline{\hspace{2cm}} + \underline{\hspace{2cm}} + \underline{\hspace{2cm}} = \underline{\hspace{2cm}}$$

Question 1   Question 2   Question 3   total essay
(0–9 score)   (0–9 score)   (0–9 score)   score

COMPOSITE SCORE

$$1.29 \times \underline{\hspace{3cm}} = \underline{\hspace{3cm}}$$

multiple-choice   weighted section I
score   score

$$3.05 \times \underline{\hspace{3cm}} = \underline{\hspace{3cm}}$$

free response   weighted section II
score   score

$$\underline{\hspace{3cm}} + \underline{\hspace{3cm}} = \underline{\hspace{3cm}}$$

weighted section I   weighted section II   composite score

You now have a number between 0 and about 150. Each year that scale is adjusted. Generally it goes like this:

0–49 = 1   50–75 = 2   76–94 = 3   95–110 = 4   112–150 = 5